The Legal Dictionary for Bad Spellers

The Legal Dictionary for Bad Spellers

Joseph Krevisky and **Jordan L. Linfield**

An Innovation Press Book

John Wiley & Sons, Inc.

New York • Chichester • Brisbane • Toronto • Singapore

Contents

Introduction

"If I don't know how to spell the word, how can I find it in the dictionary?" This lament has been the subject of cartoons, comic strips, columns by popular writers, TV sitcoms, and radio talk shows.

"It doesn't look right." Sound familiar? Most of us, regardless of age or education, face this problem sometimes, or often. Poor spelling has little to do with intelligence, level of schooling, family background, or heredity.

Presidents and princes; Ph.D.'s, L.L.D.'s, and J.D.'s; poets and professors all boast bad spellers within their groups. In fact, boast is often what these poor spellers do; they're proud of it.

So what is the recurrent problem?

The major cause is the complex pattern of English spelling and pronunciation. For example, the same letter may be pronounced several different ways. Note the pronunciation of the letter *c*

in the word *cell* (pronounced as an *s*)
in the word *cause* (pronounced as a *k*)
in the word *judicial* (pronounced as *sh*)
in the word *cello* (pronounced as *ch*)

And sometimes it is silent, as in the words *yacht, Connecticut*, and *czar*. To add to the confusion, some words are spelled alike but pronounced differently. For example, *wound*, meaning injury, is pronounced "woond," while *wound*, as in winding a clock, is pronounced "waund." Some words are pronounced alike but are spelled and defined differently:

intercession and *intersession*
heroin and *heroine*

Some words are pronounced and spelled almost alike but are defined differently:

flagrant and *flagrante*

But even more complicated is our legal language, replete with Latin and Old English. Even fewer of us study Old English than Latin these days.

So what? After all, a computer spell-checker does the work; it will quickly spot a misspelled word and provide the correct spelling.

Or will it?

First, you must be sure—even with simple misspellings—that you choose the right word from the options offered by the PC.

Second, many spell-checkers do not include words that have come into our language recently, such as *fax* or *nymble*.

Third, and this is surprising, the typical computer spell-checker used in legal offices contains very few legal terms. You can find the word *worker*, but you are unlikely to find *workers' compensation*.

Above all, no computer can catch the difference between words that look alike or sound alike. Try finding the correct *their, there,* or *they're*; or having it distinguish between *garnish* and *garnishee*. The computer will provide the options, but the choice is thrown back to you.

And what to do when you don't have a PC handy—while traveling, in the library, or when the computer is down.

The Legal Dictionary for Bad Spellers solves these problems. It provides an extensive list of words that are typically misspelled, in alphabetical order by their misspellings. Look the word up by its misspelling and you will find the correct spelling alongside it. The misspelled words are listed by their obvious misspelling: for example, *sertiorari* for *certiorari*, *gury* for *jury*. More difficult words have several variant misspellings listed to increase your chances of finding them speedily.

The corpus of the dictionary, with its wide variety of misspellings, has been collected by the authors over years among legal-brief writers and proofreaders.

The Legal Dictionary for Bad Spellers also provides the only available list of legal look-alikes and sound-alikes, which are a source of increasing confusion in legal writing.

And, finally, there is a handy quick list of correct spellings for reference if you are reasonably sure of the spelling.

How to Use This Dictionary

The Legal Dictionary for Bad Spellers is arranged in three parts. Section 1 consists of words arranged alphabetically by their incorrect spellings, with the correct spelling in the opposite column. Section 2 comprises a list of words that look alike or sound alike, with brief definitions that illustrate the differences. Section 3 is the Quick List of Correct Spellings.

If you are reasonably sure of the spelling of a word, check it in the alphabetical Quick List of Correct Spellings. If you do not find it there, check Section 1, the list of incorrect spellings with their correct spellings alongside. Try the phonetic spelling: *reck* for *wreck*, for example. Once you have found the correct spelling, be sure to examine the entire correct word carefully; for while we emphasize misspellings at the beginnings of words, we also include standard middle and ending errors such as *ant* for *ent* (as in *dependant* for *dependent*) and *ent* for *ant* (as in *defendent* for *defendant*). When asterisks (**) appear next to the correct spelling of a word in either Section 1 or Section 3, the word should be checked in Section 2, as this is a word that looks like or sounds like another word and is apt to be misused.

Suppose, for example, you are not sure how to spell *duly*. You think it is spelled *dooly* or maybe *dully*. You look up both spellings in Section 3, the Quick List of Correct Spellings. You cannot find *dooly*, but you find *dully*. You go to Section 1, Words Arranged by Their Common Misspellings. You find the incorrect spelling *dooly* with its corresponding correct spelling, *duly***. The two asterisks alert you to check the look-alikes and sound-alikes, where you find the difference between *duly* and *dully*.

SECTION 1

Words Arranged by Their Common Misspellings

A

abacy .... **abbacy**

abaitable newsence ....

.... **abatable nuisance**

abaitment .... **abatement**

abalition .... **abolition**

abandement .... **abandonment**

ab anishio .... **ab initio**

abaration .... **aberration**

ab auntiquo .... **ab antiquo**

abayance .... **abeyance**

abayence .... **abeyance**

abbaction .... **abaction**

abbandon .... **abandon**

abbandoned .... **abandoned**

abb ante .... **ab ante**

abbash .... **abash**

abbate .... **abate**

abbatement .... **abatement**

abbator .... **abator**

abbditorium .... **abditorium**

abbdomen .... **abdomen**

abbduct .... **abduct**

abbearance .... **abearance**

abb ekstra .... **ab extra**

abberation .... **aberration**

abbet .... **abet**

abbhor .... **abhor**

abbhorrent .... **abhorrent**

abbide .... **abide**

abbility .... **ability**

abb inishio .... **ab initio**

abbintra .... **ab intra**

abbiogenesis .... **abiogenesis**

abbjudication .... **abjudication**

abbjur .... **abjure****

abbjuration .... **abjuration**

abbnormal .... **abnormal**

abbode .... **abode**

abbolish .... **abolish**

abbominible .... **abominable**

abbon drot .... **à bon droit**

abb original .... **aboriginal****

abbort .... **abort**

abbortifacent .... **abortifacient**

abbortion .... **abortion**

abbortionist .... **abortionist**

abbortive .... **abortive**

abbove .... **above****

abbreviashun .... **abbreviation**

abbrige .... **abridge**

abbroad .... **abroad**

abbrochement .... **abbroachment**

  or **abroachment**

abbrupt .... **abrupt**

abbscond .... **abscond**

abbscondor .... **absconder**

abbselutely .... **absolutely**

abbsence .... **absence**

abbsentee .... **absentee****

abbsint .... **absent**

abbsolute .... **absolute**

abbsolution .... **absolution**

abbsolve .... **absolve**

abbsorbtion .... **absorption**

abbsque .... **absque**

abbstain .... **abstain**

abbstention .... **abstention**

abbstrack .... **abstract****

abbstract of record ....

.... **abstract of record**

abbstract of title .... **abstract of title**

abbstraker ... **abstracter** or **abstractor**

abbstrakshun .... **abstraction**

abbsurd .... **absurd**

abbuse .... **abuse**

abbuse of prosess .... **abuse of process**

abbusive .... **abusive**

abbut .... **abut**

abbutals .... **abuttals**

abbuter .... **abutter**

abbutment .... **abutment**

abcense .... **absence**

abcent reo .... **absente reo**

abcerd .... **absurd**

abdacate .... **abdicate**

abdatorium .... **abditorium**

abdecation .... **abdication**

abelism .... **ableism**

abetor .... **abettor**

abetter .... **abettor**

abgekt .... **abject****

abguration .... **abjuration**

abgure .... **abjure****

abjection overruled ....

.... **objection overruled**

abjeration .... **abjuration**

Incorrect	Correct	Incorrect	Correct
abjoor	**abjure****	acknolege	**acknowledge**
ablegate	**obligate**	ackochement	**accouchement**
abliterate	**obliterate**	ackoelo usque	**a coelo usque**
abloquy	**obloquy**	ackomadation	**accommodation**
abnagate	**abnegate**	ackompany	**accompany**
abolishion	**abolition**	ackompliss	**accomplice****
abovo	**ab ovo****	ackontrario	**a contrario**
abragate	**abrogate****	ackord	**accord**
abragation	**abrogation**	ackordince	**accordance**
abreviate	**abbreviate****	ackost	**accost**
abrige	**abridge**	ackount	**account**
abrigment	**abridgment**	ackounting	**accounting**
abrochement	**abroachment**	ackounts receivable	
or **abbroachment**			**accounts receivable**
absalute	**absolute**	ackrual method	**accrual method**
absenity	**obscenity**	ackrue	**accrue**
abserd	**absurd**	acksadental	**accidental**
absintee	**absentee**	ackseptance	**acceptance**
abskew	**absque**	acksepter	**acceptor**
abskew hock	**absque hoc**	acksesable	**accessible****
abskond	**abscond**	acksess	**access****
abstane	**abstain**	acksessability	**accessibility**
abstanence	**abstinence**	acksession	**accession**
abstraction of justice		acksessory	**accessory**
	obstruction of justice	ackshalize	**actualize**
abstruction	**obstruction**	ackshual	**actual**
abucive tax shelter		ackshuate	**actuate**
	abusive tax shelter	acksident	**accident**
a but	**abut**	acktionible	**actionable**
abuze	**abuse**	acktuary	**actuary**
abyuse	**abuse**	ackuiessence	**acquiescence**
abzolve	**absolve**	ackusation	**accusation**
acceed	**accede****	ackused	**accused**
accep	**accept****	ackusible	**accusable**
accesery	**accessory**	ackusor	**accuser**
accidently	**accidentally**	ackwaint	**acquaint**
accompanment	**accompaniment**	ackwaintince	**acquaintance**
accowntibility	**accountability**	ackwiesce	**acquiesce**
accrasy	**accuracy**	ackwit	**acquit**
accross	**across**	ackwittal	**acquittal**
accuman	**acumen**	aclaim	**acclaim****
accumenical	**ecumenical**	aclamate	**acclimate**
accur	**occur**	acomodate	**accommodate**
acent	**ascent****	acomplice	**accomplice****
acer	**acre**	acord	**accord**
acessed	**assessed**	acost	**accost**
acessor	**assessor**	acount	**account**
acheive	**achieve**	acountant	**accountant**
ackceleration	**acceleration**	acountable	**accountable**
ackcentuate	**accentuate**	acountible	**accountable**

Incorrect	Correct	Incorrect	Correct
acounts payible	**accounts payable**	addit	**adit****
acrage	**acreage**	addjudacate	**adjudicate**
acramony	**acrimony**	addjudacation	**adjudication**
acretion	**accretion**	addjudikatory	**adjudicatory**
acrost	**across**	addjunct	**adjunct**
acrual	**accrual**	addjuration	**adjuration**
acruel method	**accrual method**	addjust	**adjust**
acselerate	**accelerate**	addjustment	**adjustment**
acseleration clause		addjustor	**adjuster****
	acceleration clause	add lib	**ad lib**
acsessory during the act		add litem	**ad litem**
	accessory during the fact	addminister	**administer**
actavate	**activate****	addministeration	**administration**
actionible	**actionable**	addministrater	**administrator**
actis reuse	**actus reus**	addministrative	**administrative**
actus rayus	**actus reus**	addministratix	**administratrix**
acumalation	**accumulation**	addmirilty law	**admiralty law**
acumulate	**accumulate**	addmisability	**admissibility**
acurance	**occurrence**	addmissabel	**admissible**
acurate	**accurate**	addmission	**admission**
acusal	**accusal**	addmit	**admit**
acusant	**accusant**	addmitince	**admittance**
acusation	**accusation**	addmonatory	**admonitory**
acusatory	**accusatory**	addmonish	**admonish**
acuse	**accuse**	addmonishun	**admonition**
acused	**accused**	add nawseum	**ad nauseam**
acussatorial	**accusatorial**	addopt	**adopt****
adaquite	**adequate**	addoption	**adoption**
adaratus	**adiratus**	addoptive	**adoptive**
adater	**additur****	add prosequindam	
adative	**additive**		**ad prosequendam**
addalesent	**adolescent**	add queam	**ad quem**
addamant	**adamant**	add rectim	**ad rectum**
addamnam	**ad damnum**	add respondendim	
addapt	**adapt****		**ad respondendum**
add centrum	**ad centrum**	add sec	**ad seg**
add culpam	**ad culpam**	addult	**adult**
addcurium	**ad curiam**	addulteror	**adulterer**
add diem	**ad diem****	addulturate	**adulterate**
addemption	**ademption**	add valentium	**ad valentiam**
addemtion	**ademption**	add valorem tax	**ad valorem tax**
addept	**adept****	add valorim	**ad valorem**
addequate	**adequate**	addvance	**advance**
addherant	**adherent**	addvantage	**advantage**
addhere	**adhere**	addverce	**adverse****
addhesion	**adhesion**	addversery	**adversary**
add hock	**ad hoc**	addvertize	**advertise**
add hominum	**ad hominem**	addvertizement	**advertisement**
add infinitum	**ad infinitum**	addvice	**advice****
add interum	**ad interim**	addvisery	**advisory**

4

Incorrect	Correct
addvisidly	**advisedly**
addvocate	**advocate**
ade and abet	**aid and abet**
ademe	**adeem**
adenda	**addenda**
adendum	**addendum**
adgist	**agist****
adgust	**adjust**
adgustible	**adjustable**
adgustment	**adjustment**
adheer	**adhere**
adhock	**ad hoc**
adict	**addict****
adicted	**addicted**
adiment	**adamant**
adiposer	**adipocere**
adjasent	**adjacent**
adjern	**adjourn****
ad kulpam	**ad culpam**
adlay giary	**adlegiare**
ad lytem	**ad litem**
admended complaint	**amended complaint**
admended return	**amended return**
adminition	**admonition**
admision	**admission**
adresee	**addressee**
adress	**address**
ad sentrum	**ad centrum**
aduce	**adduce****
adultry	**adultery**
advakate	**advocate**
advisery	**advisory**
aerport	**airport**
aerspace	**airspace**
aethos	**ethos**
afadavit	**affidavit**
afair	**affair****
afare	**affaire****
afect	**affect****
afection	**affection**
afectus	**affectus**
aferism	**aphorism**
affadavit	**affidavit**
affermation	**affirmation**
afformentioned	**aforementioned**
afforsaid	**aforesaid**
afforshiori	**a fortiori**
afforthought	**aforethought**
affoul of	**afoul of**

Incorrect	Correct
Affrican-American	**African-American**
affter	**after**
afiant	**affiant**
afileation	**affiliation**
afilliate	**affiliate**
afinity	**affinity**
afirm	**affirm**
afirmative action	**affirmative action**
afix	**affix**
aflict	**afflict**
aforce	**afforce**
aformentioned	**aforementioned**
a forsheori	**a fortiori**
afraightment	**affreightment**
afranchise	**affranchise**
afray	**affray**
afront	**affront**
aftamath	**aftermath**
aftanoon	**afternoon**
aftarthought	**afterthought**
aftarwood	**afterward****
agensy bond	**agency bond**
aggainst	**against**
aggalma	**agalma**
aggency	**agency**
aggent	**agent**
aggervated	**aggravated**
aggio	**agio**
aggnomanation	**agnomination**
aggnomin	**agnomen**
aggotage	**agotage**
aggragate	**aggregate**
aggraphia	**agraphia**
aggree	**agree**
aggreed	**agreed**
aggreemint	**agreement**
aggreible	**agreeable**
aginst the law	**against the law**
agism	**ageism**
agnet	**agnate**
agrabusiness	**agribusiness**
agrafia	**agraphia**
agragate	**aggregate**
agrandize	**aggrandize**
agravated	**aggravated**
agreeved party	**aggrieved party**
agregation	**aggregation**
agreser	**aggressor**
agresive	**aggressive**

Incorrect	Correct	Incorrect	Correct
agression	**aggression****	aktion	**action****
agrieved	**aggrieved**	aktivate	**activate****
agust	**adjust**	aktus	**actus**
ahere	**adhere**	akwaint	**acquaint**
aijus	**aegis****	akwaintince	**acquaintance**
air-aparent	**heir apparent**	akwit	**acquit**
airess	**heiress**	alabi	**alibi**
airloom	**heirloom**	alacable	**allocable**
ajacent	**adjacent**	alagation	**allegation****
aje	**age**	alagraph	**allograph**
ajective law	**adjective law**	alagy	**allergy**
ajenda	**agenda**	alakation	**allocation****
ajent	**agent**	alamenta	**alimenta****
ajewdicate	**adjudicate**	alamony	**alimony**
ajinsy	**agency**	Alan Rule	**Allen Rule**
ajister	**agister** or **agistor****	alaquot	**aliquot**
ajoin	**adjoin****	alay	**allay****
ajournment	**adjournment****	alea	**alia****
ajudge	**adjudge**	aleamenter	**alimenta****
ajudicate	**adjudicate**	aleanate	**alienate**
ajudicater	**adjudicator**	aleanism	**alienism**
ajudication	**adjudication**	aleas	**alias**
ajunct	**adjunct**	aledge	**allege**
ajure	**adjure****	alegation	**allegation****
ajusted bases	**adjusted basis**	aleged	**alleged**
ajusted gross income		alegiance	**allegiance**
	adjusted gross income	alement	**ailment****
aker	**acre**	alergy	**allergy**
akkin	**akin**	aleviate	**alleviate**
akkwital	**acquittal**	alian	**alien**
akkwited	**acquitted**	alianage	**alienage**
aklame	**acclaim**	alianate	**alienate**
aknew	**anew**	aliance	**alliance**
aknowledge	**acknowledge**	aliatory	**aleatory**
akomadate	**accommodate**	alicable	**allocable**
aksadent	**accident**	alicution	**allocution**
akseed	**accede****	aligiance	**allegiance**
akselerate	**accelerate**	alinement	**alignment**
aksept	**accept****	alision	**allision****
akseptible	**acceptable**	alitter	**aliter****
aksess	**access****	aliviate	**alleviate**
aksessery	**accessory**	alkiholic	**alcoholic**
akshawary	**actuary**	alkohol	**alcohol**
akshionible	**actionable**	allacrity	**alacrity**
akshul	**actual**	alla giare	**allegiare**
akshun	**action****	allagy	**allergy**
aksident	**accident**	allarm	**alarm**
aksidently	**accidentally**	allbeat	**albeit**
aksiom	**axiom**	allcohol	**alcohol**
akt	**act**	allea	**alea****

Incorrect	Correct	Incorrect	Correct
alleanist	alienist	amakably	amicably
alleatory	aleatory	ambaguity	ambiguity
alledge	allege	ambalance	ambulance
alleinate	alienate	ambalate	ambulate
alleinor	alienor	ambegenic	ambigenic
allia	alia**	ambelence chaser	
allias	alias		ambulance chaser
allibi	alibi	amecks	AMEX
allien	alien	Ameracan	American
allienable	alienable	amertization	amortization
allienation	alienation	amikis kurea	amicus curiae
allienee	alienee	amiliaration	amelioration
allimenta	alimenta**	aminable	amenable
allimoney	alimony	aminible to law	amenable to law
allinment	alignment	aministrative law	
alliquot	aliquot		administrative law
alliter	aliter**	amissable	admissible
alli unde	aliunde	ammalgimation	amalgamation
alliundee	aliunde	ammalgum	amalgam
allive	alive	ammasculate	emasculate
allmaria	almaria	ammass	amass
all most	almost	ammbalatory	ambulatory
allogical	alogical**	ammbigguous	ambiguous
allott	allot**	ammbivilense	ambivalence
all teames hearez	ultimus haeres	ammblotic	amblotic
allter	alter**	ammbulence	ambulance
allteration	alteration**	ammeliorate	ameliorate
allter ego	alter ego**	ammenable	amenable
allternative minimum tax		ammend	amend**
	alternative minimum tax	ammendment	amendment
allternite	alternate	ammends	amends
allthough	although	ammenyouensis	amanuensis
allumna	alumna**	ammerce	amerce**
ally undi	aliunde	Ammerican	American
alocable	allocable	ammerse	amerce
alocation	allocation	ammertisable	amortizable
alodial	allodial	ammi	ami
alograph	allograph	ammicably	amicably
alokate	allocate	ammicus curea	amicus curiae
alonge	allonge	ammit	ambit
alot	allot**	ammnesty	amnesty
alotment	allotment	ammortize	amortize
alowance	allowance	ammotion	amotion**
alowe an appeal	allow an appeal	ammount	amount
alternitive pleading		ammplification	amplification
	alternative pleading	ammputate	amputate
alude	allude***	amoung	among
alusion	allusion**	amplafy	amplify
aluvio marris	alluvio maris	ampyatation	amputation**
aluvion	alluvion**	anafradisiac	anaphrodisiac

Incorrect	Correct
analasis	**analysis****
anals	**annals****
anamosity	**animosity**
anamus	**animus**
anatated	**annotated**
anaversery	**anniversary**
anceint	**ancient**
aneksation	**annexation**
anerky	**anarchy**
anex	**annex**
angagram	**angiogram**
angery	**angary****
angryly	**angrily**
angwish	**anguish**
anilize	**analyze****
annabollic steroid	**anabolic steroid**
annachronism	**anachronism**
annagraph	**anagraph**
annalagous	**analogous**
annalize	**analyze****
annalogy	**analogy**
annasthesea	**anesthesia**
annatation	**annotation**
annathema	**anathema**
annatomical	**anatomical**
anncestor	**ancestor**
anncillary	**ancillary**
annecdotal	**anecdotal**
annestholigist	**anesthesiologist**
annguish	**anguish**
annimosity	**animosity**
annimus	**animus**
annomaly	**anomaly**
annserable	**answerable**
anntagonize	**antagonize**
anntecedent	**antecedent**
anntedate	**antedate****
anntethisis	**antithesis**
annthrakosis	**anthracosis**
annthroppometry	**anthropometry**
annticipation	**anticipation**
anntisipitory	**anticipatory**
ano Domino	**anno Domini**
anologous	**analogous**
anology	**analogy****
anomolous	**anomalous**
anonimous	**anonymous**
anotated	**annotated**
anounced	**announced**
anouncement	**announcement**

Incorrect	Correct
anoyance	**annoyance**
ansellary	**ancillary**
anser	**answer**
ansester	**ancestor**
anshent	**ancient**
ansilery	**ancillary**
ansillery	**ancillary**
antadate	**antedate****
antadote	**antidote****
antasedent	**antecedent**
antebiotic	**antibiotic**
antedote	**antidote****
antesedant	**antecedent**
antetakeover	**antitakeover**
antetrust	**antitrust**
antimortum	**ante mortem**
antinates	**ante natus**
antinupshial	**antenuptial**
anti status quo	**ante status quo**
anual	**annual****
anuitant	**annuitant**
anuitty	**annuity**
anulled	**annulled**
anulment	**annulment**
anurism	**aneurism**
anus mirabilius	**annus mirabilis**
anuties	**annuities**
apalogy	**apology**
aparatus	**apparatus**
aparel	**apparel**
aparent	**apparent**
aparently	**apparently**
apeal	**appeal**
apear	**appear**
apelate	**appellate**
apelent	**appellant**
apellent	**appellant**
apellite	**appellate**
apend	**append**
apendage	**appendage**
apendent	**appendant**
apendises	**appendices**
apendix	**appendix**
apertain	**appertain**
apinage	**apanage** or **appanage**
aplacable	**applicable**
aplacant	**applicant**
aplacation	**application**
aplicant	**applicant**
aply	**apply**

Incorrect	Correct	Incorrect	Correct
apoint	**appoint**	arbitraitor	**arbitrator**
apointment	**appointment**	arbitter	**arbiter****
apointy	**appointee**	arearage	**arrearage**
aportion	**apportion**	areers	**arrears****
aportionment	**apportionment**	areeway	**areaway**
aposite	**apposite****	arender	**a rendre**
apostireori	**a posteriori**	arest	**arrest**
appais	**a pais****	areway	**airway**
appartment	**apartment**	argament	**argument**
appeel	**appeal**	argoomentative	**argumentative**
appeerance	**appearance**	argueable	**arguable**
appertinance	**appurtenance**	argueing	**arguing**
appikal	**apical**	argyuable	**arguable**
applee	**appellee**	arival	**arrival**
appogee	**apogee**	arkives	**archives**
appogian tides	**apogean tides**	arms length	**arm's length**
appologia	**apologia****	arogate	**arrogate****
apposteriori	**a posteriori**	arogation	**arrogation**
apprachsia	**apraxia**	arrbitor	**arbiter****
apprender	**a prendre**	arrea	**area****
appropo	**apropos**	arrere	**arere****
apraisal	**appraisal**	arrgue	**argue****
apraise	**appraise****	arrguendo	**arguendo**
apraisel	**appraisal**	arribitration	**arbitration**
aprehention	**apprehension**	arrticle	**article**
apreori	**a priori**	arrtificial persin	**artificial person**
aprize	**apprise****	arsen	**arson**
aproach	**approach**	artaficial	**artificial**
aprobation	**approbation**	artafise	**artifice**
aproove	**approve**	artikle	**article**
apropreation	**appropriation**	asail	**assail**
apropriate	**appropriate**	asailant	**assailant**
aproval	**approval**	asailible	**assailable**
aproximate	**approximate**	asaled	**assailed**
aproxximate	**approximate**	asault	**assault**
apurtain	**appertain**	asay	**assay****
apurtenance	**appurtenance**	asemble	**assemble**
aqo	**a quo**	asembly	**assembly**
aquire	**acquire**	asembly-man	**assemblyman**
aquit	**acquit**	asembly-woman	**assemblywoman**
araign	**arraign****	asennt	**ascent****
arainment	**arraignment**	asent	**assent****
arangement	**arrangement**	asert	**assert**
aray	**array**	asesment	**assessment**
arbatrage	**arbitrage**	asesment of deficiency	
arbatrajure	**arbitrageur**		**assessment of deficiency**
arbatramint	**arbitrament**	asesor	**assessor**
arbatration	**arbitration**	asess	**assess****
arbatrery	**arbitrary**	asesser	**assessor**
arbatrible	**arbitrable**	asessible	**assessable****

Incorrect	Correct	Incorrect	Correct
asets	assets	atester	attestor
aseverration	asseveration	atipical	atypical
asfyxia	asphyxia	atorn	attorn
ashure	assure**	atorney	attorney
ashurence	assurance**	atorney at law	attorney at law
asign	assign	atrabution	attribution
asignee	assignee	atribute	attribute
asine	assign	atrition	attrition
asinement	assignment	atroshus assault	atrocious assault
asines	assigns	attackted	attacked
asis	as is	attrotious	atrocious
asist	assist	aturn	attorn
asistent	assistant	audater	auditor**
asize	assize	auddit	audit**
asizer	assiser or assisor	audditer querela	audita querela
asociate	associate	autamobile	automobile
asociation	association	auter	autre**
assalt	assault	autharise	authorize
asscribe	ascribe	autharity	authority
assendants	ascendants	authentisity	authenticity
assertain	ascertain	auther	author**
assertane	ascertain	auto-optic evidence	
assessory	accessory		autoptic evidence
assessory before the fact		auxilary	auxiliary
	accessory before the fact	averrment	averment
assinine	asinine	aversarial	adversarial
asspect	aspect	aversary procseeding	
assperse	asperse		adversary proceeding
asspursion	aspersion	avertion	aversion**
asstipulation	astipulation	avincullo matrimonio	
asume	assume		a vinculo matrimonii
asumsit	assumpsit	avisement	advisement
asumtion	assumption	avisery	advisory
asurance	assurance**	avocacy	advocacy
asurtion	assertion	avocate	advocate
atach	attach**	avoidince	avoidance
atachment	attachment	avowch	avouch
atain	attain	avowel	avowal
atainder	attainder	avrage	average
ataint	attaint	avrage daily volume	
atak	attack**		average daily volume
atendent	attendant	avvails	avails
atenneris annus	a teneris annis	avvatar	avatar
aterm	a terme	avvenge	avenge
atern	attorn	avver	aver**
aterney	attorney	avverse	averse**
aterney in fact	attorney in fact	avversio	aversio**
aterny genral	attorney general	avversion	aversion**
atest	attest	avvocacy	advocacy
atestation	attestation	avvoid	avoid**

avvouch .... **avouch**
avvow .... **avow**
avvulsion .... **avulsion**
avvuncular .... **avuncular**
awate .... **await**
awdit .... **audit****
awfering .... **offering**
awktion .... **auction****
awsome .... **awesome**
awspices .... **auspices**
awthenic .... **authentic**
awthenticate .... **authenticate**

awthoratative .... **authoritative**
awtomatic .... **automatic**
awtonomous .... **autonomous**
awtopsy .... **autopsy**
awtoptik preference ....
.... **autoptic proference**
awward .... **award**
axidentally .... **accidentally**
axted .... **asked**
ayewitness .... **eyewitness**
ayl .... **ail**

B

baclog .... **backlog**
baile .... **bail****
bairer .... **bearer**
bakdating .... **backdating**
bakking .... **backing**
bak pay award .... **backpay award**
balable .... **bailable**
bale bond .... **bail bond**
baleeger .... **beleaguer**
baleiff .... **bailiff**
balement .... **bailment**
balence sheet .... **balance sheet**
baler .... **bailor**
balince .... **balance**
balistics .... **ballistics**
ballance .... **balance**
balliff .... **bailiff**
baloon .... **balloon**
baloon payment ...... **balloon payment**
balot .... **ballot**
bancrupt .... **bankrupt**
bancruptsy .... **bankruptcy**
bank reconsilliation ....
.... **bank reconciliation**
bann .... **ban****
banndit .... **bandit**
bannishment .... **banishment**
bannker .... **banker**
bannkruptsy .... **bankruptcy**
barator .... **barrator**
bare false witness . **bear false witness**
bare market .... **bear market**
barer bond .... **bearer bond**

baretry .... **barratry**
barginor .... **bargainor**
barier .... **barrier**
barister .... **barrister**
baritrous .... **barratrous**
barr .... **bar**
barr asociation .... **bar association**
barrbiterate .... **barbiturate**
barrd .... **barred**
barrgin .... **bargain**
bartir .... **barter**
basless .... **baseless**
basse .... **base****
basses .... **bases****
bassmen .... **basement**
basstard .... **bastard**
bate and switch .... **bait and switch**
batel .... **battel****
bater .... **barter**
batered .... **battered**
battary .... **battery**
baught .... **bought**
bawble .... **bauble**
bawk .... **balk**
bawrn .... **born****
bawwed .... **bawd****
baylee .... **bailee**
baysis .... **basis****
bayt .... **bait****
beaper .... **beeper**
beedel .... **bedel**
beefall .... **befall**
beefiting .... **befitting**

Incorrect	Correct	Incorrect	Correct
beefudle	befuddle	berreft	bereft
beegoten	begotten	berrer	bearer
beegruge	begrudge	berrserk	berserk
beehaf	behalf	bersa	bursa**
beehavier	behavior	bersar	bursar**
beehoof	behoof**	berth name	birth name
beelbrief	bielbrief	berthright	birthright
beens	biens**	bery	bury**
beequeeth	bequeath	beserk	berserk
beequest	bequest	besstow	bestow
beesech	beseech**	beterment	betterment
beesteality	bestiality	bet nwar	bête noir
beeyond	beyond	bettrothed	betrothed
befiting	befitting	bevrage	beverage
beger	beggar	bezoin	besoin
begget	beget**	biadegradible	biodegradable
beggin	begin	bidd	bid
begile	beguile	bidd and axed	bid and asked
begining inventory		bideing	bidding**
	beginning inventory	bider	bidder
behoovs	behooves**	big bored	Big Board
bekweeth	bequeath	biggamist	bigamist
beleaf	belief**	biggamy	bigamy
belicose	bellicose	biggot	bigot**
beligerent	belligerent	bigimist	bigamist
bellong	belong	bigimy	bigamy
belum	bellum	bilabor	belabor
bely	belie**	bi-laws	by-laws
benafactor	benefactor	bilder	builder
benaficial	beneficial	bilding	building
benifice	benefice	bilible	billable
benificiary	beneficiary	bilings	billings
benifishal	beneficial	billbos	bilboes
benifishery	beneficiary	bill of rites	Bill of Rights
benifit	benefit	bill of writes	Bill of Rights
bennaficial	beneficial	bined	bind
bennch	bench	bineding	binding
bennefishiary	beneficiary	binery	binary
bennefit	benefit	bioppsy	biopsy
bennevolense	benevolence	bisare	bizarre**
berden	burden	bisness	business
berden of prufe	burden of proof	biss	bis
bergage	burgage	bi-stander	bystander
bergess	burgess	bistowel	bestowal
bergler	burglar	blackmale	blackmail
berglery	burglary	blaim the victim	blame the victim
berial	burial	blaklist	blacklist
berking	burking	blakmale	blackmail
bern	burn**	blakout	blackout
bernout	burnout	blamless	blameless

Incorrect	Correct	Incorrect	Correct
blamme	blame	boredello	bordello
blan	bilan	bored of directors	
blanc	blank		board of directors
blancket	blanket	borow	borrow**
blassfemy	blasphemy	borower	borrower
blaytint	blatant	borrochium	burrochium
bleas	blees	borrough	borough**
bletter	bleta	bote	boat
blew coller	blue-collar**	bottim line	bottom line
blew law	blue law	boundery	boundary
blew ribbon jury	blue-ribbon jury	boundry	boundary
blew-sky law	blue sky laws	bouy	buoy**
bline trust	blind trust	bownd	bound
block voting	bloc voting	bownds	bounds
blod	blood	bowwels	bowels
blodgion	bludgeon	boxs	boxes
blok	block**	boycot	boycott
blokige	blockage	boyleroom	boiler-room
bloo-sky	blue-sky	boylerplate	boilerplate
blu-chip stock	blue-chip stock	brakage	breakage
bluf	bluff	braket	bracket
blumber	blumba	brake the law	break the law
blunnder	blunder	braking and entering	
blu-sky	blue-sky		breaking and entering
blyte	blight	brandise brief	Brandeis brief
boader	boarder**	brane	brain
bocks	box	brawd	broad**
boddly	bodily	brawdcast	broadcast
boddy	body	brawt	brought**
bodely	bodily	breatch	breach**
boggus	bogus	breef	brief**
boilerplait	boilerplate	breesh	breach
boilery	boilary	breevea	brevia
boledface	boldface	breeveate	breviate**
bonis	bonus	breth	breath**
boniss	bonus	brethalyser	breathalyzer
bonna	bona**	brethern	brethren
bonnded	bonded	brev	breve**
bonned	bond	brevvet	brevet
bonnedholder	bondholder	brevvity	brevity
bonnification	bonification	bribary	bribery
bonnus	bonus	brieb	bribe
bonsman	bondsman**	brillant	brilliant
booddle	boodle	broche	broach**
bookeeping	bookkeeping	brocken	broken
bookt	booked	brocker	broker
booky	bookie	brockerige	brokerage**
boorse	bourse**	brokage	brocage**
bootey	booty	brootum foolmen	brutum fulmen
bord	board**	broshur	brochure

Incorrect	Correct
brude	**brood**
bruse	**bruise****
bruther	**brother**
brutilise	**brutalize**
brybe	**bribe**
bryberry	**bribery**
buchel	**bushel**
budjet	**budget**
bufer	**buffer**
bugery	**buggery**
buget	**budget**
buglary	**burglary**
buillding	**building**
bul	**bull**
bulc	**bulk**
bulet	**bullet**
buletin	**bulletin**
bulion	**bullion****
bunedoggle	**boondoggle**
bunko	**bunco**
bunndle	**bundle**
burdin	**burden**

Incorrect	Correct
burreau	**bureau****
burrocracy	**bureaucracy**
burth	**berth****
busness	**business**
busyness	**business**
buted	**butted**
butress	**buttress**
buttles	**buttals**
buty	**booty**
buylaws	**by-laws**
buyproduct	**byproduct**
byannual	**biannual****
byas	**bias**
byelaws	**by-laws**
byer	**buyer**
byestander	**bystander**
bylateral	**bilateral**
byoethics	**bioethics**
byopsy	**biopsy**
bysexual	**bisexual**
byureau	**bureau****

C

Incorrect	Correct
cabanet	**cabinet**
cabatage	**cabotage**
cabbal	**cabal****
cabbinet	**cabinet**
cabel	**cable****
cach	**cache****
cadacarry	**caducary**
caddaster	**cadaster** or **cadastre**
caddaver	**cadaver**
caddere	**cadere**
caddit	**cadit****
caducer	**caduca**
cagole	**cajole**
calable	**callable**
calamy	**calumny**
caling	**calling**
callamity	**calamity**
callculate	**calculate**
callender	**calendar****
callible	**callable**
callumneator	**calumniator**
calsify	**calcify**
calumy	**calumny**

Incorrect	Correct
cammber	**camber**
cammeral	**cameral**
cammpanile	**campanile**
camoflage	**camouflage**
campane	**campaign**
camponarium	**campanarium**
camra	**camera**
canabis	**cannabis**
cancilation	**cancellation**
cander	**candor**
canen	**canon****
cannard	**canard**
canncel	**cancel**
cannonical	**canonical**
canntel	**cantel** or **cantle**
canntered	**cantered** or **cantred**
canntred	**cantered** or **cantred**
cannvas	**canvas****
cansel	**cancel**
canselation	**cancellation**
canseled	**cancelled**
canselled	**cancelled**
capatilization	**capitalization**

Incorrect	Correct	Incorrect	Correct
capital hill	**Capitol Hill**	casuality	**casualty ****
capitol crime	**capital crime**	catagorical	**categorical**
capitol gane	**capital gain**	cathater	**catheter**
capitta	**capita****	catlick	**Catholic****
cappability	**capability**	cattals	**catals**
cappacity	**capacity**	cattastrophe	**catastrophe**
cappias	**capias**	cattegorical	**categorical**
cappiater pro fine	**capiatur pro fine**	CATT scan	**CAT scan**
cappilary	**capillary**	caushin	**caution**
cappita	**capita****	cauzal	**causal****
cappital	**capital****	cauzality	**causality****
cappitula	**capitula**	cauze celebre	**causes célèbres**
cappricious	**capricious**	caviat	**caveat**
cappstone	**capstone**	cavver	**cavere**
capptation	**captation****	cavviator	**caveator**
capption	**caption****	cawcus	**caucus**
capshon	**caption****	cawsa	**causa****
caracter	**character**	cawsidicus	**causidicus**
caracter witness	**character witness**	caws-list	**causelist**
cardeogram	**cardiogram**	caws of action	**cause of action**
carees	**caries****	cawtion	**caution**
carier	**carrier****	caypax	**capax**
carless	**careless**	cayse law	**case law**
carrcanum	**carcanum**	cazual	**casual****
carrcatus	**carcatus**	cedition	**sedition**
carrcinogen	**carcinogen**	cedwee	**cestui**
carrdeopullmonery		ceed	**cede****
	cardiopulmonary	ceepi	**cepi**
carrdeovasscular	**cardiovascular**	ceera	**cera**
carrdiak	**cardiac**	ceese	**cease****
carrdiology	**cardiology**	ceizure	**seizure**
carrer	**career****	cellabate	**celibate****
carrgo	**cargo**	cellation	**celation**
carrnal	**carnal****	cell short	**sell short**
carrpay deem	**carpe diem**	cemical	**chemical**
carrta	**carta****	cemmetary	**cemetery**
carrucate	**carucate**	cenneguild	**cenegild**
carsinoma	**carcinoma**	cennsus	**census****
cartell	**cartel**	cenntal	**cental**
cary	**carry**	censership	**censorship**
casalties	**casualties**	censitive	**sensitive**
casare	**cassare**	cepeena	**subpoena**
caselode	**caseload**	ceppit	**cepit**
cash disbersement		ceptum	**septum**
	cash disbursement	cerca	**circa**
casher	**cashier**	cerch	**search**
casse	**case**	cercle	**circle**
cass forrtut	**cas fortuit**	cercuit	**circuit**
cassuistry	**casuistry**	cercumstances	**circumstances**
cassus	**casus**	cerkit	**circuit**

Incorrect	Correct
cerkit court	**circuit court**
cerrcumstantial	**circumstantial**
cerrtafiable	**certifiable**
cerrtain	**certain**
cerrtificate	**certificate**
cerrtified	**certified**
cerrtiorarri	**certiorari**
certacy	**courtesy****
certail	**curtail**
certin	**certain**
cerver	**server**
cerverence	**severance**
cesare	**cessare**
cesation	**cessation****
cesion	**cession****
cesment	**cessment**
cessions	**sessions**
ceterorim	**caeterorum**
chaccer	**chacer****
chaine	**chain**
chalenge	**challenge**
chameber	**chamber**
chammfer	**chamfer**
chammperty	**champerty**
chamot	**chamotte**
chanel	**channel**
channcer	**chancer****
chanseler	**chancellor**
chansery	**chancery****
chappter	**chapter**
chaptir 11	**Chapter 11**
charatible	**charitable**
chare	**chair**
chareman	**chairman**
chareperson	**chairperson**
charewoman	**chairwoman**
charg	**charge**
chargable	**chargeable**
chargoff	**charge-off**
charicterise	**characterize**
chark repellant	**shark repellent**
charrta	**charta****
chasstity	**chastity**
chastize	**chastise**
chatel	**chattel**
chattle	**chattel**
cheef executive	**chief executive**
cheepp	**cheap**
cheet	**cheat**
cheif	**chief****

Incorrect	Correct
chek	**check**
cheperdize	**shepardize**
Chepperds Sitations	**Shepard's Citations**
cherch	**church**
cheriff	**sheriff**
chern	**churn**
chickana	**Chicana**
chikano	**Chicano**
chiling	**chilling**
chiling effect	**chilling effect**
chort sail	**short sale**
chote leen	**choate lien**
choze	**chose****
chrive	**shrive**
churchs	**churches**
cickatricks	**cicatrix**
ciclical	**cyclical**
cinebot	**cynebote****
cinguler	**singular****
cinical	**cynical**
cirkumspect	**circumspect**
cirosis	**cirrhosis**
cirrcular	**circular**
cirrcumscribe	**circumscribe**
cirrcutous	**circuitous**
cirtax	**surtax**
cissed	**cyst**
cissta	**cista**
cittation	**citation**
cittizen	**citizen**
citty	**city**
citus	**situs**
civilan	**civilian**
civil liberty's	**civil liberties**
civvic	**civic**
civvil	**civil**
civvilius	**civilis**
clamant	**claimant**
clame	**claim**
clames	**claims**
clanish	**clannish**
clas	**class**
clauze	**clause****
clawsum	**clausum**
clayment	**claimant**
cleen	**clean**
cleeque	**clique****
cleer	**clear**
cleerence	**clearance**

Incorrect	Correct	Incorrect	Correct
cleeringhouse	**clearinghouse** or **clearing-house**	colaborration	**collaboration**
cleering house	**clearinghouse** or **clearing-house**	colapsible	**collapsible**
		colateral	**collateral**
cleint	**client**	colateral trust	**collateral trust**
clemancy	**clemency**	colatio	**collatio****
clemansy	**clemency**	colect	**collect**
cleore	**cloere**	colide	**collide**
cleptomania	**kleptomania**	colizion	**collision****
clientell	**clientele**	collibertus	**colibertus**
clinnic	**clinic****	collne	**colne**
clochure	**cloture****	collor	**color****
cloo	**clue****	collpises	**colpices**
clowd of suspicion	**cloud of suspicion**	colokate	**collocate****
		colpible	**culpable**
clowd on title	**cloud on title**	columnia	**calumnia**
clozed end	**closed-end**	colusion	**collusion****
clozing	**closing**	colyum	**column**
clurk	**clerk**	comand	**command****
clyent	**client**	comcommitant	**concomitant**
clyentele	**clientela**	comecks	**Comex**
coaddjuter	**coadjutor**	comence	**commence**
co-air	**co-heir**	comendation	**commendation**
cobliger	**co-obligor**	comenserate	**commensurate**
coconnspirator	**co-conspirator**	coment	**comment****
coddex	**codex**	comerce	**commerce**
coddification	**codification**	comersial	**commercial**
coddisil	**codicil**	comess and deffends	**comes and defends**
codefy	**codify**		
codeification	**codification**	comety	**comity****
codesil	**codicil**	comingle	**commingle**
codisilery	**codicillary**	comingling of funds	**commingling of funds**
coeequal	**coequal**		
coegsecutor	**coexecutor**	cominute	**comminute**
coehabit	**cohabit**	comission	**commission**
coejudicis	**cojudices**	comit	**commit****
coelition	**coalition**	comital	**committal**
coemmption	**coemption**	comitatur	**committitur**
coensurance	**coinsurance**	comitment	**commitment**
coerese	**coerce**	commbarrones	**combarones**
coerl	**ceorl**	commbination	**combination**
coerrtion	**coercion**	commbustable	**combustible**
cofer	**coffer**	commbustio	**combustio**
coggnitio	**cognitio****	commdomminum	**condominium**
coggnitiones	**cognitiones****	commin law	**common law**
co-hair	**co-heir**	commin stock	**common stock**
cohearance	**coherence**	commitatus	**comitatus**
coinsidance	**coincidence**	commitee of the hole	**committee of the whole**
coittus	**coitus**		
cokaine	**cocaine**	commites	**comites****
		commitisa	**comitissa**

Incorrect	Correct	Incorrect	Correct
commitiva	**comitiva**	comtestamento	
commity	**comity****	.... **cum testamento annexo**	
commpact	**compact**	comtroller	**comptroller****
commparitive	**comparative**	comune	**commune****
commpel	**compel**	comunibusanis	**communibus annis**
commpensate	**compensate**	comunication	**communication**
commpensible	**compensable**	comunis	**communis****
commpergater	**compurgator**	comunitasregne angeliae	
commperut ad deem		.... **communitas regni Angliae**	
.... **comperuit ad diem**		comunity	**community**
commpetant	**competent**	comunity property	
commpetition	**competition**	.... **community property**	
commpilation	**compilation**	comutate	**commutate**
commplainant	**complainant**	comutation	**commutation**
commplaint	**complaint**	conate	**connate**
commplement	**complement****	concanguinious	**consanguineous**
commplisity	**complicity**	conceed	**concede****
commply	**comply**	concensual	**consensual**
commposition	**composition**	concensus	**consensus****
commpound	**compound**	concensus add idem	
commprehensive	**comprehensive**	.... **consensus ad idem**	
commprize	**comprise**	concent	**consent**
commpromize	**compromise**	concerrance	**concurrence**
commpullsion	**compulsion**	concervater	**conservator**
commpulsa	**compulsa**	concideration	**consideration**
commpulsery	**compulsory**	conciderrater	**consideratur**
commpunktion	**compunction**	concilum	**consilium**
commputer	**computer**	concist	**consist**
commputis	**computus**	concistry	**consistory**
commputtation	**computation**	concklusive	**conclusive**
comodatum	**commodatum**	concubbiant	**concubeant**
comodities	**commodities**	concurant jurisdiction	
comodity	**commodity**	.... **concurrent jurisdiction**	
comon	**common****	concurant sentenses	
comonality	**commonalty****	.... **concurrent sentences**	
comoneer	**cum onere**	concurent power ...	**concurrent power**
comorintes	**commorientes**	concurr	**concur****
comotion	**commotion**	condenation	**condonation**
compatable	**compatible**	condine	**condign**
compatent party	**competent party**	condum	**condom****
compencitry	**compensatory**	conduse	**conduce**
compennsitory	**compensatory**	conect	**connect**
compergation	**compurgation**	confadential	**confidential**
compis mentus	**compos mentis**	conferance committee	
compis sue	**compos sui**	.... **conference committee**	
complaynent	**complainant**	confering	**conferring**
compleet	**complete**	confermed	**confirmed**
complie	**comply**	conferrance	**conference**
complyence	**compliance**	confeshion	**confession****
comppatint	**competent**	confeso	**confessio****

Incorrect	Correct	Incorrect	Correct
confisscater	confiscator	connsecutive	consecutive
conflickt of interest		connsent	consent
	conflict of interest	connseption	conception
confort	comfort	connsequence	consequence
confrares	confreres	connservater	conservator
congable	congeable	connsider	consider
congectio	conjectio	connsideration	consideration
congradulate	congratulate	connsinment	consignment
congresman	congressman	connsolidate	consolidate
congreswoman	congresswoman	connsonent	consonant
Congriss	Congress	connsortium	consortium
congrus	congruous	connspirasy	conspiracy
conivance	connivance	connstitutional	constitutional
conivence	connivance	connstraint	constraint
conjegal rites	conjugal rights	connstrew	construe
conjenital	congenital	connstruct	construct
conkussion	concussion	connstructive	constructive
connclude	conclude	connstuprat	constuprate
conncretion	concretion	connsultation	consultation
conncur	concur**	connsumate	consummate
conncurso	concurso	connsumer	consumer
conndem	condemn**	conntamanated	contaminated
conndictio	condictio**	conntango	contango
conndition	condition	conntemp	contempt**
connditionel	conditional	conntemplate	contemplate
conndon	condone	conntenchious	contentious
connduct	conduct	conntents	contents
connfabbulate	confabulate	conntest	contest**
connferrence	conference	conntigous	contiguous
connfes	confess**	conntinando	continuando
connfiguration	configuration	conntingency	contingency
connfinement	confinement	conntingent fee	contingent fee
connfirm	confirm	conntra	contra
connfirmatio	confirmatio**	conntrac	contract
connfiscate	confiscate	conntracter	contractor
connflict	conflict	conntradick	contradict
connformed	conformed	conntramandatio	contramandatio
connfrary	confrairie	conntramanndatim	
connfrontation	confrontation		contramandatum
connfute	confute	conntrapossition	contraposition
conngecture	conjecture	conntrary	contrary
connglommerate	conglomerate	conntravene	contravene
conngreggate	congregate	conntrefacto	contrafactio
conngress	congress	conntribbute	contribute
connjagal	conjugal	conntrite	contrite
connjoints	conjoints	conntrol	control
connjunction	conjunction	conntryvince	contrivance
connjurato	conjuratio	conntumax	contumax
connkoct	concoct	conntumely	contumely
connsanguinaty	consanguinity	connvaluted	convoluted

Incorrect	Correct	Incorrect	Correct
connvayance	conveyance	continum	continuum**
connveen	convene	contractato	contrectatio
connvention	convention	contrarywize	contrariwise
connversation	conversation	contravert	controvert
connversion	conversion	contreligato	contraligatio
connvertable	convertible	contreplaccitium	contraplacitum
connvey	convey**	contribatory	contributory
connvick	convict	contribatory negligence	
connvivium	convivium		contributory negligence
connvurge	converge	contribbutary	contributory
consealed	concealed	controled substence	
consealment	concealment		controlled substance
conseentous	conscientious	controll	control
consekwential damages		contusion	contusion
	consequential damages	conubial	connubial
conselor	counselor**	convayence	conveyance
consenses	consensus**	conveen	convene
consern	concern	conveenent	convenient
consert	concert	convenent	convenient
consesi	concessi	convursant	conversant
consesit sollver	concessit solvere	convurtable	convertible
consession	concession	conyusant	conusant
consessum	concessum	coolling-off	cooling-off
consessus	concessus**	coop detat	coup d'état
conshence	conscience	coopon	coupon
considrable	considerable	cooppertio	coopertio
consilabilum	conciliabulum	cooshant	couchant
consileation	conciliation	copa	coppa
consilum	concilium	coperate	cooperate
consine	consign**	copertus	coopertus
consious	conscious**	copiwrite	copyright
consirveter	conservator	coppartner	copartner
conspirsy	conspiracy	coppesmate	copesmate
constatt	constat**	coppralallia	coprolalia
construktion	construction	copprinciple	coprincipal
constudoe	consuetudo	coppula	copula
consul generals	consuls general	coppy	copy
consulman	councilman	coppywrite	copyright
consulwoman	councilwoman	copullate	copulate
consutudins	consuetudines	corall	corral
contajious	contagious	corect	correct
contamasy	contumacy**	corectional	correctional
contemer	contemner or contemnor	corelative	correlative
contemp	contempt**	corepis juris	corpus juris
contemt	contempt**	corespondince	correspondence**
contermand	countermand	coresspondant	co-respondent**
continnjent	contingent	coreum jewdice	coram judice
continnuence	continuance**	coreum nobiss	coram nobis
continuence	continuance**	corobborate	corroborate
continuly	continually	corperate	corporate

Incorrect	Correct	Incorrect	Correct
corpis delecti	**corpus delicti**	covinent	**covenant**
corpis jewris	**corpus juris**	covvenant	**covenant**
corppis	**corpus****	covvenenter	**covenantor**
corram	**coram**	covvert	**covert****
correnor	**coroner****	covverup	**cover-up****
corrner	**corner****	cownciler	**councilor****
corrodio habbendo		cownsellor	**counselor****
	corodio habendo	cownterclaim	**counterclaim**
corrolary	**corollary**	cowntermand	**countermand**
corrolery	**corollary**	cownteroffer	**counteroffer**
corroner	**coroner****	cownterplea	**counterplea**
corrperation	**corporation**	cownterplee	**counterplea**
corrporate	**corporate**	cowntersine	**countersign**
corrporeel	**corporeal****	co-xist	**coexist**
corrpse	**corpse****	crannage	**cranage**
corrtis	**cortis**	crannium	**cranium**
corse	**course****	crasy	**crazy**
corsor	**cursor****	cravven	**craven**
cort	**court**	cread	**creed****
corupt	**corrupt**	credable	**credible****
cosher	**kosher**	creddentials	**credentials**
cosignee	**co-assignee**	creddibility	**credibility**
cosignitory	**cosignatory**	creddit	**credit**
cossa nostre	**Cosa Nostra**	crediter	**creditor**
cossenage	**cosenage** or **cosinage**	creeate	**create**
cossignatory	**cosignatory**	creedense	**credence**
cossts	**costs**	creetin	**cretin**
cost acounting	**cost accounting**	cremmate	**cremate**
cotarrius	**cotarius**	creppusculim	**crepusculum**
coton	**cotton**	creulty	**cruelty**
cottenency	**cotenancy**	crie de paiss	
cotterminous	**conterminous**		**cri de pais** or **cry de pais**
or **coterminous**		crimenality	**criminality**
cottsettus	**cotsetus**	crimme	**crime**
coud	**could**	crimmen	**crimen**
counciler at law	**counselor-at-law**	crimminal	**criminal**
counntafeet	**counterfeit**	crimminatory	**criminatory**
counnterclaim	**counterclaim**	crimminology	**criminology**
counnty	**county**	crimnal	**criminal**
couns	**counts**	crimnal liability	**criminal liability**
counsil	**council****	cripta	**crypta**
countavale	**countervail**	crissen	**christen****
counterband	**contraband**	crissis	**crisis****
co-up	**co-op****	critasize	**criticize**
courcion	**coercion**	critcism	**criticism**
courrier	**courier****	critterion	**criterion**
courselet	**corselet**	crittic	**critic****
coursepresent	**corse-present**	cromasome	**chromosome**
courtis	**curtis**	cromosome	**chromosome**
covanent	**covenant**	croney	**crony**

Incorrect	Correct	Incorrect	Correct
cronic	**chronic**	cumpensation	**compensation**
crookd	**crooked**	cumpliance	**compliance**
cros	**cross****	cumpound	**compound**
crosclame	**cross-claim**	cumprize	**comprise**
cros-egsamination		cundemnatory	**condemnatory**
	cross-examination	cunglomerate	**conglomerate**
cros-interogatory		cunilungus	**cunnilingus**
	cross interrogatory	cunpergation	**compurgation**
cross-commplaint	**cross-complaint**	cunspirecy	**conspiracy**
crost-exsamination		cunstitutional	**constitutional**
	cross-examination	curant asets	**current assets**
crotier	**croiteir**	curency	**currency**
croun	**crown**	curent	**current**
cruce siggnati	**cruce signati**	curent liabilities	**current liabilities**
cruck	**crook**	curent rashio	**current ratio**
crule	**cruel****	curit quatuor peddibus	
cry de paiss			**currit quatuor pedibus**
	cri de pais or **cry de pais**	currative	**curative**
cryer	**crier**	currator	**curator**
cuesip number	**CUSIP number**	curratricks	**curatrix**
cuhoots	**cahoots**	curre	**cure****
cukold	**cuckold**	currensy	**currency**
cuk the evidense	**cook the evidence**	curria	**curia****
cull de sack	**cul de sac**	currtilium	**curtillium**
cullective	**collective**	cursery	**cursory****
cullminate	**culminate**	cusin	**cousin****
cullpa	**culpa**	cussip number	**CUSIP number**
cullprit	**culprit**	cusstedy	**custody**
culltavate	**cultivate**	cusstodial	**custodial**
cullusion	**collusion****	cusstodian	**custodian**
culpebillity	**culpability**	cusstody	**custody**
cumfort	**comfort**	cusstom	**custom****
cumm coopula	**cum copula**	cusstos	**custos**
cummorth	**commorth** or **comorth**	cusstuma	**custuma**
cummulative	**cumulative**	custimary	**customary**
cummunity	**community**	custim's duty	**custom duties**
cumpany	**company**	cuttanious	**cutaneous**
cumpatable	**compatible**	cuy bono	**cui bono**
cumpendium	**compendium**	cypher	**cipher**

D

Incorrect	Correct	Incorrect	Correct
daliance	**dalliance**	datta	**data**
damadges	**damages**	dauter	**daughter**
dammage	**damage**	dawter-in laws	**daughters-in-law**
dappifer	**dapifer**	dayja voo	**déjà vu**
daraine	**darrein**	dayly	**daily****
datim	**datum**	deam	**deem**

Incorrect	Correct
debach	**debauch**
debacing	**debasing**
debbatible	**debatable**
debbenture	**debenture**
debbet	**debit****
debbilitate	**debilitate**
debbit	**debet****
debbiter	**debitor**
debbitum	**debitum**
debbono etmalo	**de bono et malo**
debenny ese	**de bene esse**
debien lemort	**de biens le mort**
debreefing	**debriefing**
debtenture	**debenture**
debt sealing	**debt ceiling**
deccanatis	**decanatus**
decclare	**declare**
decclaritory	**declaratory**
deccorim	**decorum**
deccoy	**decoy**
deccree	**decree****
deceedent	**decedent****
deciet	**deceit**
decist	**desist**
decklaration	**declaration**
decklination	**declination**
deckree nesi	**decree nisi**
decmal	**decimal**
decurso	**de cursu**
ded	**dead****
dedacate	**dedicate**
dedbeat	**deadbeat****
deddi	**dedi**
deddie in deem	**de die in diem**
deddition	**dedition**
deddolo mallo	**de dolo malo**
dedduce	**deduce**
dedduction	**deduction**
dede	**deed****
dedline	**deadline**
dedlock	**deadlock**
dedly wepon	**deadly weapon**
deductabel	**deductible**
deecrettle	**decretal**
deecry	**decry**
deeface	**deface**
deefault	**default**
deefect	**defect**
deefered	**deferred**
deeficiency	**deficiency**
deeflation	**deflation**
deeflecct	**deflect**
deeformity	**deformity**
deefraud	**defraud**
deefray	**defray**
deefunc	**defunct**
deegrade	**degrade**
deehors	**dehors**
deel	**deal**
deeliberations	**deliberations**
deemand	**demand**
deeplete	**deplete**
deepreciaton	**depreciation**
deeter	**deter**
deevious	**devious**
def	**deaf**
defallcater	**defalcator**
defanite	**definite**
defawlt judgment	**default-judgment**
defayming	**defaming**
defeesable	**defeasible**
defeet	**defeat**
defemation	**defamation**
defence	**defense**
defenit	**definite****
defensable	**defensible**
defering	**deferring**
deferrance	**deference**
deffalcation	**defalcation**
deffault	**default**
deffeasance	**defeasance**
deffective	**defective**
deffend	**defend**
deffenestration	**defenestration**
deffense	**defense**
deffer	**defer****
defferential	**deferential****
defficit	**deficit**
deffience	**defiance**
deffimation	**defamation**
deffine	**define**
deffinitio	**definitio**
deffinittive	**definitive****
deffloration	**defloration**
defimation	**defamation**
defishent	**deficient**
defnit	**definite****
defrence	**deference**
defur	**defer****
deggenerate	**degenerate**

Incorrect	Correct	Incorrect	Correct
deggree	**degree****	depportation	**deportation**
dehidrate	**dehydrate**	deppose	**depose****
deis	**dies****	depposit	**deposit**
deklarent	**declarant**	deppositary	**depositary****
delapidation	**dilapidation**	depposition	**deposition**
delatteer	**de latere**	depradation	**depredation**
delicked	**delict**	depreshiation	**depreciation**
delivry	**delivery**	derect	**direct**
dell credder	**del credere**	derecter	**director**
dellegate	**delegate**	derection	**direction**
dellete	**delete**	deregalation	**deregulation**
delleterious	**deleterious**	dererogation	**derogation**
delliberate	**deliberate**	derevitive torte	**derivative tort**
dellickt	**delict**	derrain	**deraign**
dellict	**delict**	derregulate	**deregulate**
dellictum	**delictum**	derrelict	**derelict**
delligated powers	**delegated powers**	derrogation	**derogation**
dellimit	**delimit**	descovry	**discovery**
dellirious	**delirious**	descretionary	**discretionary**
delusery	**delusory**	desculpate	**disculpate**
demane	**domain****	desculpation	**disculpation**
demener	**demeanor**	desease	**decease****
demestic relations		deseased	**deceased**
	domestic relations	deseat	**deceit**
deminished capacity		desedant	**decedent****
	diminished capacity	desegnate	**designate**
demmalo	**de malo**	deseive	**deceive**
demmand	**demand**	desena	**decenna**
demmi	**demi**	desentralization	**decentralization**
demmocracy	**democracy**	deseption	**deception**
demmolish	**demolish**	desern	**discern**
demmonstrible	**demonstrable**	deshonist	**dishonest**
demmotion	**demotion**	desicion	**decision**
demmurage	**demurrage**	desicrate	**desecrate**
demmurer	**demurrer**	desinherit	**disinherit**
denagrate	**denigrate**	desision	**decision**
dennari	**denarii**	desolve	**dissolve**
dennial	**denial**	desparate	**desperate****
dennomination	**denomination**	desscription	**description**
dennsity	**density**	dessegragate	**desegregate**
dennumeration	**denumeration**	dessend	**descend****
dennunciation	**denunciation**	dessicate	**desiccate**
denny	**deny**	dessignation	**designation**
denoneciatory	**denunciatory**	desspotism	**despotism**
depleetion	**depletion**	desstroy	**destroy**
deppartment	**department**	destetute	**destitute**
deppendant	**dependent**	det	**debt****
deppendible	**dependable**	det cervice	**debt service**
deppo	**depot**	detenue	**detinue**
depponent	**deponent**	deth	**death**

dettain	detain	dieing	dying
dettection	detection	diett	diet**
dettention	detention	dietta	dieta**
detter	debtor	difacto	de facto
detterence	deterrence	difalcate	defalcate
dettereorate	deteriorate	difennso	defenso
dettermination	determination	diferal	deferral
dettinue	detinue	diference	difference**
dettour	detour**	diferent	different
dettoxify	detoxify	diferentiate	differentiate
dettract	detract	diffalt	default
dettriment	detriment	differance	difference**
deuces teecum	duces tecum	dificult	difficult
deuna part	de una parte	difil	defile
deveate	deviate	diforchiare	difforciare
develution	devolution	difuse	diffuse**
deves	dives**	diggest	digest**
devestation	devastation	diggnety	dignity
devestiture	divestiture	diggnify	dignify
devisive	divisive	diggression	digression
devolution	devolution	di incremmento	de incremento
devulge	divulge	dirijure	de rigueur
devvelop	develop	dikta	dicta
devvest	devest**	diktate	dictate
devvy	devy	dilay	delay
dew care	due care	dilicktum	delictum
dewplisity	duplicity	diligence	diligence
dew prosess	due process	dilinquency	delinquency
diacese	diocese	dilivery	delivery
dibanco	de banco	dillatory	dilatory
di bonus nonadministratis		dillema	dilemma
	de bonis non administratis	dillution	dilution**
dicca	dica	dilusion	delusion**
dicctum	dictum	dimarcation	demarcation
dicease	disseise**	dimenshia precocks	
dicern	discern		dementia praecox
dicide	decide	diminimus	de minimis
dicktim	dictum	dimise	demise**
dicline	decline	dimissery	dimissory
dicomposed	decomposed	dimize	demise**
di corpore comitatus		dimmension	dimension
	de corpore comitatus	dimmes	dismes**
dicotomy	dichotomy	dimminution	diminution
dicrease	decrease	dimmisery	dimissory
dicriminalize	decriminalize	dimonstrative	demonstrative
diductable	deductible	dimur	demur**
diease nun	dies non	dimurer	demurrer
diefy	deify	di nature brevvium	
dieing declaration			de natura brevium
	dying declaration	diniable	deniable

Incorrect	Correct	Incorrect	Correct
dinounce	denounce	disolution	dissolution
di novo	de novo	dison tort	de son tort
dipict	depict	disooitude	desuetude
dipose	depose	dispair	despair
dipositary	depositary**	disparrity	disparity
dipository	depository**	dispasition	disposition**
dippsomania	dipsomania	dispepsia	dyspepsia
dipraved	depraved	disperation	desperation
diprive	deprive	dispise	despise
diquo	de quo	dispoan	dispono
direen culpable	de rien culpable	dispoil	despoil
dirivative	derivative	dispondent	despondent
dirrect	direct	dispruf	disproof
dirrectery	directory	disputible	disputable
dirrective	directive	dissability	disability
dirress	duress	dissable	disable
disafirmance	disaffirmance	dissabuse	disabuse
disalute	dissolute	dissadvantaged	disadvantaged
disassociate	dissociate	dissafect	disaffect
disasterous	disastrous	dissaferm	disaffirm
disatisfaction	dissatisfaction	dissafirm	disaffirm
discendent	descendent	dissagree	disagree
discent	descent**	dissalow	disallow
discribe	describe	dissapear	disappear
discriminater	discriminator	dissapoint	disappoint
discription	description	dissaprobation	disapprobation
diseiser	disseisor	dissaprove	disapprove**
diseisin	disseisin	dissaster	disaster
diseizer	disseisor	dissavow	disavow
disemble	dissemble	dissbar	disbar
disemminate	disseminate	dissbarrment	disbarment
disenshion	dissension	dissburse	disburse**
disent	dissent**	disscharge	discharge
disenting opinion		dissclaimer	disclaimer
	dissenting opinion	disscloze	disclose
diseptive	deceptive	dissconcert	disconcert
disert	desert	disscontinuence	discontinuance**
disgize	disguise	disscontinuous	discontinuous**
disident	dissident	disscord	discord
disiese	disseise**	disscount	discount
disign	design	disscourage	discourage
disignare	dissignare	disscovary	discovery
disipate	dissipate	disscovert	discovert
disiplinary	disciplinary	disscovery	discovery
disire	desire	disscredit	discredit
disireable	desirable	disscreet	discreet**
diskrimmination	discrimination	disscrepency	discrepancy
diskuss	discuss	disscretion	discretion
dismisil	dismissal	disscriminate	discriminate
dismissel	dismissal	disscussion	discussion

Incorrect	Correct	Incorrect	Correct
dissdain	**disdain**	dissproof	**disproof**
dissencumber	**disencumber**	dissproove	**disprove****
dissenfranchise	**disenfranchise**	dissproportionate	**disproportionate**
dissentailment	**disentailment**	disspute	**dispute**
dissertion	**desertion**	dissputible	**disputable**
dissfavor	**disfavor**	dissqualitification	**disqualification**
dissfigure	**disfigure**	dissrate	**disrate**
dissfranchise	**disfranchise**	dissreggard	**disregard**
dissgise	**disguise**	dissreputible	**disreputable**
dissgrace	**disgrace**	dissrespect	**disrespect**
dissgruntled	**disgruntled**	dissripute	**disrepute**
dissheriter	**disheritor**	dissruptive	**disruptive**
disshonest	**dishonest**	disstance	**distance**
disshonor	**dishonor**	disstil	**distill**
dissinclination	**disinclination**	disstinct	**distinct**
dissinherison	**disinherison**	disstinguish	**distinguish**
dissinheritance	**disinheritance**	disstort	**distort**
dissinjenuous	**disingenuous**	disstrain	**distrain**
dissinsentive	**disincentive**	disstress	**distress**
dissinter	**disinter****	disstribbutive	**distributive**
dissintermediation		disstribute	**distribute**
	disintermediation	disstrick	**district**
dissintrested	**disinterested**	disstringere	**distringere**
dissinvestment	**disinvestment**	dissturbance	**disturbance**
dissjointed	**disjointed**	disterb	**disturb**
dissjunctive	**disjunctive**	distrainy	**distrainee**
dissjunctive alegation		distrayment	**distrainment**
	disjunctive allegation	distraynt	**distraint**
disslocation	**dislocation**	distrik	**district**
dissloyal	**disloyal**	disuade	**dissuade**
dissmember	**dismember**	ditail	**detail**
dissmiss	**dismiss**	diter	**deter****
dissobediance	**disobedience**	ditritus	**detritus**
dissoblige	**disoblige**	divadend	**dividend**
dissorderly	**disorderly**	divice	**device****
dissorderly condict		divirsification	**diversification**
	disorderly conduct	divise	**devise****
dissparagashio	**disparagatio**	divisee	**devisee****
dissparate	**disparate****	divolve	**devolve**
disspassionate	**dispassionate**	divorse	**divorce**
disspatch	**dispatch**	divote	**devote**
disspel	**dispel**	divurge	**diverge**
disspence	**dispense**	divvers	**divers****
disspensation	**dispensation**	divversion	**diversion**
dissplace	**displace**	divversity	**diversity**
dissplay	**display**	divvert	**divert**
disspose	**dispose**	divvestment	**divestment**
dissposess	**dispossess**	divvide	**divide**
dissposible	**disposable**	divvidend	**dividend**
dissposition	**disposition**	divvisible	**divisible**

Incorrect	Correct	Incorrect	Correct
divvision	**division**	doury	**dowry**
divvorce	**divorce**	dous'nt	**doesn't**
dizease	**disease****	dout	**doubt**
dizideratum	**desideratum**	douwable	**dowable****
dizscloser	**disclosure**	douwment	**dowment**
doccet	**docket**	dovtail	**dovetail**
doccument	**document**	Dowe	**Dow, the**
docktrine	**doctrine**	dowery	**dowry**
dockumentery	**documentary**	dowwer	**dower****
docter	**doctor**	drackonian	**draconian**
dodate	**due date**	draf	**draff****
doemain	**domain****	draine	**drain**
doggma	**dogma**	drammatic	**dramatic**
doible	**doable****	drasstic	**drastic**
doket	**docket**	drauft	**draught**
doktrinal	**doctrinal**	drawie	**drawee**
dolar	**dollar****	drawr	**drawer**
doller	**dollar****	dreco reggis	**draco regis**
dollus	**dolus**	drege	**dredge**
domane	**domain**	dreyage	**drayage**
domisiled	**domiciled**	driet-driet	**dreit-dreit**
dommesile	**domicile**	driling	**drilling**
dommestic	**domestic**	driot	**droit**
dommicile	**domicile**	drivver	**driver**
domminant	**dominant**	droun	**drown**
domminicum	**dominicum**	drugg	**drug**
domminion	**dominion**	drugist	**druggist**
domminis litis	**dominus litis**	drunkerd	**drunkard**
dommus	**domus**	dubbious	**dubious**
doneing	**dunning**	dubbitable	**dubitable**
doner	**donor**	dubbitante	**dubitante**
donnashio	**donatio****	dubble	**double****
donnatarius	**donatarius**	duble jeperdy	**double jeopardy**
donnation	**donation****	dudonem	**duodenum**
donnative	**donative**	dueodecima mannus	
donnator	**donator**		**duodecima manus**
donnis	**donis**	dueplex	**duplex**
doo	**due****	dueplicity	**duplicity**
dooly	**duly****	dues ex machine	**deus ex machina**
dorrmant	**dormant**	duety	**duty**
dorrsum	**dorsum**	dule	**duel****
dosier	**dossier**	dume	**doom**
dosile	**docile**	dumesday pill	**doomsday pill**
dossage	**dosage**	dummping	**dumping**
dottage	**dotage**	dumodo	**dummodo**
dottal	**dotal**	dumy	**dummy**
dottard	**dotard**	dunage	**dunnage**
dottation	**dotation**	dunn	**dun****
dottisa	**dotissa**	dupplicate	**duplicate**
douer	**dower****	dupplisitous	**duplicitous**

Incorrect	Correct	Incorrect	Correct
Duram Rule	**Durham rule**	dutties	**duties**
dureable	**durable**	dutty	**duty**
durrance	**durance**	duwal	**dual****
durrante	**durante**	dy	**dye****
durration	**duration**	dyagnossis	**diagnosis**
durress	**duress**	dyalisis	**dialysis**
durring	**during**	dyez	**dies****
duse	**dues****	dyvestiture	**divestiture**

E

Incorrect	Correct	Incorrect	Correct
easyly	**easily**	efemeral	**ephemeral**
eaze	**ease**	effishent	**efficient**
eb	**ebb**	eficiency	**efficiency**
ebbulience	**ebullience**	efishent	**efficient**
eccology	**ecology**	efluent	**effluent****
ecconomic	**economic****	eflux	**efflux****
ecconomise	**economize**	efraction	**effraction**
eckwity	**equity**	egaculate	**ejaculate**
eclatt	**éclat**	ege	**edge**
eclesiastic	**ecclesiastic**	egectment	**ejectment**
ecymossis	**ecchymosis**	eggregious	**egregious**
eddema	**edema**	eggress	**egress**
eddict	**edict****	eggsecutive	**executive**
eddition	**edition****	egis	**aegis****
edditus	**editus**	egsacerbate	**exacerbate**
edducational	**educational**	egsclusive	**exclusive**
edipal	**oedipal**	egspert	**expert**
edjuration	**ejuration**	ejektum	**ejectum**
eech	**each**	ejject	**eject**
ee contra	**e contra**	ejjection	**ejection****
eeduce	**educe****	ekcentricity	**eccentricity**
eegis	**aegis****	ekolallia	**echolalia**
eelection	**election**	eksaminee	**examinee**
eelemosynary	**eleemosynary**	eksample	**example**
eemasculate	**emasculate**	ekscape	**escape**
eemoluent	**emolument****	ekschange	**exchange**
eeo	**eo**	eksculpate	**exculpate**
eequivocal	**equivocal**	eksculpation	**exculpation**
eermark	**earmark**	ekscuse	**excuse**
eesement	**easement**	eksecution	**execution**
eevesdrop	**eavesdrop**	eksecutrises	**executrices**
eezement	**easement**	ekseed	**exceed****
efacacious	**efficacious**	eksemplify	**exemplify**
eface	**efface**	eksempt	**exempt**
efect	**effect****	eksept	**except****
efective	**effective**	eksess	**excess****
efectuate	**effectuate**	eksicutorship	**executorship**

Incorrect	Correct	Incorrect	Correct
eks parte	ex parte	emmenda	emenda
ekspert	expert	emmerge	emerge
ekspose	expose**	emmergency	emergency
eksposay	exposé**	emmetic	emetic
ekspostulate	expostulate	emmigrant	emigrant**
ekspromisio	expromissio	emminent doemain	
eksterritoreal	exterritorial**		eminent domain
ekstinguish	extinguish	emminent domane	eminent domain
ekstortive	extortive	emmisary	emissary
ekstricate	extricate	emmit	emit**
eksutraque part	ex utraque parte	emmolument	emolument**
ekwillise	equalize	emmpanel	empanel
eleet	elite	emmpathize	empathize
elepses	ellipsis**	emmpirical	empirical
ellaborrate	elaborate	emmplead	emplead
ellected	elected	emmploy	employ
ellective	elective	emmporium	emporium
ellectrocardiograph		emmpower	empower
	electrocardiograph	emmulate	emulate
ellectrocution	electrocution	emoshun	emotion**
ellectroensephalogram		empeechible	impeachable
	electroencephalogram	emperage	umpirage
ellectronic	electronic	emplied	implied
ellegit	elegit	emputative	imputative
elligible	eligible	empute	impute
elliminate	eliminate	emtor	emptor
ellisor jury	elisor jury	emty	empty
ellongata	elongata	enattic	enate or enatic
ellopement	elopement	encarcerate	incarcerate
elloquence	eloquence	encriminater	incriminator
elswhere	elsewhere	enculpate	inculpate**
embarass	embarrass	enculpation	inculpation
embasage	embassage	enculpatory	inculpatory
embasy	embassy	encummbrance	encumbrance
embelish	embellish	endacarditus	endocarditis
embraser	embraceor or embracer	endemure	en demeure
embreo	embryo	enemity	enmity
embrever	enbrever	enfate	enfait
embryoes	embryos	enforcable	enforceable
emfases	emphases**	enfraction	infraction
emision	emission**	enfringement	infringement
emmanate	emanate	engroce	en gros
emmbargo	embargo	enjender	engender
emmbark	embark	enjine	engine
emmbezelment	embezzlement	enjineer	engineer
emmbezle	embezzle	ennable	enable**
emmbodiment	embodiment	ennabling clause	enabling clause
emmbolism	embolism	ennact	enact
emmbrace	embrace	ennclose	enclose
emmbrasery	embracery	enncounter	encounter

Incorrect	Correct	Incorrect	Correct
enncourage	encourage	enrolement	enrollment
enncroach	encroach	enseint	enceinte
enncumber	encumber	ensephelogram	encephalogram
enncumberense	encumbrance	enss legis	ens legis
enndanger	endanger	entale	entail
enndevor	endeavor	entent	intent
enndorse	endorse**	enterbatt	entrebat
enndow	endow	enterpot	entrepôt
ennemy	enemy	enterprenuer	entrepreneur
ennergy	energy	enterrogatories	interrogatories
ennfeef	enfeoff	entierty	entirety
ennforce	enforce	entitelment	entitlement
ennfranchise	enfranchise	entrecuer	enterceur
enngage	engage	entree of judgment	
ennhanced	enhanced		entry of judgment
ennheritance	inheritance	entreety	entreaty
ennigma	enigma	entreprise	enterprise
ennitiparrs	enitia pars	entreprize	enterprise
ennjoin	enjoin	enurre	inure**
ennlarge	enlarge	envellop	envelop**
ennormity	enormity	envestigater	investigator
ennrage	enrage	enviarment	environment
ennrich	enrich	envoluntery	involuntary
ennroll	enroll	epedemic	epidemic
ennsconce	ensconce	episcene	epicene
ennseel	enseal	epitomme	epitome
ennsue	ensue	eppidural	epidural
enntail	entail	eppilepsy	epilepsy
enntendment	entendment	eppiphysis	epiphysis
ennter	enter	eppisode	episode
enntertainment	entertainment	eppistolary	epistolary
enntice	entice	eppitaf	epitaph
enntire	entire	eppoch	epoch**
enntitle	entitle	eqquip	equip
enntity	entity	eqquity	equity
enntrapment	entrapment	eqquivalent	equivalent
enntreaty	entreaty	equalibrium	equilibrium
enntrust	entrust	equallity	equality
enntry	entry	equasion	equation
ennumerated powers		equatible	equatable**
	enumerated powers	equattable	equitable**
ennummerated	enumerated	equible	equable**
ennure	inure**	equil	equal
ennviroment	environment	equilize	equalize
ennvirons	environs	equinimity	equanimity
ennvision	envision	equitible	equitable
ennvoy	envoy	equivvocate	equivocate
enpanil	empanel	erant	errant**
enphysema	emphysema	erascible	irascible**
enquest	inquest	eratic	erratic**

Incorrect	Correct	Incorrect	Correct
eratim	**erratum**	esstrepment	**estrepement**
eratta	**errata**	esstuary	**estuary**
erban	**urban****	estople	**estoppel**
ergency	**urgency**	estreap	**estrepe**
ern	**earn*****	estreet	**estreat**
erned income credit		etali et contra	**et alii è contra**
	earned income credit	et all	**et al.**
ernest	**earnest**	etalocatur	**et allocatur**
ernest money	**earnest money**	et cettera	**et cetera**
ernings	**earnings**	eteology	**etiology**
ernings per share		ethacal	**ethical**
	earnings per share	ethicks	**ethics**
eroneous	**erroneous**	et seck	**et seq.****
eror	**error****	etsick	**et sic****
errasure	**erasure**	ettaluis	**et alius**
errect	**erect****	etternal	**eternal**
errer	**error****	ettnon	**et non**
errgo	**ergo****	etuksor	**et uxor**
erristic	**eristic**	evadance	**evidence**
errode	**erode**	evadentary	**evidentiary**
erronious	**erroneous**	evalluate	**evaluate**
errotic	**erotic****	evalution	**evolution****
errupt	**erupt**	evassive	**evasive**
esartum	**essartum**	evicktion	**eviction**
escappee	**escapee**	eviddence	**evidence**
escheetor	**escheator**	evill	**evil**
esence	**essence**	evisserate	**eviscerate**
esenshal	**essential**	evok	**evoke**
eshelon	**echelon**	evry	**every**
eskwire	**esquire**	evvade	**evade**
esoign	**essoin**	evvasio	**evasio****
esscalater claws	**escalator clause**	evvent	**event**
esscalator	**escalator**	evventual	**eventual**
esscheat	**escheat**	evvict	**evict**
esscrow	**escrow**	evvidence	**evidence**
essnecy	**esnecy**	evvince	**evince**
esspousals	**espousals**	evvolved	**evolved**
essquire	**esquire**	ewebiquitus	**ubiquitous**
esstablish	**establish**	ewige	**ewage**
esstate	**estate**	exalare	**exulare**
esstate tax	**estate tax**	exalter parti	**ex altera parte**
esstimate	**estimate**	exammination	**examination**
esstimated tax	**estimated tax**	exaustion	**exhaustion**
esstop	**estop**	excede	**exceed****
esstopage	**estoppage**	excep	**except****
esstopel	**estoppel**	excercise	**exercise****
esstover	**estover**	excersise	**exercise****
esstrange	**estrange**	exchecker	**exchequer**
esstray	**estray**	excize	**excise**
esstreat	**estreat**	exclutionary rool	**exclusionary rule**

32

Incorrect	Correct	Incorrect	Correct
excollori	ex colore	explisit	explicit
excomunication	excommunication	explitive	expletive
excrament	excrement	explitory	expletory
excussatory	excusatory	exploytation	exploitation
excussible	excusable	exponnential	exponential
exdilecto	ex delicto	expozur	exposure**
exdollo mallo	ex dolo malo	exppectancy	expectancy
execcuter	executor	expremissio	expromissio
execcutive	executive	expresly	expressly
execcutrix	executrix	exprommisser	expromissor
exegence	exigence	exrated	X-rated
exegible	exigible	exray	x-ray
exellance	excellence	exrellationi	ex relatione
exemmplification	exemplification	exrigor juris	ex rigore juris
exemp	exempt	exsaminer	examiner
exemtion	exemption	exsempt	exempt
exhibbition	exhibition	exsemption	exemption
exhorbitant	exorbitant	exseptio	exceptio**
exibit	exhibit	exseption	exception**
exicuter	executor	exsesses	excesses
exicutery	executory	exsize	excise
exicutress	executress	exsize tax	excise tax
exicutricks	executrix	exsizible	excisable
exisstence	existence	extennuate	extenuate
exkavation	excavation	exterdition	extradition
exklamation	exclamation	exterrior	exterior
exklude	exclude	extinnguishment	extinguishment
exkretion	excretion	extorsion	extortion
exloccato	ex locato	extreem	extreme
exoficio	ex officio	extreemis	extremis
exort	exhort	extremmity	extremity
expattriation	expatriation	extrinnsic	extrinsic
expeddiment	expediment	extteritorrialty	exterritoriality
expeedient	expedient		or extraterritoriality**
expelee	expellee	exturnal	external
expell	expel	exumation	exhumation
expence	expense	exume	exhume
expendible	expendable	exune parti	ex una parte
expennditure	expenditure	exxagerate	exaggerate
experation	expiration	exxamen	examen**
experation date	expiration date	exxbonus	ex bonis
expergation	expurgation	exx cathedral	ex cathedra
experrtese	expertise	exx cawsa	ex causa
expiditious	expeditious	exxcept	except**
expindere	expendere	exxclusion	exclusion
expirience	experience	exxculpatory	exculpatory
explacate	explicate	exxcurie	ex curia
explaination	explanation	exxdividend	ex dividend
explaration	exploration	exxecrate	execrate
explination	explanation	exxecutary	executory

33

Incorrect	Correct
exxecute	**execute**
exxemplar	**exemplar**
exxempt	**exempt**
exx facto	**ex facto**
exx gratia	**ex gratia**
exxhibitted	**exhibited**
exxhypothese	**ex hypothesi**
exxile	**exile**
exxit	**exit**
exx malleficio	**ex maleficio**
exx mora	**ex mora**
exxonerate	**exonerate**
exxotic	**exotic****
exx parti	**ex parte**
exxpeditation	**expeditation**
exxpedite	**expedite**
exxpend	**expend**
exxpenses	**expenses**
exxperiment	**experiment**

Incorrect	Correct
exxpire	**expire****
exxplosion	**explosion**
exxport	**export**
exxposition	**exposition**
exx post factoe	**ex post facto**
exxpress	**express**
exx propreo	**ex proprio**
exxpropriation	**expropriation**
exxpulsion	**expulsion**
exxpunction	**expunction**
exxpunge	**expunge**
exxtant	**extant****
exxtent	**extent****
exxtravagant	**extravagant**
exxult	**exult**
exx volluntate	**ex voluntate**
ey	**eye****
eywitness	**eyewitness**

F

Incorrect	Correct
fabracate	**fabricate**
faccilitate	**facilitate**
faceing	**facing**
facks	**facts****
facksimile	**facsimile**
fackto	**facto****
fackultative	**facultative**
facterise	**factorize**
fagot	**faggot**
fained	**feigned****
fairo	**faro**
faite	**fait****
fakt	**fact****
fakter	**factor**
faktery	**factory**
faktion	**faction****
faktum	**factum**
fakulties	**faculties**
fakulty	**faculty**
falable	**fallible**
falacious	**fallacious**
falacy	**fallacy**
falation	**fellation**
falback	**fallback**
falce pretense	**false pretense**
fale	**fail**

Incorrect	Correct
faleure to indict	**failure to indict**
fallcare	**falcare**
fallic	**phallic**
fallsare	**falsare**
fallse	**false**
fallsification	**falsification**
fallss arest	**false arrest**
fallsus	**falsus**
falo	**fallow****
Falopian tube	**Fallopian tube**
falsafy	**falsify**
falsly	**falsely**
falss emprisonment	**false imprisonment**
falum	**fallum**
falure	**failure**
famer	**farmer**
famicide	**famacide**
familar	**familiar****
famly	**family**
famma	**fama**
fammilia	**familia****
fannatic	**fanatic**
fanntasy	**fantasy**
Fanny May	**Fannie Mae**
fansiful	**fanciful**

Incorrect	Correct	Incorrect	Correct
fare coment	**fair comment**	fedral court of claims	
fare hearing	**fair hearing**		**Federal Court of Claims**
fareness	**fairness**	fedral reserve	**Federal Reserve**
fareness doctrine	**fairness doctrine**	feduciary	**fiduciary**
fare use	**fair use**	feeat	**fiat****
farier	**farrier**	feeces	**feces****
farlew	**farleu**	feedary	**feodary**
farmaceutical	**pharmaceutical**	feef	**fief**
farrdel	**fardel**	feefer	**feoffer** or **feoffor****
fase	**face**	feelow de see	**felo de se**
faseout	**phaseout**	feelty	**fealty**
fashal	**facial****	feemale	**female**
fashist	**fascist**	feer	**fear**
fasiendo	**faciendo**	feesable	**feasible**
fasility	**facility**	feesance	**feasance****
fasinate	**fascinate**	feesibility	**feasibility**
fass	**fas****	feesor	**feasor**
fassil	**facile****	feeture	**feature**
fassinate	**fascinate**	feetus	**fetus**
fasstidious	**fastidious**	feild	**field**
fatha	**father****	fein	**fine**
fathe	**faith**	fekless	**feckless**
father-in-laws	**fathers-in-law**	felatio	**fellatio**
fattal	**fatal****	fellagus	**felagus**
fattality	**fatality**	felleny	**felony**
fattuitas	**fatuitas****	feller	**fellow****
fattum	**fatum**	fellon	**felon**
fattuous	**fatuous****	fellonice	**felonice****
faver	**favor**	fellony merder	**felony murder**
faverible	**favorable**	fellow de say	**felo de se**
favvorable	**favorable**	feloneous	**felonious****
fawlshood	**falsehood**	feloneously	**feloniously**
fawlt	**fault**	felow	**fellow****
fawtor	**fautor**	fem	**feme** or **femme**
fayker	**faker**	femme covert	**feme covert**
faytours	**faitours**	femme cuver	**feme covert**
fayvorite	**favorite**	femme soul	**feme sole**
fea	**fee**	femmicide	**femicide**
feance	**fiancé****	femminine	**feminine**
feas	**fees**	fennatio	**fenatio**
feasable	**feasible**	fennestration	**fenestration**
feasco	**fiasco**	fense	**fence**
feascos	**fiascoes** or **fiascos**	ferator	**ferrator**
feasimple	**fee simple**	fereful	**fearful**
feaunt	**fiaunt**	feret	**ferret**
fe cimple	**fee simple**	ferkin	**firkin**
fedaration	**federation**	ferm	**firm**
Fedd, the	**Fed, the**	ferma	**firma**
feddelitas	**fidelitas**	fermly	**firmly**
fedderal	**federal**	fernish	**furnish**

Incorrect	Correct	Incorrect	Correct
ferre	**ferae****	firs	**first**
ferrtillize	**fertilize**	fisk	**fisc**
ferse-degree	**first-degree**	fisscal	**fiscal****
ferther	**further****	fite	**fight**
fertherance	**furtherance**	fiteing words	**fighting words**
fertive	**furtive**	fitt	**fit**
fertum	**furtum**	fixd	**fixed**
ferum	**ferrum**	fixt costs	**fixed costs**
fesster	**fester**	fixxture	**fixture**
fesstum	**festum**	flacid	**flaccid**
fetherbedding	**featherbedding**	flagg	**flag**
fetticide	**feticide**	flaggrant delicto	**flagrante delicto**
fettid	**fetid****	flakk	**flack**
fewgatious	**fugacious**	flako	**flaco**
fewgitation	**fugitation**	flamm	**flam**
fial	**file****	flatt	**flat**
fiddelity	**fidelity**	flaygrant	**flagrant****
fiddes	**fides**	flaygrants	**flagrans****
fidducial	**fiducial**	flease	**fleece****
fidushiary	**fiduciary**	flebitis	**phlebitis**
fier	**fire**	fleksible	**flexible**
fierbug	**firebug**	flekstime	**flextime**
fierproof	**fireproof**	fligitious	**flagitious**
figgment	**figment**	flima	**flyma**
figgurehead	**figurehead**	flimmflam	**flimflam**
figgures	**figures**	flite	**flight**
fiks	**fix**	floging	**flogging**
fiktion	**fiction**	floom	**flume**
fileing	**filing****	flopy disc	**floppy disk**
fillacer	**filacer**	flor	**floor**
fillial	**filial**	flore broker	**floor broker**
fillibuster	**filibuster**	florish	**flourish**
fillius	**filius**	flote	**float**
fillshing	**filching**	flote and issue	**float an issue**
fillum	**filum****	floteing	**floating**
finanseer	**financier**	floter	**floater**
finatude	**finitude**	flottages	**flotage**
fineder's fee	**finder's fee**	flowting rate	**floating-rate**
fineding	**finding**	fluevius	**fluvius**
finil	**final**	fluks	**flux**
finishio	**finitio**	fluksus	**fluxus**
finnagle	**finagle**	fluktuate	**fluctuate**
finnance	**finance****	flumery	**flummery**
finnancial	**financial**	flumox	**flummox**
finnem fasere	**finem facere**	foalio	**folio**
finnger	**finger**	fobia	**phobia**
finnis	**finis****	foccus	**focus**
firarm	**firearm**	foder	**fodder**
firmory	**fermory**	foed	**feod**

Incorrect	Correct	Incorrect	Correct
foedal	**feodal**	forim	**forum**
foefee	**feoffee****	forin	foreign
foex	**faux****	forinsic chemistery	
foi	**foy**		**forensic chemistry**
fole	**foal**	forinsic medsin	**forensic medicine**
folger	**folgere**	forje	**forge**
folicle	**follicle**	forjery	**forgery**
follio	**folio**	forklosure	**foreclosure**
folow	**follow****	formalate	**formulate**
folowup	**follow-up**	forman	**foreman**
foly	**folly**	formela	**formula****
fondation	**foundation**	fornoledge	**foreknowledge**
fondator	**fundator**	fornowlege	**foreknowledge**
fondel	**fondle**	forquoted	**forequoted**
foneration	**foeneration**	forrensick	**forensic**
forboding	**foreboding**	forris	**foris**
forcast	**forecast**	forrum	**forum**
forclose	**foreclose**	forse	**force**
forclosure	**foreclosure**	forsee	**foresee**
forebad	**forbade**	forseeable	**foreseeable**
forebarance	**forbearance**	forseeability	**foreseeability**
forefeitable	**forfeitable**	forseeible	**foreseeable**
forefiture	**forfeiture**	forseen	**foreseen**
foregave	**forgave**	forsible	**forcible**
foregery	**forgery**	forsible entry	**forcible entry**
foreget	**forget**	forsight	**foresight**
foregive	**forgive**	forsite	**foresight**
foregonn	**forgone**	for-sited	**fore-cited**
foregot	**forgot**	forstall	**forestall**
foregoten	**forgotten**	forstarius	**forestarius**
forem	**forum**	forteori	**fortiori****
foremality	**formality**	Forth Amendment	
foremalize	**formalize**		**Fourth Amendment**
forematta brevia	**formata brevia**	forthougt	**forethought**
foremidable	**formidable**	fortut	**fortuit**
foremula	**formula****	forusfaktura	**forisfactura**
forenicate	**fornicate**	forwarned	**forewarned**
foreswear	**forswear**	fosatum	**fossatum**
Foreteenth Amendment		fose	**fosse**
	Fourteenth Amendment	fosster	**foster**
foretuitous	**fortuitous**	fotographer	**photographer**
foreward	**forward****	fourclosure	**foreclosure**
forfit	**forfeit**	fourfit	**forfeit**
forfitor	**forfeiter**	fourty	**forty****
forfiture	**forfeiture**	fownder	**founder****
forgerer	**forjurer**	fowndling	**foundling****
forgoe	**forego****	fracktious	**fractious**
forgon	**foregone**	fracshio	**fractio**
foriegn	**foreign**	fraim-up	**frame-up**

Incorrect	Correct	Incorrect	Correct
frakshional	**fractional**	fruktus	**fructus**
frakture	**fracture**	fruntage	**frontage**
framup	**frame-up**	frunteger	**frontager**
framwork	**framework**	fruntend	**front-end**
franchize	**franchise**	frute	**fruit**
franchizee	**franchisee**	frution	**fruition**
franchize tax	**franchise tax**	fryable	**friable**
franck	**franc****	fucher's contract	**futures contract**
frannchise	**franchise**	fued	**feud**
franncus	**francus**	fuedum	**feudum**
frase	**phrase****	fuel faith and credit	
frate	**freight****		**full faith and credit**
frater	**freighter**	fugative	**fugitive**
fratternal	**fraternal**	fuggator	**fugator**
frattriage	**fratriage**	fugumfesit	**fugam fecit**
frattricide	**fratricide**	fujitive	**fugitive**
fraudalent	**fraudulent**	ful	**full****
frawd	**fraud****	fule faith and credit	
frawdulant conveyence			**full faith and credit**
	fraudulent conveyance	fullminate	**fulminate**
frechet	**freshet**	fundgible	**fungible**
Freddy Mack	**Freddie Mac**	funktion	**function**
freequency	**frequency**	funndamental	**fundamental**
freeseout	**freeze-out**	funndamus	**fundamus**
freggmenta	**fragmenta**	funned	**fund**
frehold	**freehold**	funngible	**fungible**
frektum	**frectum**	furer breevis	**furor brevis**
frekwent	**frequent**	furrandi annimus	**furandi animus**
frelance	**freelance**	furriosus	**furiosus**
frend	**friend****	furst	**first**
frenneticus	**freneticus**	furst instanse	**first instance**
fressca	**fresca**	furthemore	**furthermore**
frettum	**fretum**	furtility	**fertility**
friktion	**friction**	fusstis	**fustis**
frinje	**fringe**	futchers	**futures**
frivaliss	**frivolous**	futer	**future**
frivilus	**frivolous**	futturi	**futuri**
frivvolous	**frivolous**	fyat	**fiat****
froeling	**freoling**	fyca	**FICA**
froezin asets	**frozen assets**	fyudal	**feudal**
frosen	**frozen**	fyurius	**furious**

G

Incorrect	Correct	Incorrect	Correct
gaddfly	**gadfly**	galing	**galling**
gadge	**gage****	gallvanize	**galvanize**
gaffol	**gafol**	galon	**gallon**
gagg	**gag**	galows	**gallows**

Incorrect	Correct	Incorrect	Correct
gambel	**gamble** **	gess	**guess**
gameing	**gaming**	gesstate	**gestate**
gamet	**gamut**	gettaway	**getaway**
gammbit	**gambit**	gibet	**gibbet**
ganage	**gainage**	gidance	**guidance**
gane	**gain**	gidelines	**guidelines**
ganeful	**gainful**	giggabite	**gigabyte**
gantlet	**gauntlet**	gile	**guile**
garantee	**guarantee**	gilld	**gild** **
garanter	**guarantor**	gilty	**guilty**
gardian	**guardian**	gimick	**gimmick**
gardianship	**guardianship**	ginarchy	**gynarchy**
gardien	**gardein**	Ginny May	**Ginnie Mae**
garneshment	**garnishment**	girrante	**girante**
garot	**garotte** or **garrotte** **	givaway	**giveaway**
garrage	**garage**	gizement	**gisement**
garrdianus	**gardianus**	glammer stock	**glamour stock**
garrene	**garene**	gleeba	**gleba**
garrnishee	**garnishee** **	glimer	**glimmer**
gased	**gassed** **	glos	**gloss** **
gass	**gas**	glutten	**glutton**
gavvel	**gavel**	gobldygook	**gobbledygook**
geemot	**gemot**	goddfather	**godfather**
gelld	**geld** **	goefer	**gofer**
genaral	**general** **	goeing	**going**
genarality	**generality**	goldin hancuffs	**golden handcuffs**
genaration	**generation**	goldin parishoot	**golden parachute**
genialagy	**genealogy**	gonnorea	**gonorrhea**
gennera	**genera** **	govement	**government**
genneric	**generic**	govnor	**governor**
gennerous	**generous**	govrenment	**government**
gennetic	**genetic**	govvern	**govern**
gennitalia	**genitalia**	gradduate	**graduate**
gennocide	**genocide**	graddus	**gradus**
genntes	**gentes** **	graed	**grade** **
genntiles	**gentiles**	graffed	**graft** **
gennuine	**genuine**	gramm	**gram**
gennus	**genus** **	grande larseny	**grand larceny**
genral application		grane	**grain**
	general application	granfather	**grandfather**
genralize	**generalize**	granfather claws	
genrally	**generally**		**grandfather clause**
genral oblagation		granjarus	**grangearius**
	general obligation	granje	**grange**
gentelmen	**gentlemen** **	gran-jurer	**grandjuror**
genyuine	**genuine**	gran jury	**grand jury**
geopardy	**jeopardy**	granstand	**grandstand**
gerrens	**gerens**	granter	**grantor**
gerriatrics	**geriatrics**	granty	**grantee**
gerth	**girth**	grase	**grace**

Incorrect	Correct
gratafacation	**gratification**
grattis	**gratis**
gratiss dicktim	**gratis dictum**
gratuety	**gratuity**
gratutous	**gratuitous**
graveman	**gravamen**
gravemen	**gravamen**
gravvis	**gravis**
greave	**greve****
greemium	**gremium**
greevence	**grievance**
greevous	**grievous**
greivance	**grievance**
greneback	**greenback**
grenemail	**greenmail**
gresume	**gressume**
greymail	**graymail**
grif	**griff**
grissly	**grisly**
groop	**group****
grose	**gross****
grosment	**grossement**
grothe	**growth**
grounwerk	**groundwork**

Incorrect	Correct
grownd	**ground**
growndless	**groundless**
grudje	**grudge**
grusome	**gruesome**
guage	**gauge****
guilt-eged	**gilt-edged**
gune	**goon**
gunnpoint	**gunpoint**
gurator	**jurator**
guris	**juris****
gurist	**jurist****
gurmane	**germane****
gurmanus	**germanus**
gurpi	**guerpi**
gury	**jury**
gus	**jus****
gust	**just****
gusticable	**justiciable**
gustify	**justify**
gustitia	**justitia**
guvernor	**governor**
guyde	**guide**
guyse	**guise****
gynacologist	**gynecologist**

H

Incorrect	Correct
habatancy	**habitancy**
habbendum	**habendum**
habbilis	**habilis**
habbit	**habit**
habbitual	**habitual**
habble	**hable**
habendes hominess	**habentes homines**
habess corpis	**habeas corpus**
habillitate	**habilitate**
habius korpus	**habeas corpus**
hace	**haec****
hach	**hatch**
hadship	**hardship**
haf	**half****
haffne	**hafne**
haff-truth	**half-truth**
hagle	**haggle**
hainous	**heinous****
halage	**hallage**
hale into court	**haul into court**

Incorrect	Correct
halucinate	**hallucinate**
halusinagenic	**hallucinogenic**
hamful	**harmful**
hamless	**harmless**
hancuffs	**handcuffs**
handriting	**handwriting**
handwork	**handiwork**
handycapped	**handicapped**
hangun	**handgun**
hansale	**handsale****
hansel	**handsel****
hanshake	**handshake**
hapenstance	**happenstance**
happ	**hap**
harber	**harbor**
harmles	**harmless**
harrasment	**harassment**
harrass	**harass**
harrbinger	**harbinger**
harrmony	**harmony**
harte	**heart****

Incorrect	Correct	Incorrect	Correct
harth	heart**	herriscindum	heriscindium
hauff	haugh	herrmetic	hermetic
havan	haven**	herrnia	hernia
havvoc	havoc	herroin	heroin**
hawl	haul**	herrus	herus
hazzard	hazard	her's	hers
healler	healer	hers'	hers
heares	haeres	hert	hurt
hecktare	hectare	herto	hereto
hed	head**	hertofor	heretofore
hedeless	heedless**	herunto	hereunto
hedjeboat	hedge-bote	herupon	hereupon
hedjing	hedging	herwith	herewith
hedland	headland	hesatate	hesitate
hednote	headnote	hetrosexual	heterosexual
hedway	headway	hevy-handed	heavy-handed
heematology	hematology	heyboat	hay-bote
heemofiliac	hemophiliac	hiddalgo	hidalgo
heering	hearing	hiden	hidden
heersay	hearsay	hiebrid	hybrid
heet	heat	hier	heir**
hege	hedge	hieress	heiress
hej	hedge	hierr	hire**
hejemony	hegemony	hiest	highest
helth	health	hi-flyer	high-flier**
helthy	healthy	higack	hijack
hemmatoma	hematoma	higgler	higler
hemmipledgia	hemiplegia	higherarky	hierarchy
henseforth	henceforth	highpothecry	hypothecary
henshman	henchman	highpothicate	hypothecate
hepptarchy	heptarchy	hinderence	hindrance
herafter	hereafter	hipnotic	hypnotic
heratable	heritable	hipocrasy	hypocrisy
herby	hereby	hipostasis	hypostasis
herdle	hurdle**	hipotheca	hypotheca
hereing	hearing	hipothekate	hypothecate
heresay rule	hearsay rule	hipothesis	hypothesis
heretage	heritage	hipothetical	hypothetical
herin	herein	hirarchy	hierarchy
herinafter	hereinafter	hi-risk	high-risk**
herinbefore	hereinbefore	his's	his
herinto	hereinto	hisstorical	historical**
herisy	heresy	histeria	hysteria
herminutics	hermeneutics	histery	history
hernea	hernia	histoerectomy	hysterectomy
herof	hereof	hitheto	hitherto
herrald	herald	hiway	highway
herreditery	hereditary	hocc	hoc**
herreditments	hereditaments	hojepot	hotchpot
herredity	heredity	holacaust	holocaust

Incorrect	**Correct**	Incorrect	**Correct**
holeder	**holder**	hore	**whore****
holegraphic will	**holographic will**	horible	**horrible**
holesome	**wholesome**	hormaster	**whoremaster**
holley	**wholly****	horra	**hora**
holliday	**holiday**	horrizontal	**horizontal**
hollograph	**holograph**	hosspitable	**hospitable****
hollsale	**wholesale**	hosspital	**hospital****
hom	**holm****	hosspitia	**hospitia**
homageneous	**homogeneous****	hosstage	**hostage**
homeiside	**homicide**	hosstile	**hostile****
homiside	**homicide**	hostel take-over	**hostile takeover**
hommage	**homage**	hostill wittnes	**hostile witness**
hommagium	**homagium**	housbote	**house-bote****
hommicide	**homicide**	housbreaking	**housebreaking**
hommo	**homo**	houseing	**housing**
hommologous	**homologous**	housholder	**householder**
hommosexual	**homosexual**	houskeeper	**housekeeper**
honer	**honor**	houzing	**housing**
honerary	**honorary**	hovvel	**hovel**
honisty	**honesty**	howse	**house**
honnestus	**honestus**	huey	**hui****
honnesty viver	**honeste vivere**	hukster	**huckster**
honnor	**honor**	huliganism	**hooliganism**
honrable	**honorable**	hundered	**hundred**
honymoon	**honeymoon**	hunndred	**hundred**
hooever	**whoever****	hunto	**junta****
hoomever	**whomever****	hurd	**herd****
hoonto	**junta****	huricane	**hurricane**
hoors	**hors****	huzband	**husband**
hopfuly	**hopefully**	hy	**high****
hopless	**hopeless**	hyatus	**hiatus**
hording	**hoarding**	hyegene	**hygiene**

I

Incorrect	**Correct**	Incorrect	**Correct**
ibbid	**ibid.**	idenical	**identical**
ibbidem	**ibidem**	idenntafiable	**identifiable**
iccra	**ikrah****	idenntical	**identical**
idd	**id****	ideopathic	**idiopathic**
iddem	**idem****	idiamatic	**idiomatic**
iddentic	**identic**	idiest	**id est**
iddentify	**identify**	idio	**ideo**
iddiom	**idiom**	idiology	**ideology**
iddle	**idle****	idyosincracy	**idiosyncrasy**
idea fixed	**idée fixe**	iggerance	**ignorance**
idear	**idea****	iggnite	**ignite**
IDee	**ID****	iggnominy	**ignominy**
ideel	**ideal****	iggnorance	**ignorance**

Incorrect	Correct	Incorrect	Correct
iggnoranshia	**ignorantia**	immbue	**imbue**
iggnore	**ignore**	immerality	**immorality**
ignaratio ellenshi	**ignoratio elenchi**	immitable	**imitable****
ignerent	**ignorant**	immora	**in mora**
ikkbal	**ikbal**	immortua mannu	**in mortua manu**
iladvised	**ill-advised**	immpair	**impair**
ilation	**illation**	immpanel	**impanel**
ildisposed	**ill-disposed**	immpaneling	**impaneling**
ilegal	**illegal**	immparity	**imparity**
ilegality	**illegality**	immparl	**imparl**
ilegible	**illegible****	immparlance	**imparlance**
ilegitimasy	**illegitimacy**	immpart	**impart**
ilegitimate	**illegitimate**	immpartial	**impartial**
ileviable	**illeviable**	immpartible	**impartible****
ilfated	**ill-fated**	immpechare	**impechiare**
ilgotten	**ill-gotten**	immpedients	**impediens**
ilicit	**illicit****	immpediments	**impediments**
ilimitable	**illimitable**	immpending	**impending**
iliteracy	**illiteracy**	immperative	**imperative**
ilitive	**illative**	immperfect	**imperfect**
ilness	**illness**	immplements	**implements**
ilocable	**illocable**	immplicate	**implicate**
ilogical	**illogical****	immplore	**implore**
ilucidate	**elucidate**	immports	**imports**
ilud	**illud****	immpose	**impose**
iluminate	**illuminate**	immposter	**impostor****
iluseage	**ill-usage**	immpotence	**impotence**
ilused	**ill-used**	immpressment	**impressment**
ilusion	**illusion****	immprest	**imprest****
ilusive	**illusive****	immpretiabilus	**impretiabilis**
ilusory	**illusory**	immprimatur	**imprimatur**
ilustrate	**illustrate**	immprimis	**imprimis**
imanent	**immanent****	immprisament	**imprisonment**
imatate	**imitate**	immpristi	**impristi**
imaterial	**immaterial**	immpromptu	**impromptu**
imature	**immature**	immproper	**improper**
imbezzelment	**embezzlement**	immproved	**improved**
imbonis	**in bonis**	immprovident	**improvident**
imcombustible	**incombustible**	immprudense	**imprudence**
imediate	**immediate**	immpulse	**impulse**
imemorial	**immemorial**	immpunity	**impunity****
imense	**immense**	immputation	**imputation****
imersion	**immersion**	immpute	**impute**
imigrate	**immigrate****	immputed	**imputed**
iminent	**imminent****	immyune	**immune**
immage	**image**	imobilis	**immobilis**
immagrant	**immigrant****	imoderate	**immoderate**
immbasil	**imbecile**	imolate	**immolate**
immbecile	**imbecile**	imoral	**immoral****
immbibe	**imbibe**	impail	**impale**

43

Incorrect	Correct
impanil	**impanel**
impanilment	**impanelment**
impannel	**impanel**
impare	**impair**
impari	**in pari**
imparshal	**impartial**
impeech	**impeach**
impeechment	**impeachment**
impeed	**impede**
impervius	**impervious**
implacate	**implicate**
impleed	**implead**
implyed powers	**implied powers**
implyed warrant	**implied warrant**
imposible	**impossible**
impunaty	**impunity****
impune	**impugn**
impuned	**impugned**
imput	**input**
imune	**immune**
imunity	**immunity****
imunosupresent	
	immunosuppressant
imutable	**immutable**
inabriaty	**inebriety**
inactment	**enactment**
inambigguo	**in ambiguo**
inamissable	**inadmissible**
inaplicable	**inapplicable**
inarguable	**unarguable**
inate	**innate****
inatentive	**inattentive**
incadental	**incidental**
incalcuable	**incalculable**
incarserate	**incarcerate**
incassu proviso	**in casu proviso**
inceruptable	**incorruptible**
incheef	**in chief**
incidently	**incidentally**
incider trading	**insider trading**
incinuation	**insinuation**
incipptur	**incipitur**
incistance	**insistence**
incisted	**insisted**
incloosive	**inclusive**
incom	**income**
incomon	**in common**
inconnvenience	**inconvenience**
inconsimmili cassu	
	in consimili casu

Incorrect	Correct
incontrollable	**uncontrollable**
inconventional	**unconventional**
incooperative	**uncooperative**
incoregeable	**incorrigible**
incrimanate	**incriminate**
incroach	**encroach**
incrochment	**encroachment**
or **incroachment**	
incurible	**incurrable****
indacation	**indication**
indagent	**indigent**
indagestion	**indigestion**
indalense	**indolence**
indament	**indument**
indanger	**endanger**
indangerment	**endangerment**
indases	**indices**
Indean	**Indian**
indecks	**index**
indefanite	**indefinite**
indeim	**in diem**
indellicto	**in delicto****
indemmnification	**indemnification**
indennsher	**indenture**
inderate	**indurate**
indescretion	**indiscretion**
indescriminate	**indiscriminate**
indespensible	**indispensable**
indespensible evidence	
	indispensable evidence
indevisible	**indivisible**
indifeesible	**indefeasible**
indifensable	**indefensible**
indiscrete	**indiscreet**
indiscribable	**indescribable**
indisiferible	**indecipherable**
indisium	**indicium**
indisolluble	**indissoluble**
indissposition	**indisposition**
indistructable	**indestructible**
inditee	**indictee**
inditement	**indictment**
inditible	**indictable**
indivviduely	**individually**
indoobitable	**indubitable**
indorsment	**endorsement**
or **indorsement**	
indukt	**induct**
indurance	**endurance**
indusement	**inducement**

Incorrect	Correct
indy	**inde**
Indyan	**Indian**
ineebriate	**inebriate**
inegsact	**inexact**
inegscambio	**in excambio**
inegstremus	**in extremis**
inelegible	**ineligible****
inepptitude	**ineptitude**
inequal	**unequal**
iner	**inner**
inesential	**inessential** or **unessential**
iness	**in esse**
iness dejure	**in est de jure**
inextennso	**in extenso**
inexxitu	**in exitu**
inexxorible	**inexorable**
infaci curia	**in facie curiae**
infact	**in fact**
infalable	**infallible**
infammia	**infamia**
infanite	**infinite**
infegare	**infugare**
infekshus	**infectious**
inferi	**in fieri**
infering	**inferring**
informative	**infirmative**
infermity	**infirmity**
infero	**in foro**
inferrance	**inference**
inferstructure	**infrastructure**
infertunuim	**infortunium**
inffarable	**inferable**
infimous	**infamous**
infincy	**infancy**
infireor	**inferior**
inflaggrante delecto	**in flagrante delicto** or **flagrante delicto**
inflamable	**inflammable**
inflamatory	**inflammatory**
inflamible	**inflammable**
inflammed	**inflamed**
inflewance pedling	**influence peddling**
infoedo	**in feodo**
infoffment	**infeoffment**
infranchible	**infrangible**
infrawdem	**in fraudem**
infre	**infra****
infrence	**inference**
inful	**in full**

Incorrect	Correct
infur	**infer****
infuture	**in futuro**
ingect	**inject**
ingenner	**in genere**
ingergitate	**ingurgitate**
ingquest	**inquest**
ingrateful	**ungrateful**
ingunction	**injunction**
ingurious	**injurious**
inhabbitant	**inhabitant**
inhac party	**in hac parte**
inherater	**inheritor**
inheratricks	**inheritrix**
inheretence tax	**inheritance tax**
inherrater	**inheritor**
inherrent	**inherent**
inherritence	**inheritance**
inhirant powers	**inherent powers**
iniluctible	**ineluctable**
inirant	**inerrant**
iniscapable	**inescapable**
inishal public offering	**initial public offering**
inixaustable	**inexhaustible**
inixcusible	**inexcusable**
injenious	**ingenious****
injenuitas	**ingenuitas**
injenuity	**ingenuity**
injer	**injure****
injerry	**injury****
injest	**ingest**
injoin	**enjoin**
injustiss	**injustice**
inkausa	**in causa**
inkautious	**incautious**
inker	**incur**
inkerrect	**incorrect**
inkersion	**incursion**
inkind	**in kind**
inklosher	**inclosure**
inklude	**include**
inklukate	**inculcate****
inkognito	**incognito**
inkoherent	**incoherent**
inkomendam	**in commendam**
inkomensurate	**incommensurate**
inkompatible	**incompatible**
inkomplete	**incomplete**
inkomunicado	**incommunicado**
inkonsiderable	**inconsiderable**

Incorrect	Correct	Incorrect	Correct
inkonsideration	**in consideration**	inncitu	**in situ**
inkontestability	**incontestability**	innclose	**inclose** or **enclose**
inkontinence	**incontinence**	innclusion	**inclusion**
inkontractibus	**in contractibus**	inncome	**income**
inkorperation	**incorporation**	inncompetent	**incompetent**
inkorporamus	**incorporamus**	inncomprehensable	
inkote	**inchoate**		**incomprehensible**
inkradullity	**incredulity**	innconceivable	**inconceivable**
inkrease	**increase**	innconclusive	**inconclusive**
inkrementum	**incrementum**	inncongruity	**incongruity**
inkriminatory	**incriminatory**	innconsequential	**inconsequential**
inkumbrence	**incumbrance**	innconsistent	**inconsistent**
inkurea	**in curia**	inncontrovertible	**incontrovertible**
inkustodial egis	**in custodia legis**	inncorigible	**incorrigible**
inkweirendo	**inquirendo**	inncorporate	**incorporate**
inkwest	**inquest**	inncredulous	**incredulous**
inkwiry	**inquiry**	inncriminate	**incriminate**
in lawe	**in law**	inncumbent	**incumbent**
inlocco	**in loco**	inncumber	**incumber**
inlytem	**in litem**	inndebitatus	**indebitatus**
inmeedia rest	**in medias res**	inndeed	**indeed**
innability	**inability**	inndelable	**indelible****
inn absenchia	**in absentia**	inndelacate	**indelicate****
innaccesible	**inaccessible**	inndemify	**indemnify**
innaction	**inaction**	inndemnity	**indemnity**
innacurate	**inaccurate**	inndemonstrable	**indemonstrable**
innadaquate	**inadequate**	inndent	**indent**
innadmisable	**inadmissible**	inndenter	**indentor**
innadverseum	**in adversum**	innderect	**indirect**
innadvertance	**inadvertence**	inndesent	**indecent**
innadvisable	**inadvisable**	inndetedness	**indebtedness**
inn aleeno solo	**in alieno solo**	inndex	**index**
innalienable	**inalienable**	inndicative	**indicative**
inn allio loco	**in alio loco**	inndict	**indict****
innalterable	**inalterable**	inndignity	**indignity**
innane	**inane****	inndiktio	**indictio**
inn apicabus juris	**in apicibus juris**	inndipendant	**independent**
innapropriate	**inappropriate**	inndisia	**indicia**
inn as much as	**inasmuch as**	inndisision	**indecision**
innaticulo	**in articulo**	inndisstinguishable	
innaudible	**inaudible**		**indistinguishable**
innauspicious	**inauspicious**	inndistanter	**indistanter**
innbanco	**in banco**	inndistinctive	**indistinctive**
inn camara	**in camera**	inndite	**indict****
inncapacitated	**incapacitated**	innditerminate	**indeterminate**
inn capita	**in capita**	inndividual	**individual**
inncarserate	**incarcerate**	inndivissum	**indivisum**
innchartar	**inchartare**	inndorse	**indorse** or **endorse**
innchote	**inchoate**	inndorser	**indorser**
inncidious	**insidious**	innduce	**induce**

Incorrect	Correct
innducia	induciae
inndulgence	indulgence
inndustrial	industrial
innedible	inedible**
inneducible	ineducable
innefective	ineffective
innefectual	ineffectual
inneficient	inefficient
innelastic	inelastic
innept	inept**
innequable	inequable
innequality	inequality
innequity	inequity**
innerference	interference
innert	inert
innestimable	inestimable
innevitable	inevitable
innexactitude	inexactitude
innexecutible	inexecutable
innexistant	inexistent
innexpedient	inexpedient
innexpensive	inexpensive
innexperience	inexperience
innexplicable	inexplicable
innfaciendo	in faciendo
innfadility	infidelity
innfans	infans
innfantacide	infanticide
innfatuate	infatuate
innfection	infection
innferior	inferior
innferrential	inferential
innfidelis	infidelis
innfine	in fine
innfinitesmal	infinitesimal
innfinitim	infinitum
innfirm	infirm
innflame	inflame
innflation	inflation
innflect	inflect**
innflikt	inflict**
innfluence	influence
innformal	informal
innformation	information
innformed	informed
innforment	informant
innformer	informer
innfraction	infraction
innfrequent	infrequent
innfringment	infringement

Incorrect	Correct
innfusion	infusion
inngenuous	ingenuous**
inngery	injury**
inngratatude	ingratitude
inngress	ingress
inngrossater	ingrossator
innguinal	inguinal
innhabit	inhabit
innhallant	inhalant
innhere	inhere
innherit	inherit
innhibition	inhibition
innhock	in hoc
innhuman	inhuman**
innimacal	inimical**
innimatible	inimitable**
inninfinitim	in infinitum
inninitio	in initio
inniquity	iniquity**
innitial	initial
innitiate	initiate
innitiative	initiative
inn joor	in jure**
innjudico	in judicio
innjudishus	injudicious
innjunction	injunction
innjuries	injuries
innjustice	injustice
innjus voccare	in jus vocare
innkrement	increment
innlaw	in-law
innlimine	in limine
innmalem partem	
	in malam partem
innmate	inmate**
innmedico	in medico
innoculate	inoculate**
inn omnibus	in omnibus
innoperable	inoperable
innotice	in notis
inn otre droite	in autre droit
innpatiendo	in patiendo
innpersonaum	in personam
inn perrpetuity	in perpetuity
innpleno lumina	in pleno lumine
innpound	impound
innprender	in prender
innprincipio	in principio
innpropria	in propria
innquest	inquest

Incorrect	Correct	Incorrect	Correct
innquisition	inquisition	innteligence	intelligence
innrem	in rem	inntemperate	intemperate
innsane	insane	inntence	intense**
innsannity	insanity	inntend	intend
innscription	inscription	inntent	intent
innsecure	insecure	innter	inter**
innseminate	inseminate	innteragency	interagency**
innsensable	insensible	innter bank	interbank
innsergent	insurgent	inntercede	intercede
innsert	insert**	innterchangable	interchangeable
innsider	insider**	innter conjudges	inter conjuges
innsignificant	insignificant	inntercourse	intercourse
innsinsere	insincere	innterdit	interdict
innsinuate	insinuate	innteress	interesse**
innsistent	insistent	innterest	interest**
innsobriety	insobriety	innterface	interface
inn so far	insofar	innterfer	interfere
innsolation	insolation	innterlinnation	interlineation
innsolence	insolence	innterlocking	interlocking
inn solido	in solido	innterlocutory	interlocutory
inn solo	in solo	innterlopers	interlopers
innsolvent	insolvent**	inntermariage	intermarriage
innspect	inspect	inntermedle	intermeddle
innspecter	inspector	innterminus	in terminis
innssure	insure**	inntermitent	intermittent
innstability	instability	inntermixture	intermixture
innstall	install	innternal	internal
innstalment	installment	innternational	international
innstigate	instigate	innteroggatory	interrogatory
innstill	instill	innterpolate	interpolate**
innstince	instance**	innterpose	interpose
innstinctive	instinctive	innterpretation	interpretation
innstitution	institution	inntersection	intersection**
innstruct	instruct	inntersperce	intersperse
innstrument	instrument**	innterstate	interstate**
innstrumenta	instrumenta**	innterstises	interstices
innsubordination	insubordination	innterstishial	interstitial
innsubstantial	insubstantial	innterval	interval
innsuficcient	insufficient	innterveen	intervene
innsulate	insulate	innterview	interview
innsullar	insular	inntervivos	inter vivos
innsult	insult	inn tesstimonium	in testimonium
innsuportable	insupportable	inntestate	intestate**
innsupresible	insuppressible	inntimate	intimate
innsurence	insurance**	inntimmidate	intimidate
inntack	intact	inntol and utol	intol and uttol
inntangible	intangible	inntollerible	intolerable
inntegration	integration	inn toto	in toto
inntegrity	integrity	inntoxikated	intoxicated
inntejer	integer	inntra	intra**

Incorrect	Correct	Incorrect	Correct
inntractible	intractable	inovation	innovation
inntrafiddem	intra fidem	inpact	impact
inntransijent	intransigent	inpays	in pais
inntraparties	intra parietes	inpeach	impeach
inntrastate	intrastate**	inpecunious	impecunious
inntrautterine	intrauterine	inpeeechment	impeachment
inntreeg	intrigue	inpel	impel
inntricate	intricate	inpenitent	impenitent
inntrinsik	intrinsic	inperil	imperil
inntromision	intromission**	inpermisible	impermissible
inntruder	intruder	in persenum	in personam
inntrusion	intrusion	inpersonal	impersonal
inntrust	intrust	inpersonation	impersonation
innundation	inundation	inperturbable	imperturbable
innure	inure**	inpetuous	impetuous
innurtness	inertness	inpetus	impetus
innvagle	inveigle	inpignorata	impignorata
innvalidation	invalidation	inpinge	impinge
innvalide	invalid	inplacable	implacable
innvaluble	invaluable	inplant	implant
innvariable	invariable	inplead	implead
innvasion	invasion	inplied	implied
innvective	invective	inport	import
innvent	invent	inportune	importune
innventer	inventor**	inposts	imposts
innventis	inventus	inpoverish	impoverish
innverse	inverse	inpracticable	impracticable**
innvest	invest**	inpregnable	impregnable
innvestagate	investigate	inpregnate	impregnate
innvestature	investiture	inprescriptible	imprescriptible
innvestigation	investigation	inpressible	impressible
innvestment	investment	inpression	impression
innveterate	inveterate	inprest	imprest**
innvidious	invidious**	inprison	imprison
innvigorate	invigorate	inprobable	improbable
innvinculus	in vinculis	inpropriety	impropriety
innvisible	invisible	inprovement	improvement
innvitation	invitation	inprovise	improvise
inn vitro	in vitro	inpulsive	impulsive
inn vivo	in vivo	inpuned	impugned
innvoice	invoice	inpurity	impurity
innvoke	invoke	inpute	impute
innvoluntary	involuntary	inqwest	inquest
innvolve	involve	in ree	in re
innvulnerable	invulnerable	in reebus	in rebus
inny	any	inrichment	enrichment
inoccuous	innocuous	insamull	insimul
inocence	innocence	insendiary	incendiary
inopperitive	inoperative	insentive	incentive
inosense	innocence**	inseption	inception

Incorrect	Correct
insertitude	**incertitude**
insesent	**incessant**
insest	**incest**
insestuos	**incestuous****
inshmaree claws	**inchmaree clause**
inshurable	**insurable**
inshured	**insured**
insidense	**incidence****
insidently	**incidentally**
insipient	**incipient**
insission	**incision**
insite	**incite****
insiter	**inciter****
in sitoo	**in situ**
insivile	**incivile**
insize	**incise**
inspektion	**inspection**
inspite	**in spite**
in status quo	**in statu quo**
instatute	**institute**
insted	**instead**
insterment	**instrument****
insterpar	**instirpare**
in sterpeas	**in stirpes**
instetorial	**institorial**
instink	**instinct**
instintanious	**instantaneous**
instintly	**instantly**
instrement	**instrument****
instruktion	**instruction**
insuficient evidance	
	insufficient evidence
inta allia	**inter alia**
intagrate	**integrate**
intalokutory	**interlocutory**
intamacy	**intimacy**
intaparres	**inter pares****
intaspousal	**interspousal**
intaracial	**interracial**
intaregnim	**interregnum**
intarogatories	**interrogatories**
intarogee	**interrogee**
intaruption	**interruption**
intasession	**intercession****
intelectual property	
	intellectual property
intenshional	**intentional**
interduce	**introduce**
interlockutory	**interlocutory**
intermeddiary	**intermediary**

Incorrect	Correct
interogation	**interrogation**
interpeter	**interpreter**
interpleed	**interplead**
interr allios	**inter alios**
interrment	**interment****
interrvener	**intervenor**
intersede	**intercede**
intervenous	**intravenous**
interversion	**introversion**
inter-vireus	**intra vires**
intesstasy	**intestacy**
intesstate	**intestate****
intierty	**entirety**
intollerance	**intolerance**
intradict	**interdict**
intramediate	**intermediate**
intrapleeder	**interpleader**
intrapment	**entrapment**
intraposed	**interposed**
intravention	**intervention**
intredict	**interdict**
intrest	**interest****
intrested	**interested**
intrim	**interim**
inturn	**intern****
inturnal	**internal**
inturnal revvenue code	
	Internal Revenue Code
inturnment	**internment**
inturprete	**interpret**
intute	**intuit**
inuendo	**innuendo**
inumerible	**innumerable**
inurtia	**inertia**
in uttero	**in utero**
in vakuo	**in vacuo**
invester	**investor**
invialible	**inviolable**
invilable	**inviolable**
invity	**invitee**
involantery	**involuntary**
involuntery manslaughter	
	involuntary manslaughter
in wittness wheroff	
	in witness whereof
iotta	**iota**
ippso fakto	**ipso facto**
ipse jure	**ipso jure**
ipsi dixit	**ipse dixit**
irational	**irrational**

Incorrect	Correct	Incorrect	Correct
irbane	**urbane****	ireverense	**irreverence**
ireconsilable	**irreconcilable**	irevocable	**irrevocable**
irecoverible	**irrecoverable**	irigation	**irrigation**
ireducable	**irreducible**	iritable	**irritable**
ireedemable	**irredeemable****	irrascible	**irascible**
irefutible	**irrefutable**	irrate	**irate**
iregular	**irregular**	irregardless	**regardless**
irelevent	**irrelevant**	irrevelant	**irrelevant**
iremedeable	**irremediable****	irronsafe clause	**iron-safe clause**
iremmisible	**irremissible**	isalate	**isolate****
irepeelible	**irrepealable**	ishew	**issue**
ireperable	**irreparable**	ishuable	**issuable**
ireplevable	**irrepleviable**	isne	**eisne**
ireproachible	**irreproachable**	isshue	**issue**
iresistable	**irresistible**	itemmize	**itemize**
iresolluble	**irresoluble**	itim	**item**
iresolvible	**irresolvable**	itinnerary	**itinerary**
irespective	**irrespective**	itterate	**iterate**
iresponsable	**irresponsible**	ittinerant	**itinerant**
iretreivable	**irretrievable**	itts	**its** or **it's****

J

Incorrect	Correct	Incorrect	Correct
jacktivation	**jactitation**	jestation	**gestation**
jaktavus	**jactivus**	jestum	**gestum**
jaktus	**jactus**	jetison	**jettison**
jale	**jail**	jewdishel	**judicial**
janator	**janitor**	jewer	**juror****
jaridical	**juridical**	jewist	**jurist**
jayewalking	**jay walking**	jewlry	**jewelry**
Jayne Doe	**Jane Doe**	jist	**gist****
Jayson clause	**Jason clause**	jober	**jobber**
jenatals	**genitals**	jointer	**jointure**
jender	**gender**	Jon Dough	**John Doe**
jender newtral	**gender-neutral**	joodicater	**judicator**
jene splicing	**gene splicing**	joodicature	**judicature**
Jenks Act	**Jencks Act**	jooish	**Jewish**
jenocide	**genocide**	joonta	**junta****
jenre	**genre**	joonyer	**junior**
jens	**gens****	joora	**jura****
jentry	**gentry**	jooridical	**juridical**
jepardy	**jeopardy**	jooris consult	**jurisconsult**
jeperdise	**jeopardize**	joorisprudance	**jurisprudence**
jerisprudance	**jurisprudence**	joovenile	**juvenile**
jermane	**germane**	josle	**jostle**
jernal	**journal**	jouer	**jouir**
jerrymander	**gerrymander**	joure	**jour**
jersume	**gersume**	joynder	**joinder**

Incorrect	Correct
joyn issue	**join issue**
joynt	**joint**
joynt-air	**joint heir**
joynt tenensy	**joint tenancy**
joynt tortfeesors	**joint tort-feasors**
judacato	**judicatio**
judacible	**judicable**
juddacatory	**judicatory**
juddicare	**judicare**
juddicial	**judicial**
juddikium	**judicium**
judicial notiss	**judicial notice**
judishiary	**judiciary**
judix	**judex**
juedichus	**judicious**
juedicis	**judices**
juge	**judge**
jugement	**judgement** or **judgment**
jugguler	**jugular**
jugstapose	**juxtapose**
juice	**jus****
jujmentel laps	**judgmental lapse**
jump bale	**jump bail**

Incorrect	Correct
junkit	**junket**
junktion	**junction**
junnier	**junior**
junque	**junk**
juree	**jure****
jurer	**juror****
juret	**jurat**
jurnal entree	**journal entry**
jurral	**jural**
jurrare	**jurare**
jurrat	**jurat**
jurris	**juris**
jurrisdiction	**jurisdiction**
jurusprudence	**jurisprudence**
jushtishible	**justiciable**
juss	**jus****
jusstice	**justice**
jusstification	**justification**
justishible	**justiciable**
justiss of the piece	**justice of the peace**
juvinile	**juvenile**

K

Incorrect	Correct
kangeroo court	**kangaroo court**
kanvas	**canvas****
kapable	**capable**
karnal	**carnal****
kay	**quay****
kaya	**kaia**
kealage	**keelage**
keecard	**keycard**
keeman insurance	**key man insurance**
Keeoh plan	**Keogh Plan**
kenel	**kennel**
kenledge	**kentledge**
Keny method	**Kenny method**
keue	**queue****
keus	**keyus**
kewpon	**coupon**
key estate	**que estate**
kiddnapping	**kidnapping**
kikback	**kickback**
kiler	**killer**
Killberg doctrine	**Kilberg doctrine**
kinderd	**kindred**

Incorrect	Correct
kintel	**kintal** or **kintle**
kirb	**curb**
kiropodist	**chiropodist**
kith	**kyth**
kitting	**kiting**
kneesee prius	**nisi prius**
knifpoint	**knifepoint**
knites	**knights****
knockious	**noxious**
knocksal	**noxal**
knohow	**know-how**
knolege	**knowledge**
knollegible	**knowledgeable**
knowvation	**novation**
knowverint	**noverint**
kode	**code** or **Code**
kognovit	**cognovit**
koodos	**kudos**
korpus juris	**corpus juris**
kost	**cost**
krool	**cruel****
kue	**queue****
kuipon	**coupon**

Incorrect	Correct	Incorrect	Correct
kuliana	**kuleana**	kwench	**quench**
kurf	**kerf**	kwere	**quaere****
kurnel	**kernel****	kwerens	**quaerens**
kwa	**qua**	kwerilous	**querulous**
kwack	**quack**	kwery	**query****
kwadrant	**quadrant**	kwesstus	**quaestus**
kwadrennium	**quadrennium**	kwest	**quest**
kwadripartite	**quadripartite**	kwestio	**quaestio**
kwadripledgia	**quadriplegia**	kwestion	**question**
kwadripleggic	**quadriplegic**	kwestionable	**questionable**
kwadruplet	**quadruplet**	kweya	**quia**
kwae	**quae****	kwibble	**quibble**
kwagmire	**quagmire**	kwick	**quick**
kwalification	**qualification**	kwickening	**quickening**
kwalified	**qualified**	kwid pro quo	**quid pro quo**
kwalify	**qualify**	kwiet	**quiet****
kwality	**quality**	kwietude	**quietude**
kwallitative	**qualitative**	kwietus	**quietus**
kwalm	**qualm**	kwintesense	**quintessence**
kwantatative	**quantitative**	kwintesential	**quintessential**
kwantim	**quantum**	kwirk	**quirk**
kwantity	**quantity**	kwisotic	**quixotic**
kwarantine	**quarantine**	kwit	**quit**
kwarelsome	**quarrelsome**	kwitclaim	**quitclaim**
kwarrel	**quarrel**	kwitrent	**quit rent**
kwarry	**quarry****	kwittance	**quittance**
kwart	**quart**	kwitter	**quitter**
kwarter	**quarter**	kwizical	**quizzical**
kwarterly	**quarterly**	kwod	**quod**
kwash	**quash**	kworum	**quorum**
kwashing	**quashing**	kwota	**quota****
kwasi	**quasi**	kwotable	**quotable**
kwasi-judishal	**quasi-judicial**	kwotation	**quotation**
kwaver	**quaver**	kwote	**quote****
kwee bono	**cui bono**	kwotidian	**quotidian**
kweens	**queen's**	kwuare	**quare**
kweezy	**queasy**	kyage	**keyage**
kwell	**quell**		

L

Incorrect	Correct	Incorrect	Correct
labbyrinth	**labyrinth**	laggaman	**lage-man**
labeal	**labial****	lakonic	**laconic**
laber	**labor**	lakta	**lacta**
lable	**label****	lakuna	**lacuna**
labratory	**laboratory**	lakus	**lacus**
labrinthine	**labyrinthine**	laman	**layman**
ladeing	**lading**	lamm	**lam**
lagg	**lag**	lanfill	**landfill**

53

Incorrect	Correct	Incorrect	Correct
langauge	language	leat	leet
lanlady	landlady	leate	leaute
lanlord	landlord	lecks	lex
Lannam Trademark Act		lecks non scripta	lex non scripta
	Lanham Trademark Act	lecks terray	lex terrae
lannguish	languish	ledgem	legem
lanreve	land-reeve	ledgend	legend
lans	lands	ledgislative	legislative
lapadge	lappage	ledgist	legist
lappidation	lapidation	ledgitime	legitime
lappse	lapse**	lee	lea**
lapptop	laptop	leedership	leadership
lapsd	lapsed	leeding	leading
large a complaint	lodge a complaint	leegal	legal
larjess	largess or largesse**	leegalism	legalism
larsenous	larcenous	leegalistic	legalistic
larseny	larceny	leegist	legist
laserate	lacerate	leekage	leakage
lashess	laches**	leel	leal
lasivious	lascivious	leelty	lealte
latatude	latitude	leen	lien**
latemotif	leitmotif	leener	lienor
lattent	latent	leese	lease
latteral	lateral	leesion	lesion
lattina	Latina**	leesure	leisure
lattino	Latino**	leethal	lethal
lattitat	latitat	leeve	leave
lattrocination	latrocination	leeyen	lean**
lavvish	lavish	legalise	legalize
lawbraker	lawbreaker	legallese	legalese
lawdatory	laudatory	legecy	legacy
lawdinum	laudanum	legel aid society	Legal Aid Society
lawdum	laudum	leger	ledger
lawfil	lawful	legeslation	legislation
lawfullness	lawfulness	legesy	legacy
law jurnal	law journal	legetery	legatary
lawnch	launch	leggacy	legacy
lawnder	launder	leggare	legare
lawnder money	launder money	leggatum	legatum
lawndring	laundering	legges	leges**
law revue	law review	leggislate	legislate
lawsoot	lawsuit	leggwork	legwork
laxaty	laxity	legil eagel	legal eagle
layborer	laborer	legilise	legalize
laye	ley**	legilism	legalism
layety	laity	legill remedy	legal remedy
layof	layoff	legil services corporation	
leage	league		Legal Services Corporation
leashold	leasehold	legitee	legatee
leassback	leaseback	legiter	legator

Incorrect	Correct	Incorrect	Correct
legitery	**legatary**	libill	**libel**
leguly	**legally**	libillee	**libelee**
leige	**liege**	libity	**liberty**
lejislater	**legislator**	lible	**liable****
lejit	**legit**	libral	**liberal**
lejitimicy	**legitimacy**	libre	**libber****
lejjer	**ledger**	liccer	**liquor**
lejjerdemain	**legerdemain**	liccet	**licet**
leks domisilii	**lex domicilii**	lickwidation	**liquidation**
leks forry	**lex fori**	liebellent	**libelant**
leksis	**Lexis**	lieing	**lying**
lekss	**lex**	lienn	**lien****
leks scripta	**lex scripta**	lier	**liar**
lemmon law	**lemon law**	lifhold	**lifehold**
lenniency	**leniency**	ligalisation	**legalization**
lerned	**learned**	ligality	**legality**
lesa	**lessa****	ligance	**ligeance**
lesee	**lessee****	liggare	**ligare**
leser	**lessor****	liggation	**legation****
lessay fare	**laissez-faire**	liggius	**ligius**
lessemajesty	**lese majesty**	light pendent	**lite pendente**
leter	**letter**	ligitimasy	**legitimacy**
leter of the law	**letter of the law**	ligiture	**ligature**
letigible	**litigable**	likible	**likable** or **likeable**
letigious	**litigious**	liklihood	**likelihood**
leveable	**leviable**	likness	**likeness**
levie	**levee****	likwid	**liquid**
levrage	**leverage**	lim	**limb****
levrejed bi-out	**leveraged buyout**	limatation	**limitation**
levridge	**leverage**	limitted	**limited**
levvant et coushant		limmit	**limit**
	levant et couchant	linaments	**lineaments**
levvee	**levy****	Linberg Act	**Lindbergh Act**
levveraged buyout		linckage	**linkage**
	leveraged buyout	linee	**linea**
levvy	**levy****	lingaul	**lingual**
leeter	**liter** or **litre****	liniage	**lineage****
lex citus	**lex situs**	linient	**lenient**
lex lowci	**lex loci**	linier	**linear**
liason	**liaison**	linnage	**linage****
libb	**lib**	linneal	**lineal**
libbation	**libation**	linup	**lineup****
libbel	**libel****	liquadate	**liquidate**
libber	**liber****	liquiddity	**liquidity**
libberate	**liberate**	lirra	**lira**
libberties	**liberties**	lisense	**license**
libbido	**libido**	lisentous	**licentious**
libbra	**libra**	lisetmess	**licitness**
libellent	**libelant**	lisit	**licit**
libery	**library**	liss	**lis****

Incorrect	Correct	Incorrect	Correct
lissting	**listing**	lonjevity pay	**longevity pay**
litagate	**litigate**	lonsharking	**loansharking**
litagater	**litigator**	loo	**lieu****
litagent	**litigant**	loockout	**lookout****
litering	**littering**	lood	**lewd**
litoral	**littoral****	loozer	**loser**
litorary	**literary**	losen	**loosen**
litracy	**literacy**	lott	**lot**
litteral	**literal****	louphole	**loophole**
littigant	**litigant**	Loyd's	**Lloyd's**
littigationist	**litigationist**	loyil	**loyal**
littigous	**litigious**	loyulty	**loyalty**
littmus test	**litmus test**	lubbricant	**lubricant**
livible	**livable** or **liveable**	lucer	**lucre**
livlihood	**livelihood**	luddicrous	**ludicrous**
livstock	**livestock**	lugage	**luggage**
livvery	**livery**	luggubrious	**lugubrious**
livvid	**livid**	lukrative	**lucrative**
livving	**living**	luksurious	**luxurious**
lobbeeing	**lobbying**	lummen	**lumen**
lobbotomise	**lobotomize**	lummina	**lumina**
lobying	**lobbying**	lunicy	**lunacy**
lobyist	**lobbyist**	lunitic	**lunatic**
loccal	**local****	lunje	**lunge**
lockative calls	**locative calls**	lunsh	**lunch**
loddgings	**lodgings**	lurning dissability	
lodgic	**logic**		**learning disability**
lodjer	**lodger**	lurrid	**lurid**
loggjam	**logjam**	lushous	**luscious**
loging	**logging**	lusid	**lucid**
loitre	**loiter**	lusst	**lust**
loiyer	**lawyer**	luter	**looter**
lojical	**logical**	luxxury	**luxury**
lojistics	**logistics**	ly	**lie****
lokality	**locality**	lyability	**liability**
lokate	**locate**	lybelous	**libelous**
loko parentes	**loco parentis**	lycensee	**licensee**
lokus	**locus**	lyeing	**lying**
lokwacious	**loquacious**	lyenee	**lienee**
longinimity	**longanimity**	lynchpin	**linchpin**
longterm	**long-term** or **long term****		

M

Incorrect	Correct	Incorrect	Correct
macculate	**maculate**	Macnaughton rule	**M'Naghten Rule**
machavellan	**Machiavellian**	maddams	**mesdames**
macko	**macho**	maddness	**madness**
MacNab-Mallery rule		maffia	**Mafia**
	McNabb-Mallory Rule	mafyoso	**mafioso**

magastrate	**magistrate**	mallevolence	**malevolence**
magesty	**majesty**	mallfeeser	**malfeasor**
maggic	**magic**	mallfunction	**malfunction**
maggistral	**magistral**	mallicious	**malicious**
maggna carta	**Magna Carta**	mallign	**malign**
or **Magna Charta**		mallinger	**malinger**
maggna culpe	**magna culpa**	mallnutrition	**malnutrition**
maggnanimous	**magnanimous**	mallo	**malo**
maggnat	**magnate****	mallpractiss	**malpractice**
maggnify	**magnify**	mallum	**malum**
magistrait	**magistrate**	Malory rule	**Mallory Rule**
magizine	**magazine**	malpractiss	**malpractice**
magnatude	**magnitude**	maltreetment	**maltreatment**
magnim oppus	**magnum opus**	mamary	**mammary**
magolomania	**megalomania**	mame	**maim****
maidden	**maiden**	mamogram	**mammogram**
maihim	**mayhem**	Man Act	**Mann Act**
majarity	**majority**	manafacture	**manufacture**
majer	**major**	manafest	**manifest****
majesterial	**magisterial**	manafesto	**manifesto****
majestracy	**magistracy**	managable	**manageable**
majister	**magister**	manage a trios	**ménage à trois**
majjisterial	**magisterial**	manamit	**manumit****
majjority	**majority**	mandamiss	**mandamus**
makination	**machination**	mandetory	**mandatory****
makismo	**machismo**	manditary	**mandatary****
maksamum	**maximum**	maneac	**maniac****
malace	**malice**	maneframe	**mainframe**
malajusted	**maladjusted**	maneline	**mainline**
malato	**mulatto**	maner	**manner****
maldamer	**mal de mer**	manestream	**mainstream**
maleable	**malleable**	mannacles	**manacles**
maleise	**malaise**	mannage	**manage****
maleorder	**mail order**	mannbote	**manbote**
malestrom	**maelstrom**	manndamis	**mandamus**
malevirsation	**malversation**	manndate	**mandate**
malfaction	**malefaction**	manndatory	**mandatory****
malfeesance	**malfeasance**	mannhandle	**manhandle**
maliss	**malice**	mannia	**mania****
maliss aforthought		mannic	**manic****
malice aforethought		mannifestation	**manifestation**
malitious	**malicious**	mannifold	**manifold**
malkonduct	**malconduct**	mannipulate	**manipulate**
malla	**mala****	mannumision	**manumission**
malladapted	**maladapted**	mannuscrip	**manuscript**
malladies	**maladies**	manoever	**maneuver**
malladroit	**maladroit**	manour	**man-hour**
mallady	**malady**	manprise	**mainprise**
mallcontent	**malcontent**	manshion	**mansion**
malldistribution	**maldistribution**	manslawter	**manslaughter**

Incorrect	Correct	Incorrect	Correct
man's rea	**mens rea**	matramonial	**matrimonial**
mantain	**maintain**	matraside	**matricide**
mantenance	**maintenance**	matreark	**matriarch**
mantikulate	**manticulate**	matrelineal	**matrilineal**
mantil	**mantel** or **mantle**	matteria	**materia****
manuel	**manual**	matternity	**maternity**
marage	**marriage****	mattrikulate	**matriculate**
marajuana	**marijuana**	mattrix	**matrix**
marass	**morass**	matture	**mature**
maratime	**maritime**	maturrity	**maturity**
marc	**mark****	mavin	**maven**
marganal	**marginal**	mawl	**maul****
marjin	**margin**	maxum	**maxim**
marjin account	**margin account**	mayer	**mayor**
markitable	**marketable**	maynage a trois	**ménage à trois**
markupp	**markup**	maynly	**mainly**
marqe	**marque****	Mcnaughton rule	**M'Naghten Rule**
marrathon	**marathon**	meating	**meeting**
marrauder	**marauder**	mecanick's lean	**mechanic's lien**
marre	**mare**	Medacade	**Medicaid**
marrina	**marina**	medacal	**medical**
marrine	**marine**	Medacare	**Medicare**
marrital	**marital****	medatate	**meditate**
marrxist	**Marxist**	meddiate	**mediate**
marschal	**marshal****	meddical	**medical**
marshal law	**martial law**	meddicolegal	**medico-legal**
marter	**martyr**	medean	**median**
martius	**maritus**	medecation	**medication****
marvellous	**marvelous**	medesin	**medicine**
mas	**mass**	mediocer	**mediocre**
masachism	**masochism**	medle	**meddle****
masacre	**massacre**	medlesome	**meddlesome**
masage	**massage****	meedium	**medium**
mase	**mace**	meeger	**meager** or **meagre**
mashinery	**machinery**	meens	**means**
masif	**massif****	meer	**mere**
masive	**massive****	meese	**mese**
maskerade	**masquerade**	meets and bounds	
masproduced	**mass-produced**		**metes and bounds**
massculine	**masculine**	meetus	**metus****
massicre	**massacre**	meggabite	**megabyte**
masstektomy	**mastectomy**	mekanic	**mechanic**
massuse	**masseuse**	meladiction	**malediction**
masterbate	**masturbate**	meleor	**melior**
mastry	**mastery**	mellankolia	**melancholia**
masure	**masseur**	mellee	**melee**
matearial	**material****	memarandum	**memorandum**
materation	**maturation**	memior	**memoir****
maternel	**maternal**	memmber	**member**
matoority	**maturity**	memmbrum	**membrum**

Incorrect	Correct	Incorrect	Correct
memmery	memory**	mesureable	measurable
memmorial	memorial	metefor	metaphor
memry	memory**	metemorefosis	metamorphosis
menapause	menopause	methadology	methodology
mendacant	mendicant	methedone	methadone
meneal	menial	metrapolitan	metropolitan
menice	menace	metta	meta**
menndashus	mendacious	mettabolism	metabolism
menns	mens**	mettalic	metallic
menntition	mentition	mettastisis	metastasis
menopolise	monopolize	mette	mete**
mense	mensa**	metter	meter**
menseez	menses**	mettric system	metric system
menser	mensor	Mexacan divorce	Mexican divorce
mentel	mental	mezanine	mezzanine
menticapus	mente captus	miakulpa	mea culpa
mentil angwish	mental anguish	miander	meander
mentill crewlty	mental cruelty	micerfilm	microfilm
Meranda Rule	Miranda Rule	micraprocesser	microprocessor
merandise	Mirandize	microconomics	microeconomics
meratocracy	meritocracy	micronalisis	microanalysis
merc	Merc	middcourse	midcourse
mercantill law	mercantile law	middelman	middleman
merchint	merchant	midiation	mediation
merder	murder	midle	middle
merderes	murderess	miegrant	migrant
merdrum	murdrum	miggratory	migratory
merdur	murder	mikrostructure	microstructure
meretorious	meritorious	milatery	military
merjer	merger	milige	milage or mileage
merkable	mercable	milimeter	millimeter
merkantile	mercantile	milionaire	millionaire
merkat	mercat	millitant	militant
merly	merely	millitate	militate
merrchandize	merchandise	milstones	milestones
merrciles	merciless	mimmic	mimic
merretricious	meretricious	minamal	minimal
merrit	merit	minature	miniature
merrits	merits	mineful	mindful
mersenary	mercenary	mineing	mining
mershandize	merchandise	mineset	mindset
mersiful	merciful	minimmum	minimum
mersy of the court		minis	minus
	mercy of the court	miniscule	minuscule
mesen	mesne**	minite	minute**
messege	message**	minites	minutes**
messwich	messuage**	minitory	minatory
mestiso	mestizo	minner	miner**
mesuage	messuage**	minneral	mineral
mesure	measure	minnimise	minimize

Incorrect	Correct	Incorrect	Correct
minnister	**minister**	misshandle	**mishandle**
minnits	**minutes****	missfit	**misfit**
minnor	**minor****	missjoinder	**misjoinder**
minnority	**minority**	missjudge	**misjudge**
miror	**mirror**	misslable	**mislabel**
Mirranda rule	**Miranda Rule**	missmanage	**mismanage**
misalocation	**misallocation**	missmatch	**mismatch**
misaplication	**misapplication**	missnomer	**misnomer**
misaprehension	**misapprehension**	missogenation	**miscegenation**
miscarrege	**miscarriage**	missplace	**misplace**
mischiff	**mischief**	missprison of felony	
misderection	**misdirection**		**misprision of felony**
misdyagnose	**misdiagnose**	missprizon	**misprision**
miselaneous	**miscellaneous**	missquote	**misquote**
misgided	**misguided**	missrepresentation	
mishapp	**mishap****		**misrepresentation**
mishelgemot	**michel-gemot**	missricital	**misrecital**
misinnform	**misinform**	misstake	**mistake**
misinnterprete	**misinterpret**	misstreat	**mistreat**
misives	**missives**	misstress	**mistress**
miskalculate	**miscalculate**	misstrial	**mistrial**
miskonception	**misconception**	misstrust	**mistrust**
miskonstrue	**misconstrue**	missuse	**misuse**
miskreant	**miscreant**	mistatement	**misstatement**
mislayed	**mislaid**	misterious	**mysterious**
misleeding	**misleading**	mistic	**mystic**
misojiny	**misogyny**	misunnderstand	**misunderstand**
misrable	**miserable**	mitagate	**mitigate**
misreeding	**misreading**	mitagation	**mitigation**
misry	**misery**	mitegating	**mitigating**
missadventure	**misadventure**	mith	**myth**
missadvise	**misadvise**	mitimus	**mittimus**
missapply	**misapply**	mittigation	**mitigation**
missapropriation	**misappropriation**	mixd	**mixed**
missbegotten	**misbegotten**	mixter	**mixture**
missbehavior	**misbehavior**	mize	**mise**
misscariage	**miscarriage**	mizerer	**miserere**
misschance	**mischance**	mizprison of felony	
misschievous	**mischievous**		**misprision of felony**
missconduct	**misconduct**	mobil	**mobile**
missdeed	**misdeed**	moc	**mock**
missdemeenent	**misdemeanant**	mocion	**motion**
missdemenor	**misdemeanor**	modacum	**modicum**
missdimienant	**misdemeanant**	moddel	**model****
missfeaser	**misfeasor**	modderate	**moderate**
missfeesance	**misfeasance**	moddest	**modest**
missfile	**misfile**	mode ed former	**modo et forma**
missfortune	**misfortune**	modefy	**modify**
missgiving	**misgiving**	model legacy	**modal legacy**

Incorrect	Correct
modis	**modus**
modren	**modern**
modrenise	**modernize**
modurn	**modern**
modyular	**modular**
moedem	**modem**
moffioso	**mafioso**
moity	**moiety**
molify	**mollify**
mollest	**molest**
momenntum	**momentum**
mommentery	**momentary**
mommentus	**momentous**
monagomous	**monogamous**
monament	**moniment**
monatery	**monetary****
monetory	**monitory****
monicism	**monachism**
monilith	**monolith**
monita	**moneta**
monnandy	**monandry**
monnopoly	**monopoly**
monnopsomy	**monopsony**
monstans di driot	
	monstrans de droit
monsterous	**monstrous**
mony	**money**
monyuments	**monuments****
Moodees	**Moody's**
mooreage	**moorage**
moote	**moot****
moovable	**movable** or **moveable**
moovant	**movant** or **movent****
moppup	**mop-up**
morabund	**moribund**
morater in lege	**moratur in lege**
morda	**moerda**
moreatorium	**moratorium**
morefine	**morphine**
Moreman	**Mormon**
moreon	**moron**
moretality	**mortality**
moreteis cawsa	**mortis causa**
moretorium	**moratorium**
morg	**morgue**
morgage	**mortgage****
morgagor	**mortgagor****
morgege	**mortgage****
morover	**moreover**

Incorrect	Correct
morrell	**moral****
morrer	**mora**
morres	**mores**
morrose	**morose**
morse	**mors**
morte	**mort**
mortemain	**mortmain**
mortgegy	**mortgagee****
mortil	**mortal**
mortman	**mortmain**
mortuous	**mortuus**
morturary	**mortuary**
moshion	**motion**
motavate	**motivate**
motercycle	**motorcycle**
mother-in-laws	**mothers-in-law**
motte	**mote**
mottive	**motive****
mottor vehicle	**motor vehicle**
movment	**movement**
movvent	**movant** or **movent****
mowse	**mouse**
mowthpiece	**mouthpiece**
moyety	**moiety**
muchual fund	**mutual fund**
mudle	**muddle**
muger	**mugger**
muggshot	**mug shot**
mulc	**mulct**
muler	**mulier**
mulibrity	**muliebrity**
mullct	**mulct**
mulltafarious	**multifarious**
mulltiple	**multiple**
mulltitude	**multitude**
multapplicity	**multiplicity**
multe	**multa**
multelateral	**multilateral**
multenational	**multinational**
multepurpose	**multipurpose**
munisiple bond	**municipal bond**
munitia	**minutia****
munndane	**mundane**
munnements	**muniments****
munnicipal	**municipal**
munnificient	**munificent**
murale	**morale****
murcatum	**mercatum**
murger	**merger**

Incorrect	Correct
murrderor	**murderer**
mursy	**mercy**
musem	**museum**
musster	**muster**
mutalate	**mutilate**
muteable	**mutable**
muteal fund	**mutual fund**
mute case	**moot case**

Incorrect	Correct
muttation	**mutation**
muttatus mutandis	
	mutatis mutandis
muttuel	**mutual**
mynable	**minable** or **mineable**
myunitions	**munitions**
myute	**mute****

N

Incorrect	Correct
nacent	**nascent**
nacker	**knacker**
naedir	**nadir**
NAFFTA	**NAFTA**
namless	**nameless**
narate	**narrate**
naritive	**narrative**
narck	**narc** or **nark**
narkosis	**narcosis**
narrcoanalysis	**narcoanalysis**
narrcotics	**narcotics**
narsisism	**narcissism**
nashional	**national**
Nassdack	**NASDAQ**
natcheralization	**naturalization**
natchura brevum	**natura brevium**
nateral	**natural**
nateralise	**naturalize**
natonalization	**nationalization**
nattive	**native**
naturlise	**naturalize**
naut	**naught**
navagible	**navigable**
navvagate	**navigate**
navval	**naval****
nawseah	**nausea**
nawtical	**nautical**
naybor	**neighbor**
nayborhood	**neighborhood**
nayder	**nadir**
naytive american	**Native American**
nayve	**knave**
nebuelous	**nebulous**
neccesity	**necessity**
nedless	**needless**
nedy	**needy**
neegro	**Negro**
neejerk	**knee-jerk**

Incorrect	Correct
neemo	**nemo**
neesi prius	**nisi prius**
neether party	**neither party**
nefew	**nephew**
neggate	**negate**
negglagent	**negligent**
negglect	**neglect**
negglegance	**negligence**
neggotible	**negotiable**
negitive	**negative**
negitive cash flo	**negative cash flow**
neglagence	**negligence**
negociable	**negotiable**
negroe	**Negro**
nehil	**nihil**
neiborhood	**neighborhood**
neice	**niece**
nekrophilia	**necrophilia**
nell	**knell**
nemisis	**nemesis**
nemly	**namely**
nepatism	**nepotism**
Nepoleonic Code	**Napoleonic Code**
nere	**near**
nereby	**nearby**
neresighted	**nearsighted**
nerture	**nurture****
nerveous	**nervous**
nesesery	**necessary**
neshence	**nescience**
nett	**net**
nettwork	**network**
neutrilise	**neutralize**
nevvertheless	**nevertheless**
newclear	**nuclear**
newsense	**nuisance**
newtral	**neutral**
nexxt	**next**

Incorrect	Correct
nexxus	**nexus**
niccotine	**nicotine**
NICE	**NYSE**
nich	**niche**
nieve	**naive**
ni exiat	**ne exeat**
nifareous	**nefarious**
NIFE	**NYFE**
nife	**knife**
nigation	**negation**
nigotiate	**negotiate**
nikname	**nickname**
nill	**nil**
nimphomania	**nymphomania**
ninty	**ninety**
niophyte	**neophyte**
nisety	**nicety**
nissi	**nisi****
nite	**night**
nivete	**naivete**
nobless oblige	**noblesse oblige**
nock	**knock**
nockious	**noxious**
nocksal	**noxal**
noeload	**no-load**
noestrike clause	**no-strike clause**
noffault	**no-fault**
nokternal	**nocturnal**
nol and void	**null and void**
noledge	**knowledge**
nole prosqui	**nolle prosequi**
nollens vollens	**nolens volens**
nollo contendre	**nolo contendere**
nollpros	**nol pros**
nomanate	**nominate**
nomenee	**nominee**
nomethic	**nomothetic**
nomin	**nomen**
nomminal	**nominal**
nonaddmision	**non-admission**
nonapearance	**non-appearance**
nonaquiesense	**nonacquiescence**
nonasessible	**non-assessable**
noncomepetitive	**noncompetitive**
noncunforming uses	**nonconforming use**
noncupate	**nuncupate**
noncyumalative	**noncumulative**
nondescrimanatory	**nondiscriminatory**

Incorrect	Correct
nondiductable	**nondeductible**
nondilevery	**non-delivery**
nonditachable	**non-detachable**
nonebalable	**non-bailable**
nonecomital	**noncommittal**
nonecompismentes	**non compos mentis**
nonecomplience	**noncompliance**
nonecontinuos	**non-continuous**
nonefeeser	**nonfeasor**
nonegotiable	**non-negotiable**
nonegsistent	**nonexistent**
noneintervention	**non-intervention**
nonejudgmental	**nonjudgmental**
nonelegal	**nonlegal**
nonensurable risk	**noninsurable risk**
none pros	**non pros**
nonesoot	**nonsuit**
nonfeesance	**nonfeasance**
nonforrfitable	**non-forfeitable**
nonfunktional	**non-functional**
nonkontribution	**noncontribution**
nonn	**non****
nonnability	**non-ability**
nonnacceptance	**non-acceptance**
nonnage	**non-age**
nonndiscloser	**non-disclosure**
nonnentity	**nonentity**
nonnintercourse	**non-intercourse**
nonnmerchantible title	**non-merchantable title**
nonnparil	**nonpareil**
nonnpayment	**nonpayment**
nonnprofit	**non-profit**
nonnsense	**nonsense**
nonobbservince	**nonobservance**
nonpartasan	**nonpartisan**
nonrezidence	**non-residence**
nonricourse	**nonrecourse**
nonsekuiter	**non sequitur**
nonstuck	**non-stock**
nontennure	**non-tenure**
nonusser	**non-user**
nonwaver agreement	**non-waiver agreement**
nood	**nude**
nopar	**no-par**
no parr value	**no-par value**
noremative	**normative**

norrmal	**normal**	nukleus	**nucleus**
nosent	**nocent**	nukular	**nuclear**
noshion	**notion**	nula bona	**nulla bona**
nosstrum	**nostrum**	nulafy	**nullify**
nosupport	**non-support**	nul and void	**null and void**
notafy	**notify**	nulification	**nullification**
noteable	**notable**	nulity	**nullity**
noteing	**noting**	nully prosekway	**nolle prosequi**
notery	**notary**	nulywed	**newlywed**
notiss	**notice**	nummerous	**numerous**
notta	**nota**	numology	**nomology**
nottariel	**notarial**	nun abstant verdict	
nottary public	**notary public**		**non obstante veredicto**
nottation	**notation**	nun cumpis mentis	
nottice	**notice**		**non compos mentis**
nottorious	**notorious**	nunderection	**non-direction**
nottwithstanding	**notwithstanding**	nundescript	**nondescript**
notworthy	**noteworthy**	nunk pro tunk	**nunc pro tunc**
novilty	**novelty**	nunlegal	**nonlegal**
novis homo	**novus homo**	nunncio	**nuncio**
novvation	**novation**	nunproseequiter	**non prosequitur**
novvel	**novel**	nun sequiter	**non sequitur**
novvice	**novice**	nurotic	**neurotic**
nowingly	**knowingly**	Nurrenburg defense	
nown	**known**		**Nuremberg defense**
noxus	**noxious**	nurvous	**nervous**
nuborn	**newborn**	nusance	**nuisance**
nucular	**nuclear**	nutral	**neutral**
nudea	**nuda**	nyif	**naif**
nudem pactim	**nudum pactum**	nyuclear	**nuclear**
nuggatory	**nugatory**		

O

oassis	**oasis**	obbreption	**obreption**
obaisance	**obeisance**	obbserve	**observe**
obay	**obey**	obbsolete	**obsolete**
obbediance	**obedience**	obbsruction	**obstruction**
obbese	**obese**	obbstanate	**obstinate**
obbfiscatory	**obfuscatory**	obbstant	**obstante**
obbit	**obit**	obbtrusive	**obtrusive**
obbiter dictum	**obiter dictum**	obbtuse	**obtuse****
obbituary	**obituary**	obbviate	**obviate**
obbjection	**objection**	obbvious	**obvious**
obblate	**oblate**	obderacy	**obduracy**
obbligation	**obligation**	obfascate	**obfuscate**
obblige	**oblige****	obgective	**objective**
obbliquity	**obliquity**	obgergate	**objurgate**
obblivious	**oblivious**	objec	**object****

Incorrect	Correct	Incorrect	Correct
oblagate	**obligate**	ofspring	**offspring**
oblegation	**obligation**	oh besoin	**au besoin**
obleger	**obliger** or **obligor****	oh contraire	**au contraire**
obleque	**oblique**	olefactory	**olfactory**
oblige	**obligee****	olligopoly	**oligopoly**
obliggatory	**obligatory**	ologopsomy	**oligopsony**
obragation	**obrogation**	omcology	**oncology**
obsalesent	**obsolescent**	ommen	**omen**
obsene	**obscene**	ommision	**omission**
obsesion	**obsession**	ommit	**omit****
obsiquios	**obsequious**	ommnipotent	**omnipotent**
obskure	**obscure**	omnabus	**omnibus**
obstettrics	**obstetrics**	omnepresense	**omnipresence**
obsticle	**obstacle**	omnishent	**omniscient**
obtane	**obtain**	on bank	**en banc**
obtension	**obtention**	on-block	**en bloc**
obzerbant	**observant**	oner	**owner**
ocasion	**occasion**	onesty	**honesty**
occer	**occur**	onfare	**unfair**
occular	**ocular**	on-going	**ongoing**
occurance	**occurrence**	onis	**onus**
oclude	**occlude**	on mass	**en masse**
ocult	**occult**	onnanism	**onanism**
ocupant	**occupant**	onnerous	**onerous**
ocupy	**occupy**	onnes probandy	**onus probandi**
ocurance	**occurrence**	on root	**en route**
ocurred	**occurred**	on vie	**en vie**
ocyupation	**occupation**	oparate	**operate**
oddor	**odor**	opeate	**opiate**
odeous	**odious**	openend	**open-end**
oderless	**odorless**	openning	**opening**
odjob	**odd job**	opertune	**opportune**
odlot	**odd lot**	ophtometrist	**optometrist**
oellti	**owelty**	opin	**open**
ofal	**offal****	opinon	**opinion**
ofen	**often**	oponent	**opponent**
ofender	**offender**	opose	**oppose**
ofer	**offer**	oppasite	**opposite****
oferer	**offeror**	opperable	**operable**
ofer of proof	**offer of proof**	oppinion	**opinion**
offcoler	**off-color**	oppium	**opium**
offence	**offense**	opptimmum	**optimum**
offrecord	**of record**	oppus	**opus**
ofgrade	**off-grade**	oprate	**operate**
ofhand	**offhand**	oprative	**operative**
ofice	**office**	opress	**oppress**
oficial	**official**	oprobrious	**opprobrious**
oflimits	**off-limits**	opshion	**option**
ofright	**of right**	opshun	**option**
ofset	**offset**	optamal	**optimal**

Incorrect	Correct	Incorrect	Correct
opthalmolagist	**ophthalmologist**	outsett	**outset**
optimmism	**optimism**	out side	**outside**
optishan	**optician**	outtcome	**outcome**
opugn	**oppugn**	outter	**outer**
orbitt	**orbit**	outtgrowth	**outgrowth**
ordaine	**ordain**	outtlaw	**outlaw**
ordanary	**ordinary**	outtlay	**outlay**
ordane	**ordain**	outtlive	**outlive**
ordeel	**ordeal**	outtstanding	**outstanding**
ordenance	**ordinance****	ovadraw	**overdraw**
ordinery income	**ordinary income**	ovarrian	**ovarian**
oregan	**organ**	ovature	**overture**
oreganization	**organization**	ovedue	**overdue****
orfan	**orphan**	overal	**overall****
orfice	**orifice**	overasessment	**overassessment**
orignal	**original**	overate	**overrate**
orijinal	**original**	overberden	**overburden**
orjy	**orgy**	overchage	**overcharge**
orkestrate	**orchestrate**	overcom	**overcome**
orral	**oral****	over-develop	**overdevelop**
orrder	**order**	overdosse	**overdose**
orrganic	**organic**	over-draft	**overdraft**
orrigin	**origin**	overeach	**overreach**
orrthodox	**orthodox**	overegstend	**overextend**
orthoepaedics	**orthopedics**	overenphasise	**overemphasize**
osillate	**oscillate**	over-estimate	**overestimate**
osstensable	**ostensible**	over-flow	**overflow**
osstentation	**ostentation**	overhawl	**overhaul**
ossteopath	**osteopath**	overhed	**overhead**
ostrisize	**ostracize**	overhere	**overhear**
oth	**oath**	overide	**override**
otre	**autre****	overlae	**overlay**
our's	**ours**	overlode	**overload**
ours'	**ours**	over look	**overlook**
outberst	**outburst**	over power	**overpower**
outbrake	**outbreak**	over-see	**oversee**
outgoe	**outgo**	oversimmplify	**oversimplify**
outige	**outage**	oversite	**oversight**
outloock	**outlook**	oversyte	**oversight**
outlore	**outlaw**	over the counter	**over-the-counter**
outlorry	**outlawry**	overthrow	**overthrow**
outmodded	**outmoded**	over time	**overtime**
outofcourt	**out-of-court**	over turn	**overturn**
outofpocket	**out-of-pocket**	overule	**overrule**
out patent	**outpatient**	overun	**overrun**
outpawring	**outpouring**	over-use	**overuse**
outputt	**output**	over-value	**overvalue**
outraje	**outrage**	overwelm	**overwhelm**
outreech	**outreach**	ovim	**ovum**
outrite	**outright**	ovvation	**ovation**

ovvercompensate ..... **overcompensate**
ovverlap .... **overlap**
ovvert .... **overt**
oweing ....**owing**
owener .... **owner**
owster .... **ouster**

owtlet .... **outlet**
owtline .... **outline**
oxegenize .... **oxygenize**
oyar .... **oyer**
oyyez........................... **oyez**

P

paccare .... **pacare**
packige .... **package**
pacsregis .... **pax regis**
pactim .... **pactum**
padloc .... **padlock**
paganate .... **paginate**
paidin ....**paid-in**
paidup .... **paid-up**
pail of the law .... **pale of the law**
paiment .... **payment**
paiss .... **pais** or **pays**
pakt .... **pact****
paktum .... **pactum**
paliate .... **palliate**
pallatable............... **palatable**
pallimoney .... **palimony**
pallpable .... **palpable**
pallpitate .... **palpitate**
pallsy................... **palsy**
palltry......................... **paltry**
palyative .... **palliative**
panal .... **panel**
panalation .... **pannellation**
pandamonum .... **pandemonium**
pandict .... **pandect**
panestaking .... **painstaking**
panicy .... **panicky**
pannache ....**panache**
panndemic.................... **pandemic**
pannder ....**pander**
pannel .... **panel**
pannick .... **panic**
pannoply .... **panoply**
panphlet ....**pamphlet**
papparazi........... **paparazzi**
papper .... **paper**
Papp smear .... **Pap smear**
paracide................ **parricide**
paradime .... **paradigm**
paradocks............ **paradox**

parafernalia .... **paraphernalia**
parafrase .... **paraphrase**
para-legal ....**paralegal**
parammour .... **paramour**
paraproffesional ...... **paraprofessional**
parchmint .... **parchment**
parden .... **pardon**
paree passu .... **pari passu**
parentel .... **parental**
paress .... **pares****
parilegel ....**paralegal**
parilize .... **paralyze**
parinoia .... **paranoia**
parisis................ **paresis**
parisite .... **parasite**
parlament .... **parliament**
parollee .... **parolee****
parr........................ **par**
parrachute .... **parachute**
parragon .... **paragon**
parragraph ....**paragraph**
parralel ....**parallel**
parralisis .... **paralysis**
parrameter .... **parameter**
parramount .... **paramount**
parraph .... **paraph**
parrdon .... **pardon**
parrens .... **parens****
parrent .... **parent**
parr issue .... **par issue**
parrity .... **parity****
parrlay ....**parlay****
parrokial................**parochial**
parrol................ **parol****
parrole .... **parole****
parrs .... **pars****
parrticulers .... **particulars**
parrtner .... **partner**
parsamony .... **parsimony**
parsel................ **parcel**

Incorrect	Correct	Incorrect	Correct
parsener	**parcener**	payso	**peso**
parshal	**partial**	payter	**pater**
partable	**partible**	paytria	**patria**
parteis	**parties**	peasful	**peaceful**
partener	**partner**	pecable	**peccable**
particculer	**particular**	pecadilo	**peccadillo**
partishun	**partition**	pecant	**peccant**
partisipate	**participate**	pecculation	**peculation**
partisipatory	**participatory**	peccuniary	**pecuniary**
partizan	**partisan**	peckadilo	**peccadillo**
party's litigant	**parties litigant**	peculliar	**peculiar**
parvalue	**par value**	peddantic	**pedantic**
pary	**parry**	pedderasty	**pederasty**
parya	**pariah**	peddestrian	**pedestrian**
pasable	**passable****	pedeatrician	**pediatrician**
pasage	**passage**	pedegree	**pedigree**
pascive activity	**passive activity**	pedement	**pediment**
pascive income	**passive income**	pedler	**peddler**
pase	**pace**	peece	**peace****
pasenger	**passenger**	peeple	**people**
pasible	**passible****	pegorative	**pejorative**
pasify	**pacify**	peicework	**piecework**
pasim	**passim**	peida ter	**pied-à-terre**
pasive	**passive**	peir	**pier****
pasport	**passport**	pelf	**pelfe**
pass book	**passbook**	pelmel	**pell-mell**
passerbys	**passers-by**	penatentiary	**penitentiary**
passige	**passage**	pendancy	**pendency**
patens	**patiens****	pendennte lit	**pendente lite**
patern	**pattern**	pendense	**pendens**
pathalogical	**pathological**	pendent light	**pendente lite**
patint	**patent****	penelty	**penalty**
patramony	**patrimony**	penery	**penury**
patrelineal	**patrilineal**	penetent	**penitent**
patremoney	**patrimony**	penil	**penal****
patrenage	**patronage**	penile law	**penal law**
pattent	**patent****	penilty	**penalty**
pattentee	**patentee**	pennalize	**penalize**
patternity	**paternity**	pennance	**penance****
pattricide	**patricide**	pennetrable	**penetrable**
paturnal	**paternal**	pennitentiary	**penitentiary**
pauner	**pawner** or **pawnor**	pennology	**penology**
pawcity	**paucity**	pennsion	**pension**
pawnography	**pornography**	pennumbra doctrine	
pawper	**pauper**		**penumbra doctrine**
payible	**payable**	pennury	**penury**
payof	**payoff**	penoyer rule	**Pennoyer Rule**
payolla	**payola**	Pensylvania rule	
payote	**peyote**		**Pennsylvania Rule**
payshence	**patience**	pention	**pension**

penus	penis	perpertrater	perpetrator
peranum	per annum	perpettual	perpetual
per bona	pro bono	perpietery	proprietary
percedure	procedure	perport	purport**
perchase	purchase	perpose	purpose
perchiser	purchaser	perposeful	purposeful
percievable	perceivable	perposly	purposely
perculiar	peculiar	perprize	purprise
percuream	per curiam	perquasites	perquisites
percurer	procurer	perquod	per quod
perdoorable	perdurable	perraccidents	per accidens
per dyem	per diem	perr adventure	peradventure
pere	peer**	perrcapita	per capita
perectrum	per rectum	perrcentile	percentile
pereodical	periodical	perremption	peremption
perequisite	prerequisite**	perremtory	peremptory
peres	peers	perrenial	perennial
perferate	perforate	perrfect	perfect
perfer charges	prefer charges	perrform	perform
perference	preference	perrifrasis	periphrasis
perfess	profess	perril	peril
perfesser	professor	perriod	period
perfiddious	perfidious	perrish	perish
perforse	perforce	perrjury	perjury
perfuse	profuse	perrmissive	permissive
pergation	purgation	perrmit	permit
perging	purging	perrplex	perplex
periferal	peripheral	perrsevere	persevere
perjer	perjure	perrsonel	personnel**
perlieu	purlieu	perrspicacious	perspicacious**
perlific	prolific	perrverbal	per verba
perliminary	preliminary	persay	per se
perloin	purloin	perscript	prescript
permatation	permutation	perse	purse
permiable	permeable	perseeds	proceeds
perminent	permanent	persent	percent
permisable	permissible	persentment	presentment
permision	permission	perseption	perception
permissadventure	per misadventure	perser	purser
permitee	permittee	personel	personal**
permy et pertoot	per my et per tout	personna	persona**
pernency	pernancy	persoot	pursuit
perogative	prerogative	perspectus	prospectus
perose	per os	perspikuous	perspicuous**
perotre vee	per autre vie	persuant	pursuant
perpart	purpart**	persue	pursue
perpatrate	perpetrate	persuer	pursuer
perpatuities	perpetuities	persuit	pursuit
per pays	per pais	persumption	presumption
perpensity	propensity	pertant key	pur tant que

Incorrect	Correct	Incorrect	Correct
pertend	**pretend****	pirimid skeme	**pyramid scheme**
pertenent	**pertinent**	piromania	**pyromania**
pertou et nonpermy		pirracy	**piracy**
	per tout et non per my	pirric	**pyrrhic**
pervayer	**purveyor**	pistel	**pistol****
perveyance	**purveyance**	pitance	**pittance**
pervided	**provided**	pitee	**pity**
perview	**purview****	pititioner	**petitioner**
perviso	**proviso**	pittfal	**pitfall**
peryear	**per year**	pityfull	**pitiful**
pessticide	**pesticide**	pityless	**pitiless**
pessuer	**pursuer**	pius	**puis**
pesurable wares	**pessurable wares**	pius uses	**pious uses**
petit assize	**petite assize**	pixx jury	**pix jury** or **pyx jury**
pettisio princio	**petitio principii**	plagery	**plagiary**
pettit	**petit****	plain close man	**plainclothesman**
pettition	**petition**	plajiarize	**plagiarize**
pettyfogger	**pettifogger**	plakit	**placit**
pety	**petty****	planed	**plaint****
petyfogger	**pettifogger**	planetiff	**plaintiff****
preeview	**preview****	planetiv	**plaintive****
phalic	**phallic**	plann	**plan**
pharmasist	**pharmacist**	plantiff	**plaintiff****
pharrmacology	**pharmacology**	plase	**place**
phelander	**philander**	plasebo	**placebo**
phillanthropy	**philanthropy**	plasser	**placer**
phillistine	**philistine**	platatude	**platitude**
phillosopher	**philosopher**	platoh	**plateau**
phinomemon	**phenomenon**	platt	**plat****
phiric	**pyrrhic**	plattform	**platform**
phiseotherapy	**physiotherapy**	plattonic	**platonic**
phisician	**physician**	plauzible	**plausible**
phisycal	**physical****	plawsable	**plausible**
phyric	**pyrrhic**	pleadding	**pleading**
picpocket	**pickpocket**	plee	**plea**
pielit	**pilot**	plee barginning	**plea bargaining**
pijeon hole	**pigeonhole**	pleed	**plead**
piket	**picket**	pleeder	**pleader**
piks jury	**pix jury** or **pyx jury**	pleed gilty	**plead guilty**
pilage	**pillage**	pleedings	**pleadings**
pilar	**pillar**	plege	**pledge**
pilery	**pillory**	pleger	**pledger** or **pledgor**
piller	**pillar**	pleni	**plene**
pillfer	**pilfer**	plennary	**plenary**
pillotage	**pilotage**	plennepotentiary	**plenipotentiary**
pinacle	**pinnacle****	plesur	**pleasure**
pionage	**peonage**	plevvin	**plevin**
piqque	**pique****	ploiy	**ploy**
piramid	**pyramid**	ploorilism	**pluralism**
piramiding	**pyramiding**	plott	**plot**

Incorrect	Correct
plowback	**plow back**
plucenta	**placenta**
plueral	**plural****
plummer	**plumber**
plurelism	**pluralism**
plurrality	**plurality**
plyable	**pliable**
poche	**poach**
pocker	**poker**
podeum	**podium**
poizin pill	**poison pill**
poket	**pocket**
pol	**poll****
polety	**polity****
poliandry	**polyandry**
poligamy	**polygamy**
polittics	**politics**
pollemic	**polemic**
pollice	**police**
pollicy	**policy****
pollished	**polished**
polliticly correct	**politically correct**
pollygraph	**polygraph**
pollyopsiny	**polyopsony**
polly polly	**polypoly**
polutant	**pollutant**
pompus	**pompous**
ponde	**pound**
pondrable	**ponderable**
ponntif	**pontiff**
ponse scheme	**Ponzi scheme**
pontifficate	**pontificate**
pooch money	**push money**
poolling	**pooling**
poosher	**pusher**
poppulace	**populace**
poppular	**popular**
poppullation	**population**
populer	**popular**
popurri	**potpourri**
porcion	**portion****
poreover	**pour-over**
poretent	**portent****
pornagraphic	**pornographic**
porpose	**propose**
porrous	**porous**
porrtray	**portray**
portentious	**portentous**
portfollio	**portfolio**
portible	**portable**

Incorrect	Correct
portige	**portage**
portil to partil act	
	Portal-to-Portal Act
portoin	**portion**
Porto Riccan	**Puerto Rican**
posative cash flo	**positive cash flow**
posdate	**postdate**
posess	**possess**
posibility	**possibility****
posible	**possible****
posnatal	**postnatal**
posnuptil	**postnuptial**
pospartum	**postpartum**
pospone	**postpone**
possi	**posse**
possition	**position**
possted	**posted**
possteriority	**posteriority**
possterity	**posterity**
posteage	**postage**
postel	**postal**
posthipnotic	**posthypnotic**
post morrtem	**postmortem**
postopperative	**postoperative**
postrial	**post-trial**
postruamatic	**posttraumatic**
postumous	**posthumous**
postyalate	**postulate**
posure	**poseur****
poteable	**potable**
pottent	**potent**
pottential	**potential**
pounse	**pounce**
pouwers	**powers**
povverty	**poverty**
powwer	**power**
poynts	**points**
poysen pill	**poison pill**
poyson	**poison**
pozession	**possession**
pozitive	**positive**
practacable	**practicable****
practicle	**practical****
practicly	**practically**
practise	**practice****
practiss law	**practice law**
prafanity	**profanity**
praksis	**praxis****
prare	**prayer****
praseworthy	**praiseworthy**

Incorrect	Correct	Incorrect	Correct
preapism	priapism	preform	perform
prebatio	probatio**	preformance bond	
precentense	pre-sentence		performance bond
precentment	presentment**	prefrence	preference
precerser	precursor	prefur	prefer**
preciding	presiding	pregnency	pregnancy
preciding judge	presiding judge	pregudice	prejudice
precipe	praecipe	prehaps	perhaps
preconndition	precondition	prejjudicial	prejudicial
preddacate	predicate**	prejuge	prejudge
preddatary	predatory	prejury	perjury
preddate	predate	prekatory	precatory
predditermin	predetermine	prelimminary	preliminary
predesesser	predecessor	prellude	prelude
predial	praedial	prelocutor	prolocutor
predicction	prediction	premarrital	premarital
predisspose	predispose	premer	premier**
preeamble	preamble	preminent	preeminent
preecaution	precaution	premmeditate	premeditate
preeclude	preclude	premmises	premises**
preeconceive	preconceive	premonnitary	premonitory
preefabricate	prefabricate	premptery	peremptory**
preematur	premature	premption	preemption
preemium	premium	premyum	premium
preemonition	premonition	prenattal	prenatal
preemptory	peremptory	prenicious	pernicious
preepaid	prepaid	prennder	prender or prendre
preepayment	prepayment	prenthisis	parenthesis
preepense	prepense	preocupancy	preoccupancy
preeponderence	preponderance	preoripetente	priori petenti
preescription	prescription	preorrdain	preordain
preesent	present	prepietry	propriety
preeserve	preserve**	prepperation	preparation
preesipitous	precipitous	prepposterus	preposterous
preesume	presume	presadent	precedent
preetax	pretax	prescence	prescience
preetence	pretense	presedent	president
preetext	pretext**	preseeding	preceding**
preetrial	pre-trial	presege	presage
preevail	prevail	presennter	presenter
preevaricator	praevaricator	presept	precept
preevent	prevent	presevation	preservation
prefekt	prefect**	preshus	precious
prefered	preferred	presinkt	precinct
prefering	preferring	presipe	precipe
preferrance	preference	presise	precise**
prefesser	professor	presistent	persistent
prefface	preface	pressdent	president
preffer	prefer**	pressentation	presentation

Incorrect	Correct
presside	**preside**
president of the United States ...	**President of the United States**
presumibly	**presumably**
presumtious	**presumptuous**
presumtive	**presumptive**
presupose	**presuppose**
presur	**pressure**
prettention	**pretention**
pretterlegal	**preter legal**
prettermit	**pretermit**
pretuim	**pretium**
preturminal	**preterminal**
prevade	**pervade**
preverse	**perverse**
preversely	**perversely**
previso	**proviso**
prevvalent	**prevalent**
prevvaracation	**prevarication**
prevvention	**prevention**
prevy	**privy**
prezence	**presence****
prezently	**presently**
prezentment	**presentment**
pricarious	**precarious**
primaface	**prima facie**
primative	**primitive**
prime fasha	**prima facie**
primmadona	**prima donna**
primmage	**primage**
primmary	**primary**
prinsipal	**principal****
prinsipel	**principle****
priscribe	**prescribe****
prise	**price**
prisiding judge	**presiding judge**
prisin	**prison**
prissoner	**prisoner**
privalege	**privilege**
privalege comunication	
	privileged communication
privalejed	**privileged**
privee	**privy**
privees	**privies**
priveous	**previous**
privicy	**privacy**
privite	**private**
privitize	**privatize**
privlege	**privilege**

Incorrect	Correct
privviledged	**privileged**
privvity	**privity**
prize earnings ratio	
	price earnings ratio
pro indivviso	**pro indiviso**
probait	**probate**
probait judge	**probate judge**
probashion	**probation****
probbability	**probability**
probbate	**probate**
probblem	**problem**
probety	**probity**
probible	**probable**
probible caws	**probable cause**
probitive	**probative**
problimatical	**problematical**
probly	**probably**
probonno	**pro bono**
proccurater	**procurator**
proccure	**procure**
proceedure	**procedure**
prochien	**prochein**
prochoise	**prochoice**
procksy	**proxy**
proclaime	**proclaim**
proclimation	**proclamation**
proconcillio	**pro consilio**
proconfeso	**pro confesso**
proconnsul	**proconsul**
procrasstanate	**procrastinate**
procrusstian	**procrustean**
procter	**proctor**
procurment	**procurement**
prodagal	**prodigal**
proddigous	**prodigious**
prodduct	**product**
prodegy	**prodigy**
proditer	**proditor**
producsion	**production**
produse	**produce**
proe	**pro**
proefakto	**pro facto**
proegressive	**progressive**
proemtor	**pro emptore**
proeponent	**proponent**
proerata	**pro rata**
proe solid	**pro solido**
proetuberent	**protuberant**
profecy	**prophecy**

Incorrect	Correct	Incorrect	Correct
profer	**proffer****	proposision	**proposition****
profesional	**professional**	proppaganda	**propaganda**
proffane	**profane**	proppagate	**propagate**
proffesion	**profession**	propper	**proper****
profficient	**proficient**	proppinquety	**propinquity**
proffit	**profit****	propportionate	**proportionate**
proffound	**profound**	propposal	**proposal**
profitts	**profits**	proppound	**propound**
proforma	**pro forma**	proppter	**propter****
profylatic	**prophylactic**	propreiter	**proprietor**
proggeniter	**progenitor**	propryeter	**proprietor**
proggnosis	**prognosis**	proregation	**prorogation**
proggram	**program**	prorenate	**pro re nata**
proggresion	**progression**	prorrog	**prorogue****
prohibbit	**prohibit**	prosacuter	**prosecutor**
prohibbitory	**prohibitory**	prosacutorial	**prosecutorial**
proibition	**prohibition**	prosay	**pro se****
projeny	**progeny**	prosede	**proceed****
projject	**project**	prosedural	**procedural**
proklivity	**proclivity**	prosee	**pro se****
prolacide	**prolicide**	proseeding	**proceeding**
proleggato	**pro legato**	proseequiter	**prosequitur**
proless	**proles**	prosess	**process**
prolixxity	**prolixity**	prosesser	**processor**
prollapse	**prolapse**	proskee	**prosequi**
prollepsis	**prolepsis**	prospectiss	**prospectus**
prolliferate	**proliferate**	prosperety	**prosperity**
prollongation	**prolongation**	prosprous	**prosperous**
prologgue	**prologue**	prosscribed	**proscribed**
promalgate	**promulgate**	prossecute	**prosecute****
promascuty	**promiscuity**	prossecuter	**prosecutor**
promisory note	**promissory note**	prosspective	**prospective****
promminent	**prominent**	prosspectus	**prospectus**
prommiscuous	**promiscuous**	prossper	**prosper**
prommise	**promise**	prosstrate	**prostrate****
promissory	**promissory****	prostatute	**prostitute**
prommote	**promote**	prosthises	**prosthesis**
promt	**prompt**	protannto	**pro tanto**
pronnouncment	**pronouncement**	protemm	**pro tem**
pronotory	**pronotary**	protempere	**pro tempore**
pronounse	**pronounce**	protesstando	**protestando**
pronunnciation	**pronunciation**	protesstation	**protestation**
proofe	**proof****	prothonnetery	**prothonotary**
proov	**prove****	prototipe	**prototype**
propely	**properly**	protrakt	**protract**
propety	**property**	protrood	**protrude**
prophetec	**prophetic**	prottaganist	**protagonist**
propishiate	**propitiate**	prottection	**protection**
propitous	**propitious**	prottege	**protegé****
proposesor	**pro possessore**	prottest	**protest**

Incorrect	Correct	Incorrect	Correct
prottestent	**Protestant**	pufery	**puffery**
prottocol	**protocol**	puggnacious	**pugnacious**
prouler	**prowler**	puine	**puisne****
provacative	**provocative**	pujilist	**pugilist**
provacoture	**provocateur**	puling	**pulling**
proveable	**provable**	pulite	**polite**
provinsial	**provincial**	pullmonary	**pulmonary**
proviser	**provisor**	pullsater	**pulsator**
provissional	**provisional**	pullution	**pollution**
provocke	**provoke**	pulmanery	**pulmonary**
provosed	**provost**	pumel	**pummel**
provvide	**provide**	punashible	**punishable**
provvince	**province**	punative	**punitive**
provvision	**provision**	pungtuation	**punctuation**
provvocation	**provocation**	punishmint	**punishment**
prowd	**proud**	punktilious	**punctilious**
proxamate	**proximate**	punktuation	**punctuation**
proximmity	**proximity**	punndit	**pundit**
proxxy	**proxy**	punngent	**pungent**
prozaic	**prosaic**	punnishable	**punishable**
pruddence	**prudence**	punnishment	**punishment**
pruedent	**prudent**	puntilious	**punctilious**
pruerent interest	**prurient interest**	puny judge	**puisne judge**
prymacy	**primacy**	puppil	**pupil**
pryme	**prime**	purchise	**purchase**
prymer	**primer**	purety	**purity**
pryor	**prior**	purgitive	**purgative**
pryority	**priority**	purility	**puerility**
pryse court	**prize court**	purjury	**perjury**
pseudacysis	**pseudocyesis**	purks	**perks**
psichedelic	**psychedelic**	purloo	**purlieu**
psichoanalist	**psychoanalyst**	purnansy	**pernancy**
psicopath	**psychopath**	purose	**per os**
psikology	**psychology**	purpisless	**purposeless**
psudo	**pseudo**	purposful	**purposeful**
psycophant	**sycophant**	purposse	**purpose****
psykotherapy	**psychotherapy**	purrity	**purity**
psynod	**synod**	purrparty	**purparty**
pubberty	**puberty**	purrport	**purport****
pubblic	**public****	purrsu	**pursue**
pubblicity	**publicity**	purrsuant	**pursuant**
pubblish	**publish**	purrus iddiot	**purus idiota**
pubic law	**public law**	purrveyor	**purveyor**
publacist	**publicist**	pursecute	**persecute****
publicher	**publisher**	purson	**person**
publick	**public****	pursonality	**personality****
publickly	**publicly**	pursonalty	**personalty****
pucher	**pusher**	pursuade	**persuade**
puedicity	**pudicity**	pursuint	**pursuant**
puenitive	**punitive**	purtain	**pertain**

purterbation	**perturbation**	pweblo	**pueblo**
purvayance	**purveyance**	pyramania	**pyromania**
purvert	**pervert**	pyrimidding	**pyramiding**
purvew	**purview****	pyrramid	**pyramid**
pusilannimous	**pusillanimous**	pyrromania	**pyromania**
pusuit	**pursuit**	pyunitive	**punitive**
putitive	**putative**	pyure	**pure****
puttative	**putative**	pyusilaninous	**pusillanimous**
puttrid	**putrid**	pyutrid	**putrid**
putts and calls	**puts and calls**		

Q

qeu estate	**que estate**	quarrantine	**quarantine**
qeurelous	**querulous**	quarrter	**quarter**
qeury	**query****	quartige	**quartage**
quac	**quack**	quarto de post	**quarto die post**
quach	**quash**	quary	**quarry****
quaddrant	**quadrant**	quassi	**quasi**
quaddripartite	**quadripartite**	quaterly	**quarterly**
quaddriplegic	**quadriplegic**	quavver	**quaver**
quaddriplejia	**quadriplegia**	quazi	**quasi**
quaddroon	**quadroon**	quee	**quae****
quaddruplacation	**quadruplication**	queans	**queen's**
quaddruplet	**quadruplet**	queare	**quare****
quadrenium	**quadrennium**	queazy	**queasy**
quadriumverate	**quadrumvirate**	queesy	**queasy**
quaf	**quaff**	quel	**quell**
quaggmire	**quagmire**	queralous	**querulous**
qualafication	**qualification**	quere	**quaere****
qualafier	**qualifier**	querens	**quaerens**
qualafy	**qualify**	querk	**quirk**
quallatative	**qualitative**	quert	**quart**
quallified	**qualified**	quescent	**quiescent**
quallify	**qualify**	quesshionable	**questionable**
quallity	**quality**	quesst	**quest**
quam	**qualm**	quesstion	**question**
quamdo	**quamdiu**	quesstionable	**questionable**
quanndo acciderent		questinable	**questionable**
	quando acciderint	questio	**quaestio**
quanntity	**quantity**	questor	**quaestor**
quanntum	**quantum**	questour	**quaestor**
quantative	**quantitative**	quetus	**quietus**
quante minorris	**quanti minoris**	queu	**queue****
quar	**quare****	quey	**quay****
quarel	**quarrel****	queysay judical	**quasi-judicial**
quarela	**querela****	quible	**quibble**
quarellsome	**quarrelsome**	quidd pro quo	**quid pro quo**
quarintine	**quarantine**	quidpro quo	**quid pro quo**

Incorrect	Correct
quieetis	quietus
quiett	quiet**
quik	quick
quikening	quickening
quiksotic	quixotic
quinch	quench
quinntesence	quintessence
quinntuplet	quintuplet
quintesential	quintessential
quitare	quietare
quitence	quittance
quiter	quitter
quitince	quittance
quitt	quit**
quittan	qui tam
quittclaim	quitclaim
quittrent	quit rent
quitude	quietude
quitus	quietus

Incorrect	Correct
quizical	quizzical
quoannimo	quo animo
quodd	quod
quod hoc	quoad hoc
quorim	quorum
quorrum	quorum
quoshent verdict	quotient verdict
quoteable	quotable
quotta	quota**
quottation	quotation
quotte	quote**
quottidian	quotidian
quya	quia
qwackery	quackery
qwadripartitis	quadripartitus
Qwaker	Quaker
qwee	quae
qwessta	questa
qwo waranto	quo warranto

R

Incorrect	Correct
rabbid	rabid
rabees	rabies
rabi	rabbi
rabinnical	rabbinical
raceism	racism
raceist	racist
rachet	ratchet
raciall	racial
rackit	racket**
radacals	radicals
raddar	radar
raddiation	radiation
raddicals	radicals
raddioactive	radioactive
raddius	radius
raddon	radon
rade	raid
radeal	radial
radeant	radiant
radeation	radiation
radeoactive	radioactive
radeology	radiology
rader	raider
radiactive	radioactive
radialogy	radiology
radikal	radical

Incorrect	Correct
raffel	raffle
rafish	raffish
rafle	raffle
raftige	raftage
raice	race
raign	reign**
raillage	railage
raillroad	railroad
railway laber act	Railway Labor Act
railwey	railway
raip	rape
rairly	rarely
rait	rate
raize	raise**
raje	rage
rak	rack**
rakateer	racketeer
raket	racket**
raketearing	racketeering
rakoff	rake-off
rakrent	rack-rent
ralage	railage
ralehead	railhead
raleroad	railroad
raleside	railside

Incorrect	Correct	Incorrect	Correct
raleway	railway	rassism	racism
ramafication	ramification	rassling	wrestling
ramafy	ramify	rassure	rasure
ramefy	ramify	ratabble	ratable
rammble	ramble	ratafication	ratification
rammbunctious	rambunctious	rateable	ratable
rammification	ramification	ratefy	ratify
rammpant	rampant	rateing	rating
rammshakle	ramshackle	ratening	rattening
rampint	rampant	rath	wrath
ranbunctuous	rambunctious	ratiffication	ratification
ranck	rank	rationel	rational**
rancker	rancor	rationnal	rationale**
randomm	random	rationnilization	rationalization
ranemaker	rainmaker	ratpayer	ratepayer
rangle	wrangle**	rattable	ratable
ranje	range	ratte	rate
ranjer	ranger	rattification	ratification
ranncerous	rancorous	ratting	rating
ranncid	rancid	rattional	rational**
ranndom	random	rattione	ratione
rannking	ranking	raunnchy	raunchy
rannsack	ransack	ravasher	ravisher
rannsom	ransom	ravige	ravage
ransak	ransack	ravinous	ravenous
ranselman	rancelman	ravvage	ravage
ransid	rancid	ravvish	ravish
ransomm	ransom	rawnchy	raunchy
rapcher	rapture	rayder	radar
rapeist	rapist	raydon	radon
raporte	rapport**	rayp	rape
rapp	rap**	rayse	raze**
rappe	rape**	raysing	raising
rapperoshment	rapprochement	raysism	racism
rappid	rapid	reabilitate	rehabilitate
rappine	rapine	reachible	reachable
rappist	rapist	reacktor	reactor
rappsheet	rap sheet	reacter	reactor
raprochement	rapprochement	reactionery	reactionary
raptur	rapture**	read herring	red herring
rar	raw	reafer	refer
rarefide	rarefied	reafirm	reaffirm
rarified	rarefied	reajurn	readjourn
rarly	rarely	reajustmint	readjustment
rashial	racial	reaktion	reaction
rashio	ratio	reaktionary	reactionary
rashional	rational**	realese	release
rasing	raising	realise	realize**
rasion	ration	realitty	reality**
rasist	racist	reall	real**

Incorrect	Correct
reallign	**realign**
reallised gain	**realized gain**
reallism	**realism**
reallty	**realty****
realot	**reallot**
realter	**Realtor****
reaply	**reapply**
reaportionment	**reapportionment**
reapraise	**reappraise**
reaquired	**reacquired**
reaquisition	**reacquisition**
reargament	**reargument**
rearr	**rear**
rearrgument	**reargument**
reasaning	**reasoning**
reasearch	**research**
reasert	**reassert**
reasess	**reassess**
reashurance	**reassurance**
reasine	**reassign**
reason deter	**raison d'être**
reassesment	**reassessment**
reasurance	**reassurance**
reatach	**reattach**
reave	**reeve**
reazon	**reason**
reazonable	**reasonable**
rebbate	**rebate****
rebbel	**rebel**
rebbuff	**rebuff**
rebbutel	**rebuttal**
rebelion	**rebellion**
rebild	**rebuild**
rebis sic stantabuss	**rebus sic stantibus**
rebuf	**rebuff**
rebutal	**rebuttal**
rebuter	**rebutter**
rebutt	**rebut**
rebuttible	**rebuttable**
rebuttle	**rebuttal**
recalment	**recallment**
recanition	**recognition**
recapcher	**recapture**
recappitalization	**recapitalization**
recappitulate	**recapitulate**
reccipprocal	**reciprocal**
recclesness	**recklessness**
reccomend	**recommend**
reccompensible	**recompensable**

Incorrect	Correct
recconaisance	**reconnaissance**
recconcile	**reconcile**
recconfirm	**reconfirm**
recconsider	**reconsider**
recconvay	**reconvey**
recconversion	**reconversion**
reccount	**recount**
reccoupment	**recoupment**
reccourse	**recourse**
reccover	**recover****
reccovery	**recovery****
reccreant	**recreant**
recctify	**rectify**
reccumbent	**recumbent**
reccuperate	**recuperate**
reccusants	**recusants**
reccuse	**recuse****
reccycle	**recycle**
receed	**recede**
receetor	**receiptor**
receeve	**receive**
receever	**receiver**
recemendation	**recommendation**
recepptive	**receptive**
recerd	**record**
recicle	**recycle**
recievable	**receivable**
recieve	**receive**
recievor	**receiver**
recievorship	**receivership**
recitle	**recital**
reckant	**recant**
reckening	**reckoning**
reckfree	**wreckfree**
recklamation	**reclamation**
recluse	**recluse**
reckognise	**recognize**
reckognition	**recognition**
reckondite	**recondite**
reckonsideration	**reconsideration**
reckonstruct	**reconstruct**
reckord	**record**
reckourse	**recourse**
reckreant	**recreant**
reckreation	**recreation**
reckrudesense	**recrudescence**
recktal	**rectal**
recktum	**rectum**
reckuperato	**recuparatio**
reckusation	**recusation**

Incorrect	Correct
reckwisition	reacquisition
reclamant	reclaimant
reclame	reclaim
reclesly	recklessly
reclimation	reclamation
recloose	recluse**
recognisance	recognizance
recomence	recommence
recomend	recommend
recomit	recommit
recon	reckon
reconise	recognize
reconize	recognize
reconnduction	reconduction
reconnsign	reconsign
reconntinuence	recontinuance
reconnversion	reconversion
reconnveyance	reconveyance
reconoiter	reconnoiter
reconsilable	reconcilable
recoop	recoup
recordor	recorder
recovrible	recoverable
recovver	recover**
recovvery	recovery**
recrimminating	recriminating
recrimmination	recrimination
recrost-examination	recross examination
recrute	recruit
rectel	rectal
recter	rector
rectery	rectory
rectesincurie	rectus in curia
rectiffication	rectification
rectiffy	rectify
rectim	rectum
recupperate	recuperate
recuzation	recusation
recuze	recuse**
recyusal	recusal
redalent	redolent
reddemise	redemise
reddemtion	redemption
reddetermination	redetermination
reddhanded	red handed
reddhibitory	redhibitory
reddiscount	rediscount
redditus	reditus
reddlining	redlining

Incorrect	Correct
reddolent	redolent
reddout	redout
reddress	redress
reddundancy	redundancy
redduplicate	reduplicate
redeamable	redeemable
redellivery	redelivery
redeme	redeem
redenda	reddenda
redendum	reddendum
redessesin	redisseisin
redetus	reditus
redevellop	redevelop
redevvelop	redevelop
redgistration	registration
redhering	red herring
redibition	redhibition
rediculous	ridiculous
redily	readily
redistrick	redistrict
reditermine	redetermine
redition	reddition
redoose	reduce
redought	redoubt**
redresment	redressment
redubers	redubbers
reducable	reducible
reducktion	reduction
reduckto ad abserdim	reductio ad absurdum
redundent	redundant
reduse	reduce
redy and wiling	ready and willing
ree	re
reeaction	reaction
reealocate	reallocate
reealot	reallot
reebut	rebut
reebutal	rebuttal
reecal	recall
reecalcitrant	recalcitrant
reecant	recant
reecapitulate	recapitulate
reecapter	recapture
reecaption	recaption
reeceivable	receivable
reecently	recently
reeceptive	receptive
reecess	recess
reech	reach

Incorrect	Correct	Incorrect	Correct
reeclaim	reclaim	reeflect	reflect
reecluse	recluse	reeform	reform
reeco	RICO	reeformitory	reformatory
reecodification	recodification	reefrain	refrain
reecognisance	recognizance	reefresh	refresh
reecoil	recoil	reefund	refund
reecolect	recollect	reefurbish	refurbish
reeconcile	reconcile	reefusal	refusal
reeconessance	reconnaissance	reegard	regard
reeconsider	reconsider	reegarding	regarding
reeconsiliation	reconciliation	reegent	regent
reeconstruck	reconstruct	reegon	region
reeconstrucktion	reconstruction	reegrant	regrant
reeconveen	reconvene	reegress	regress
reeconventional	reconventional	reegret	regret
reeconversion	reconversion	reegroup	regroup
reeconvict	reconvict	reehash	rehash
reecord	record	reehearing	rehearing
reecording	recording	reeify	reify**
reecount	recount	reeimburse	reimburse
reecourse	recourse	reeiterate	reiterate
reecover	recover**	reejection	rejection
reecovree	recoveree**	reejenerative	regenerative
reecriminate	recriminate	reejoinder	rejoinder
reecruit	recruit	reelapse	relapse
reecumbent	recumbent	reeleaf	relief
reecuperation	recuperation	reelease	release
reedeem	redeem	reelent	relent
reedemption	redemption	reel estate tax	real estate tax
reeders	readers	reeliance	reliance
reedevelop	redevelop	reelingquish	relinquish
reedisaysin	redisseisin	reelism	realism
reediscount	rediscount	reelity	reality
reedistribution	redistribution	reelive	relive**
reedistrict	redistrict	reelize	realize**
reedjourn	readjourn	reellect	reelect
reedjustment	readjustment	reelocation	relocation
reedmitance	readmittance	reelty	realty**
reed only memory	read-only memory	reeluctant	reluctant
reedouble	redouble	reemand	remand
reedoubt	redoubt**	reemark	remark
reedout	read-out	reemburse	reimburse
reedraft	redraft	reemise	remise
reedress	redress	reemiss	remiss
reeduce	reduce	reemission	remission
reeduction	reduction	reemit	remit
reedundant	redundant	reemmploy	reemploy
reefinance	refinance	reemorse	remorse
reefirmation	reaffirmation	reemote	remote
		reemoval	removal

Incorrect	Correct	Incorrect	Correct
reen	**rien**	reesponsive	**responsive**
reencarnate	**reincarnate**	re establish	**reestablish**
reencorporate	**reincorporate**	reestorative	**restorative**
reencounter	**rencounter**	reestore	**restore**
reeneg	**renege**	reestraint	**restraint**
reenegotiable	**renegotiable**	reestrayning order	
reenforce	**reinforce**		**restraining order**
reenounse	**renounce**	reestrict	**restrict**
reenstate	**reinstate**	reestrictive	**restrictive**
reensurance	**reinsurance**	reesultent	**resultant**
reenvesment	**reinvestment**	reetail	**retail**
reenvest	**reinvest**	reetaning	**retaining**
reenvigorate	**reinvigorate**	reetard	**retard**
reeopen	**reopen**	reetorical	**rhetorical**
reeorder	**reorder**	reetraction	**retraction**
reepay	**repay**	reetreat	**retreat**
reepeal	**repeal**	reetrial	**retrial**
reeplace	**replace**	reeunite	**reunite**
reeplead	**replead**	reeus	**reus**
reeplenish	**replenish**	reevaluashion	**reevaluation****
reeplete	**replete**	reevere	**revere**
reeplevin	**replevin**	reeverification	**reverification**
reepligare	**replegiare**	reeverse	**reverse**
reeply	**reply**	reevest	**revest**
reepo	**repo**	reevindicate	**revindicate**
reeport	**report**	reevive	**revive**
reepose	**repose**	reevoke	**revoke**
reeposses	**repossess**	reevolt	**revolt**
reepression	**repression**	reevolving	**revolving**
reeprieve	**reprieve**	reeward	**reward**
reeproach	**reproach**	reework	**rework**
reeproduce	**reproduce**	reexammination	**reexamination**
reepudiation	**repudiation**	reexxport	**reexport**
reepugnant	**repugnant**	reezone	**rezone**
reepulse	**repulse**	refering	**referring**
reepurchase	**repurchase**	refermation	**reformation**
reesalable	**resalable**	referree	**referee****
reesemble	**resemble**	referrence	**reference****
reeside	**reeside**	refery	**referee****
reesidual	**residual**	refewtation	**refutation**
reesind	**rescind**	reffer	**refer****
reesiprocate	**reciprocate**	refferee	**referee****
reesist	**resist**	refference	**reference****
reesite	**recite**	refferendum	**referendum**
reesonable	**reasonable**	reffinment	**refinement**
reesonible dout	**reasonable doubt**	refform	**reform**
reesourceful	**resourceful**	refformatory	**reformatory**
reespect	**respect**	reffrain	**refrain**
reespectable	**respectable**	reffreshing	**refreshing**
reespondant	**respondent**	reffuge	**refuge**

Incorrect	Correct	Incorrect	Correct
reffunds	refunds	regullation A	Regulation A
reffuse	refuse	reguvenate	rejuvenate
reffusel	refusal	regyularity	regularity
refinnance	refinance	rehabbilitate	rehabilitate
refirm	reaffirm	rehabilittation	rehabilitation
refleksive	reflexive	rehersal	rehearsal
reflektion	reflection	rehipothecation	rehypothecation
refraine	refrain	reiffy	reify**
refraktion	refraction	reinacct	reenact
refrence	reference	reinberse	reimburse
refujee	refugee	reing	reign**
refuns	refunds	reinntegration	reintegration
refurance	reference	reinshurer	reinsurer
refuttation	refutation	reishue	reissue
refyoutation	refutation	reiterrate	reiterate
refyugee	refugee	reitterate	reiterate
refyutation	refutation	rejec	reject
regalation	regulation	rejement	regiment**
regailia	regalia	rejency	regency
regalarize	regularize	rejenerate	regenerate
regashio	rogatio	rejester	register
regect	reject	rejia via	regia via
regeem	regime	rejicide	regicide
regel	regal	rejime	regime**
regelar	regular	rejina	regina
regemen	regimen**	rejional	regional
regergitate	regurgitate	rejistered	registered
regestrant	registrant	rejjoinder	rejoinder
reggale	regale	rejjoining grattis	rejoining gratis
reggard	regard	rejoyce	rejoice
reggeneration	regeneration	rejoyn	rejoin
reggicide	regicide	rejuvvenate	rejuvenate
reggister	register	rek	reck**
reggistry	registry	rekalcitrant	recalcitrant
reggret	regret	rekall	recall
reggula	regula**	rekant	recant
reggular	regular**	rekapitulate	recapitulate
reggulate	regulate	rekkolection	recollection
reggulation	regulation	rekless	reckless
reglar	regular**	reknown	renown
regoin	rejoin	rekontrol	recontrol
regres	regress	rekordim	recordum
regrescive tax	regressive tax	rekrimination	recrimination
regrett	regret	reks	rex**
regulait	regulate	rektum	rectum
reguleable	regulable	rekwest	request
reguler	regular	rekwire	require
regulers	regulars	rekwisite	requisite
regullarize	regularize	rekwite	requite
regullate	regulate	relagate	relegate

Incorrect	Correct
relaksatio	relaxatio
relaps	relapse
relashionship	relationship
relashun	relation
relaited	related
relaiter	relater
relaxxant	relaxant
relayter	relator**
relect	reelect
releef	relief
releese	release
rele estate	real estate
releeve	relieve
releif	relief
releive	relieve
relenntless	relentless
relesse	releasee
reletive	relative
relevent	relevant
relible	reliable
relicshion	reliction
relie	rely
relience	reliance
religgious	religious
relign	realign
relijion	religion
relivancy	relevancy
rellapse	relapse
rellate	relate
rellations	relations
rellative	relative
rellatrix	relatrix
rellaxar	relaxare
rellease	release
relledge	reallege
rellegate	relegate
rellent	relent
rellevant	relevant
relliable	reliable
rellick	relic
rellief	relief**
relligion	religion
rellinquish	relinquish
rellish	relish
rellocate	relocate
relluctance	reluctance
relly	rely
relm	realm
relokation	relocation
reluctent	reluctant

Incorrect	Correct
reluktance	reluctance
relyable	reliable
remady	remedy
remander	remainder
remanes	remains
remarage	remarriage
remariage	remarriage
remarkeable	remarkable
remarkible	remarkable
remary	remarry
remeddy	remedy
remedees	remedies
rememmber	remember
remend	remand
remenisent	reminiscent
remenneration	remuneration
remenstrate	remonstrate
remidial	remedial
remidies	remedies
reminise	reminisce
remision	remission
remitee	remittee
remitel	remittal
remitence	remittance
remititer	remittitur**
remitt	remit
remittment	remitment
remize	remise
remmainder	remainder
remmains	remains
remmand	remand
remmark	remark
remmedial	remedial
remmember	remember
remminice	reminisce
remmiss	remiss
remmit	remit
remmiter	remitter**
remmitor	remittor**
remmnant rule	remnant rule
remmodel	remodel
remmonstrance	remonstrance
remmorse	remorse
remmote	remote
remmove	remove
remmunerate	remunerate
remoddle	remodel
remonnetisation	remonetization
remoov	remove
remors	remorse

Incorrect	Correct	Incorrect	Correct
remorsful	**remorseful**	repatreation	**repatriation**
remorsless	**remorseless**	repeel	**repeal**
removeal	**removal**	repeet	**repeat**
remploy	**reemploy**	repell	**repel**
renact	**reenact**	repentent	**repentant**
renagade	**renegade**	reperchase	**repurchase**
renasance	**renaissance**	repetoire	**repertoire**
rence	**rents**	repitition	**repetition**
rench	**wrench**	replase	**replace**
rendayavous	**rendezvous**	replecate	**replicate**
reneg	**renege**	repleed	**replead****
reneggotiation	**renegotiation**	repleet	**replete****
renegotition act	**Renegotiation Act**	replege	**repledge**
renevare	**renovare**	replevable	**repleviable**
renevate	**renovate**	replevee	**replevy**
renewel	**renewal**	replevvin	**replevin**
rengal years	**regnal years**	replevviser	**replevisor**
rennaissance	**renaissance**	replie	**reply**
rennder	**render**	reporrtedly	**reportedly**
renndevous	**rendezvous**	reposess	**repossess**
renndition	**rendition**	repossesion	**repossession**
rennegotiate	**renegotiate**	reposte	**riposte**
rennew	**renew**	repoze	**repose**
rennewal	**renewal**	reppairs	**repairs**
rennounce	**renounce**	repparable	**reparable**
rennovate	**renovate**	reppartee	**repartee**
rennt	**rent**	reppatriation	**repatriation**
rennunciation	**renunciation**	reppay	**repay**
rennvoy	**renvoi**	reppeal	**repeal**
renominate	**renominate**	reppeat	**repeat**
renoun	**renown**	reppel	**repel**
renstatement	**reinstatement**	reppent	**repent**
rensured	**reinsured**	reppetition	**repetition**
rentible	**rentable**	repplacment	**replacement**
rentige	**rentage**	reppleador	**repleader**
rentrol	**rent-roll**	repplenish	**replenish**
rentry	**reentry**	repplevin	**replevin**
renue	**renew**	repplica	**replica**
renumerate	**remunerate**	repplicant	**replicant**
renunnsiation	**renunciation**	repplikate	**replicate**
renvest	**reinvest**	reppo	**repo**
reoabsent	**reo absente**	repporter	**reporter**
reoppen	**reopen**	repportioment	**reapportionment**
reorginise	**reorganize**	repprehend	**reapprehend**
reorginize	**reorganize**	repprehensable	**reprehensible**
reorrder	**reorder**	reppres	**repress**
reorrganization	**reorganization**	reppresent	**represent**
repare	**repair**	repprimand	**reprimand**
reparration	**reparation**	repprisal	**reprisal**
reparty	**repartee**	repproach	**reproach**

85

Incorrect	Correct	Incorrect	Correct
repprobate	**reprobate**	resavoir	**reservoir**
repproduction	**reproduction**	reseant	**resiant**
repprove	**reprove**	resedance	**residence****
reppublic	**republic**	resedence	**residence****
reppudiate	**repudiate**	reseed	**recede**
reppugnant	**repugnant**	reseever	**receiver**
reppulsive	**repulsive**	resegnation	**resignation**
repputable	**reputable**	resegragate	**resegregate**
reppute	**repute**	reseivable	**receivable**
reprabation	**reprobation**	reseivership	**receivership**
repraise	**reappraise**	resemmblence	**resemblance**
repramand	**reprimand**	resently	**recently**
repreeve	**reprieve**	reseptakle	**receptacle**
represenative	**representative**	resepter	**receptor**
representer	**representor**	reseption	**reception**
representitive	**representative**	reserch	**research**
represive	**repressive**	resergent	**resurgent**
repressentation	**representation**	resesion	**recession**
reprezentative	**representative**	resess	**recess**
reprisel	**reprisal**	resession	**recession**
represisentee	**representee**	resetlement	**resettlement**
reprizes	**reprises**	residduery	**residuary**
reproch	**reproach**	residdum	**residuum**
reproduse	**reproduce**	residense	**residence****
reproov	**reprove**	residivism	**recidivism**
repubblican	**republican**	residuel	**residual**
repubblish	**republish**	residuo	**residua**
republikan	**republican**	resieser	**resseiser**
repudeater	**repudiator**	resillient	**resilient**
repugnency	**repugnancy**	resind	**rescind**
repugnnant	**repugnant**	resine	**resign****
repullsion	**repulsion**	resinee	**resignee**
reputible	**reputable**	resipiant	**recipient**
reputtation	**reputation**	resiprocal	**reciprocal**
reputted	**reputed**	resiprocity	**reciprocity**
repyutable	**reputable**	resisery	**rescissory**
reqquest	**request**	resision	**rescission**
reqquisition	**requisition**	resistence	**resistance**
requier	**require**	resital	**recital**
requirment	**requirement**	reskript	**rescript**
requittal	**requital**	reskue	**rescue**
requizition	**requisition**	resorce	**resource**
reqwire	**require**	resoreces	**resources**
rere	**rear**	resourcefull	**resourceful**
rerite	**rewrite**	respecktive	**respective**
resadent	**resident**	respectible	**respectable**
resail	**resale**	respectivly	**respectively**
resaleable	**resalable**	respekt	**respect**
resalution	**resolution**	respondant	**respondent**
resavation	**reservation**	respondenchia	**respondentia**

responnsibility .... **responsibility**
responsable .... **responsible**
ress .... **res**
resscue .... **rescue**
resseance .... **resiance**
ressearch .... **research**
ressegnation .... **resignation**
ressegregation .... **resegregation**
resseprocity .... **reciprocity**
ressert .... **reassert**
resserve .... **reserve**
resset .... **reset**
ressidential .... **residential**
ressign .... **reassign**
ress ippsa loquiter .... **res ipsa loquitur**
ressisting .... **resisting**
ress judicata .... **res judicata**
ressling .... **wrestling**
ressolute .... **resolute**
ressolution .... **resolution**
ressort .... **resort**
resspit .... **respite**
ressplendant .... **resplendent**
resspond .... **respond**
resspondant .... **respondent**
resspondeat superior ....
.... **respondeat superior**
resst .... **rest****
resstitution .... **restitution**
resstricted .... **restricted**
resstrictive .... **restrictive**
ressts .... **rests**
ressurect .... **resurrect**
restablish .... **reestablish**
resterant .... **restaurant**
restetution .... **restitution**
restor .... **restore**
restrainning .... **restraining**
restrane .... **restrain**
restraneing order .... **restraining order**
restrick .... **restrict**
restrictiv .... **restrictive**
restriktion .... **restriction**
restruccture .... **restructure**
resullting .... **resulting**
resumons .... **resummons**
resumtion .... **resumption**
resurance .... **reassurance**
resussitate .... **resuscitate**
retachment .... **reattachment**

retadation .... **retardation**
retainner .... **retainer**
retakeing .... **retaking**
retale .... **retail**
retalliatory .... **retaliatory**
retane .... **retain**
retaned .... **retained**
retaught .... **retort**
retayner .... **retainer**
retecent .... **reticent**
retern .... **return**
retier .... **retire**
retiry .... **retiree**
retoric .... **rhetoric**
retortion .... **retorsion**
retrac .... **retract**
retracksit .... **retraxit**
retracktion .... **retraction**
retractive .... **retroactive**
retreave .... **retrieve**
retrebution .... **retribution**
retreet .... **retreat**
retreeve .... **retrieve**
retreival .... **retrieval**
retreive .... **retrieve**
retresede .... **retrocede**
retrespective .... **retrospective**
retribbutive .... **retributive**
retrie .... **retry**
retroggresion .... **retrogression**
retryal .... **retrial**
rett .... **rette**
rettailer .... **retailer**
rettainer .... **retainer**
rettaliation .... **retaliation**
rettardate .... **retardate**
rettention .... **retention**
retticense .... **reticence**
rettirement .... **retirement**
rettort .... **retort**
rettribution .... **retribution**
rettro .... **retro**
rettroactive .... **retroactive**
rettrogression .... **retrogression**
rettrosession .... **retrocession**
rettrospecction .... **retrospection**
rettry .... **retry**
retturn .... **return**
returnible .... **returnable**
returny .... **returnee**

Incorrect	Correct	Incorrect	Correct
revacable	**revocable**	rexamination	**reexamination**
revallorize	**revalorize**	rexchange	**reexchange**
revalluate	**reevaluate**	rexport	**reexport**
revealation	**revelation**	reyunion	**reunion**
revecation	**revocation**	rezadue	**residue**
reveel	**reveal****	rezemble	**resemble**
reveer	**revere**	rezervation	**reservation**
reveiw	**review**	rezide	**reside**
revelant	**relevant**	rezidence	**residence****
revell	**revel****	reziduary	**residuary**
revellatory	**revelatory**	rezign	**resign**
revelution	**revolution**	reziliency	**resiliency**
revenew	**revenue**	rezistance	**resistance**
revennues	**revenues**	rezoneing	**rezoning**
revenue ruling	**Revenue Ruling**	rezort	**resort**
reverbrate	**reverberate**	rezult	**result**
revers	**reverse**	rezumay	**résumé****
reversable	**reversible**	rezume	**resume****
reversell	**reversal**	rhetoricle	**rhetorical**
reversoner	**reversioner**	rhythim	**rhythm**
revewable	**reviewable**	ri	**re**
revinues	**revenues**	riallocate	**reallocate****
reviver	**revivor**	riballed	**ribald****
revize	**revise**	ricco	**RICO**
revizer	**revisor**	ricepient	**recipient**
revrence	**reverence**	richard row	**Richard Roe**
revullsion	**revulsion**	richual	**ritual**
revursal	**reversal**	rickoshay	**ricochet**
revursion	**reversion**	ricktus	**rictus**
revvalidate	**revalidate**	ricognisance	**recognizance**
revveal	**reveal****	ridance	**riddance**
revvel	**revel****	riddendum	**reddendum**
revvendication	**revendication**	ridder	**rider**
revvenge	**revenge**	riddicule	**ridicule**
revverberate	**reverberate**	riddince	**riddance**
revverence	**reverence**	ridgid	**rigid**
revverify	**reverify**	ridicullous	**ridiculous**
revversal	**reversal**	rief	**reif****
revversionery	**reversionary**	riefy	**reify****
revverter	**reverter**	rienforce	**reinforce**
revvision	**revision**	rienstate	**reinstate**
revvisit	**revisit**	riet	**riot**
revvitalize	**revitalize**	rieve	**reve**
revvivel	**revival**	riger	**rigor**
revvoke	**revoke**	rigerous	**rigorous**
revvolutionery	**revolutionary**	riggidity	**rigidity**
revvolver	**revolver**	rightfull	**rightful**
revvultion	**revulsion**	right-off	**write-off**
revvurt	**revert**	rightono	**right to know**
rewward	**reward**	righttful	**rightful**

Incorrect	Correct	Incorrect	Correct
righttoo work	right to work	rober	robber
riging the market		robery	robbery
	rigging the market	rocbotom	rock bottom
rigling	ridgeling	rodd	rod
rigognizance	recognizance	rodebed	roadbed
rigressive	regressive	rodeway	roadway
rigts	rights	rod of land	rood of land
rilate	relate	roebust	robust
rilegious	religious	Roeman law	Roman law
rimemberance	remembrance	roescolored	rose-colored
ringging	ringing	roge	rogue
rinkle	wrinkle	roggare	rogare
riottous	riotous	roggatory letters	rogatory letters
riparya	riparia	roggery	roguery
riple effect	ripple effect	roi	roy
riplevin	replevin	rolback	rollback
ripness doctrin	ripeness doctrine	roldup	rolled up
rippa	ripa	roleback	rollback
ripparian	riparian	role call	roll call
ripute	repute	roling	rolling
riseing of court	rising of court	rollmodel	role model
riserve	reserve	rolover paper	roll-over paper
risskay	risqué	rols	rolls
risolve	resolve	roman cathalic	Roman Catholic
rispect for law	respect for law	romanntic	romantic
rissk	risk	romanse	romance
rist	wrist	rommance	romance
rit	writ	rong	wrong
ritedown	write-down**	rongdoor	wrongdoer
ritein	write-in**	rongfill	wrongful
riteoff	write-off**	roobell	ruble
riteous	righteous	roobrick	rubric
riteto life	right-to-life	rooky	rookie
riteup	write-up	rool	rule
rithm	rhythm	roolet	roulette
riting	writing	rool of law	rule of law
ritte	rite**	roommer	roomer**
ritten	written	roote	root**
ritt of certiori	writ of certiorari	roothless	ruthless
rituel	ritual	rootine	routine
rivil	rival	rorshak test	Rorschach test
rivised	revised	rosster	roster
rivolver	revolver	roten clause	rotten clause
rivvalry	rivalry	rotta	rota
rivver	river	rottate	rotate
robb	rob	rotte	rote**
robbes	robes	roudy	rowdy
Robbinson Patmen		roussed	roust
	Robinson-Patman	routeen	routine
robbry	robbery	routte	route**

Incorrect	Correct
rownd	**round**
rowsing	**rousing**
royallties	**royalties**
royel	**royal**
royilty	**royalty**
royl	**roil****
royyal	**royal**
rubbric	**rubric**
rubecon	**Rubicon**
rubela	**rubella**
ruber	**rubber**
ruddimintary	**rudimentary**
rudementery	**rudimentary**
rudness	**rudeness**
ruen	**ruin**
rues de gare	**ruse de guerre**
ruinnous	**ruinous**
rukus	**ruckus**
ruleing	**ruling**
rulling	**ruling**
rulls	**rules**
rumage	**rummage**

Incorrect	Correct
rumer	**rumor****
rummadger	**rummager**
rumminate	**ruminate**
rummor	**rumor****
rummpus	**rumpus**
rummrunning	**rumrunning**
runate	**ruinate**
runer	**runner**
runing	**running**
runnaway	**runaway**
runndown	**rundown**
runnin	**run-in**
run of	**runoff**
run of the mil	**run-of-the-mill**
runous	**ruinous**
ruotously	**routously**
ruptcher	**rupture**
Rushian roulet	**Russian roulette**
russler	**rustler**
russticum forum	**rusticum forum**
ryitously	**riotously**
ryoter	**rioter**

S

Incorrect	Correct
sabath	**Sabbath**
sabatical	**sabbatical**
sabatoge	**sabotage**
sabbotage	**sabotage**
sabiture	**saboteur**
sacade	**saccade**
saccarin	**saccharin**
saccrilege	**sacrilege**
sacered	**sacred**
sacersanct	**sacrosanct**
sacharine	**saccharine**
sackerdotal	**sacerdotal**
sackerin	**saccharin**
sackramentum	**sacramentum**
sackriledge	**sacrilege**
sackrossankt	**sacrosanct**
sacrafice	**sacrifice**
sacrifise	**sacrifice**
sacus	**saccus**
saddism	**sadism**
saddomasochism	**sadomasochism**
sadeism	**sadism**

Incorrect	Correct
sadomasakist	**sadomasochist**
safconduck	**safe-conduct**
safcracker	**safecracker**
safdeeposit	**safe deposit**
safegard	**safeguard**
saffe	**safe**
safguard	**safeguard**
safings	**savings**
safkeeping	**safekeeping**
safty	**safety**
sagaccity	**sagacity**
sagesdella lei	**sages de la ley**
saggacious	**sagacious**
saggamen	**sagaman**
sailers	**sailors**
saill	**sail**
saime	**same**
saintely	**saintly**
sakerine	**saccharine**
sakke	**sake**
sakrament	**sacrament**
sakred	**sacred**

Incorrect	Correct	Incorrect	Correct
saleable	**salable**	sanktion	**sanction**
salery	**salary**	sanktuary	**sanctuary**
saling	**sailing**	sannatorium	**sanatorium**
sallable	**salable**	sannity	**sanity**
sallacious	**salacious**	sanse	**sans**
sallary	**salary**	sanwich lease	**sandwich lease**
salles	**sales**	sarcasstic	**sarcastic**
sallic law	**Salic Law**	sargeant	**sergeant**
salline	**saline**	sarjenty	**serjeanty**
salloon	**saloon**	sarkasm	**sarcasm**
sallubrious	**salubrious**	sarrcasm	**sarcasm**
sallus	**salus**	sarrdonic	**sardonic**
sallutary	**salutary**	sashiate	**satiate**
sallute	**salute**	satable	**satiable**
sallvage	**salvage****	satalite	**satellite**
sallvation	**salvation**	satasfactory	**satisfactory**
sallve	**salve****	saterate	**saturate**
sallvo	**salvo***	saterday nite special	
Sally May	**Sallie Mae**		**Saturday night special**
saloot	**salute**	satinism	**Satanism**
salsman	**salesman**	satisfactery	**satisfactory**
salspeeple	**salespeople**	satisfye	**satisfy**
salswomin	**saleswoman**	satissfied	**satisfied**
salutery	**salutary**	sattanic	**satanic**
saluttation	**salutation**	sattelite	**satellite**
salvadge	**salvage****	sattire	**satire****
salver	**salvor****	sattirical	**satirical**
salvuss pledgius	**salvus plegius**	sattisfaction	**satisfaction**
samarritan	**Samaritan**	savagin	**sauvagine**
sammpler	**sampler**	sassiety	**society****
sampel	**sample**	savagry	**savagery**
sampleing	**sampling**	saveing	**saving**
sanatarium	**sanitarium**	saveings	**savings**
sanatary	**sanitary**	saviorfair	**savoir-faire****
sanatation	**sanitation**	savita	**saevitia**
sanatise	**sanitize**	savvagery	**savagery**
sanaty	**sanity**	savy	**savvy**
sanbag	**sandbag**	sawdoff	**sawed-off**
sancktum	**sanctum**	sawnter	**saunter**
sancshon	**sanction**	sawrce	**source****
sanctamonious	**sanctimonious**	sayle	**sale**
sanctuery	**sanctuary**	sayne	**sane**
saneorage	**seigniorage**	saypient	**sapient**
sangtion	**sanction**	sayve	**save**
sangwin	**sanguine**	scabb	**scab**
sanitery	**sanitary**	scabbrous	**scabrous**
sanitorium	**sanatorium**	scafold	**scaffold**
sankefin	**saunkefin**	scalle	**scale**
sanktimonious	**sanctimonious**	scalled	**scald**

Incorrect	Correct
scallper	**scalper**
scammp	**scamp**
scandle	**scandal**
scandlous matter	**scandalous matter**
scarr	**scar****
scarse	**scarce****
scattological	**scatological**
scavvenger	**scavenger**
sceince	**science**
scennario	**scenario**
sceptic	**skeptic**
schedduled	**scheduled**
schemmatic	**schematic**
schitzophrenia	**schizophrenia**
schizm	**schism**
scholer	**scholar**
schollership	**scholarship**
scholroom	**schoolroom**
schoollhouse	**schoolhouse**
scid	**skid**
scienntist	**scientist**
scinntila	**scintilla**
scin search	**skin search**
scipp bale	**skip bail**
scoflaw	**scofflaw**
scopafiliac	**scopophiliac**
scorr	**score**
scottfree	**scot-free**
scrall	**scrawl**
screme	**scream**
screwtable	**scrutable**
scripp	**scrip****
scripped	**script****
scrivvener	**scrivener**
scrole	**scroll**
scrootinize	**scrutinize**
scrupyulous	**scrupulous**
scruteable	**scrutable**
scruteny	**scrutiny**
scruttable	**scrutable**
scruttiny	**scrutiny**
scurility	**scurrility**
scurulous	**scurrilous**
seald	**sealed**
sealling	**sealing****
sease and decist	**cease and desist**
seazonal	**seasonal**
sebbstomania	**sebastomania**
sebordinated	**subordinated**
sebregation	**subrogation**

Incorrect	Correct
sebstantive	**substantive**
sec	**seck****
seccondary	**secondary**
seccretary	**secretary**
secction	**section**
seccular	**secular**
seccundim	**secundum**
seccure	**secure**
seceed	**secede**
secends	**seconds**
secklude	**seclude**
seckond	**second**
secktarian	**sectarian**
secktion	**section**
seckular	**secular**
seckundum	**secundum**
secondegree	**second-degree**
secondery	**secondary**
seconhand	**second-hand**
secratariat	**secretariat**
secreet	**secrete****
secresy	**secrecy**
secretery	**secretary**
secretery genral	**secretary-general**
secrett	**secret****
sectionel	**sectional**
seculer	**secular**
secureties	
... Securities (Act, Commission)	
securred	**secured**
sedd	**said** or **sed**
seddation	**sedation**
seddatoanima	**sedato animo**
seddentary	**sedentary**
seddimentation	**sedimentation**
seddition	**sedition**
sedduction	**seduction**
sedementation	**sedimentation**
sedentery	**sedentary**
sedetive	**sedative**
sedooce	**seduce**
seducctive	**seductive**
seebed	**seabed**
seeced	**secede**
seeclusion	**seclusion**
seecrecy	**secrecy**
seecrete	**secrete****
seekus	**secus**
seel	**seal**
seelect	**select**

Incorrect	Correct
seelection	selection
seels	seals
seemen	seamen or semen**
seeniority	seniority
seenyer	senior
seequella	sequela
seequence	sequence
seequester	sequester
seeshore	seashore
seesin	seisin**
seesina	seisina
seesonal	seasonal
seeward	seaward
seeworthy	seaworthy
seeze	seize**
segeragate	segregate
seggment	segment
seggregate	segregate
segmint	segment
segnor	seignior
segragation	segregation
seige	siege
seinor	seignior
seiser	seizor
seishure	seizure
seklusion	seclusion
sekret	secret**
sekt	sect**
sekta	secta
sektarien	sectarian
sekularizm	secularism
sekurity	security
sekwelle	sequelae
sekwestation	sequestration
selec	select
seler	seller
selfagrandizement	self-aggrandizement
selfconshus	self-conscious
selfdeeling	self-dealing
self-defence	self-defense
self-deffence	self-defense
selfdepprecating	self-deprecating
selfdeseption	self-deception
selfdesstruction	self-destruction
selfditermination	self-determination
selfemmployment	self-employment
selfevedent	self-evident
selffaccusation	self-accusation

Incorrect	Correct
selfhelp	self-help
selfimmposed	self-imposed
selfinncrimination	self-incrimination
selfinnduced	self-induced
selfinnsurance	self-insurance
selfinterrest	self-interest
selfliquiddating	self-liquidating
selfreggulating	self-regulating
selfresstraint	self-restraint
selfriteous	self-righteous
selfsurving	self-serving
seliciter	solicitor
sellectman	selectman
sellfcontraddictery	self-contradictory
sembel	semble
semeannual	semiannual
semeing	seeming
sememonthly	semimonthly
semenal	seminal
semenary	seminary**
semeofficial	semiofficial
semi-automatic	semiautomatic
semi-legal	semilegal
seming	seeming
semiskiled	semiskilled
semi-weekly	semiweekly
semmblance	semblance
semmen	semen**
semmiconscious	semiconscious
semminal	seminal**
semmination	semination
semmiprivate	semiprivate
semmperparatus	semper paratus
semyearly	semiyearly
senario	scenario
sencus	census**
senet	senate
senier	senior
senillity	senility
senitor	senator
sennage	senage
sennate	senate
sennesence	senescence
sennile	senile
sennior	senior
sennit	Senate
senniter	senator
sennsational	sensational

Incorrect	Correct	Incorrect	Correct
sennses	**sensus****	serees	**series**
sennsible	**sensible**	serejoin	**surrejoin**
sennsive	**censive**	sereptition	**surreptition**
senntence	**sentence**	serface	**surface**
senntient	**sentient**	serfeit	**surfeit**
sensative	**sensitive**	serff	**serf**
senser	**censor****	sergeon	**surgeon**
sensery	**sensory**	sergicle	**surgical**
sensetive	**sensitive**	sergint	**sergeant**
sensitare	**censitaire**	sergon genneral	**Surgeon General**
sensorship	**censorship**	seriattum	**seriatim**
sensyual	**sensual**	serjin	**surgeon**
sentena	**centena**	serly	**surly****
sentenceing	**sentencing**	sermise	**surmise**
sentenel	**sentinel**	sermount	**surmount**
sentense	**sentence**	sername	**surname**
sentensia	**sententia**	serpass	**surpass**
sentree	**sentry**	serplus	**surplus**
senyor	**senior**	serprise	**surprise**
separrable	**separable**	serrender	**surrender**
sepeage	**seepage**	serriately	**seriately**
sepeena	**subpoena**	serries	**series****
sepena dushes tecum		serrious	**serious****
	subpoena duces tecum	serrogate	**surrogate**
seperate	**separate**	serrological	**serological**
seperior court	**superior court**	serrvant	**servant**
seperration	**separation**	serrvitude	**servitude**
sepi	**cepi**	sersher	**searcher**
sepose	**suppose**	sertax	**surtax**
sepp	**SEP**	sertificate	**certificate**
sepperation	**separation**	sertified	**certified**
sepptum	**septum**	sertified check	**certified check**
sepratists	**separatists**	sertified public acountent	
sepreem court	**Supreme Court**		**certified public accountant**
sepress	**suppress**	sertin	**certain**
sepulker	**sepulcher**	sertiorari	**certiorari**
sequense	**sequence**	serv	**serve**
sequesstrater	**sequestrator**	servailance	**surveillance**
sequils	**sequels**	servent	**servient**
ser	**sir****	servint	**servant**
serated	**serrated**	servise	**service**
serch	**search**	servisible	**serviceable**
serch and siezure		serviss	**service**
	search and seizure	servive	**survive**
sercharge	**surcharge**	servivirship	**survivorship**
serch worrent	**search warrant**	ses	**sess**
sercumstantial	**circumstantial**	sesession	**secession**
sereal	**serial****	seshio	**sessio**
serebut	**surrebut**	seshion	**session****
serebutter	**surrebutter**	sesi	**seisi**

Incorrect	Correct	Incorrect	Correct
sesion	session**	shermen antetrust act	
sessation	cessation**		Sherman Antitrust Act
sestain	sustain	sherrif	sheriff**
setelment	settlement	shevage	chevage
setle	settle	shicanery	chicanery
setler	settler**	shicano	Chicano
setlor	settlor**	shier	shire
setof	set-off**	shiffting	shifting
sett	set	shiling	shilling
settback	setback**	shiper	shipper
seudograph	pseudograph	shiping	shipping
seveer	severe**	shipp	ship
severel	several	shippment	shipment
severence	severance	shipreck	shipwreck
severety	severity	shister	shyster
severraly	severally	shok	shock
sevirable	severable	shoor	sure**
sevrable	severable	shoote	shoot**
sevral	several	shopkeper	shopkeeper
sevrance	severance	shopooks	shop-books
sevver	sever**	shopp	shop
sevverance	severance	shopplifting	shoplifting
sevvere	severe	shorchange	shortchange
sewwer	sewer	shorr	shore
sexuel	sexual	shorterm	short-term
sexx	sex**	shortt	short
shafft	shaft	shott	shot
shaimful	shameful	show caws	show cause
shakdown	shakedown	shreek	shriek**
shakle	shackle	shrubb	shrub
shal	shall	shurely	surely**
shamefull	shameful	shurety	surety
shamm	sham	shurity	surety
shamperter	champertor	shut-down	shutdown
shanghy	shanghai	sibarite	sybarite
shapup	shape-up**	sicc	sic**
shareiff	sheriff**	sichoanalisis	psychoanalysis
sharholder	shareholder	sichopathology	psychopathology
sharlatan	charlatan	sichuate	situate
sharowner	shareowner	sicofant	sycophant
sharre	share**	sicotherapy	psychotherapy
shawt sale	short sale	sicuritees	securities
shaydy	shady	siditious	seditious
shecanna	Chicana	sidwalk	sidewalk
sheild laws	shield laws	sience	science
shellter	shelter	sienter	scienter
sheperdise	shepardize	si eta est	si ita est
Shepperds Sitations		sieze	seize**
	Shepard's Citations	siezure	seizure
sherk	shirk**	sifalitic	syphilitic

Incorrect	Correct
siggnal	**signal**
siggnatory	**signatory**
siggnet	**signet**
siggnificant	**significant**
signafication	**signification**
signe	**sign****
signefy	**signify**
signifficant	**significant**
signiffy	**signify**
signiture	**signature**
sik	**sick****
siknes	**sickness**
sikotic	**psychotic**
sikout	**sickout**
silabus	**syllabus**
silance	**silence**
silense	**silence**
silicet	**scilicet**
silint	**silent**
sillence	**silence**
sillent	**silent**
sillicet	**solicit**
sillver	**silver**
silogism	**syllogism**
silvan	**sylvan**
simalarity	**similarity**
simbolic	**symbolic**
simbolize	**symbolize**
simetry	**symmetry**
similcum	**simul cum**
similer	**similar**
simillar	**similar**
simmilter	**similiter**
simmony	**simony**
simmple	**simple**
simmplex	**simplex**
simmulate	**simulate**
simmultaneous	**simultaneous**
simoney	**simony**
simpathetic strike	
	sympathetic strike
simpel	**simple**
simpithy	**sympathy**
simplissiter	**simpliciter**
simpplicity	**simplicity**
simtoms	**symptoms**
simullated	**simulated**
simulltaniously	**simultaneously**
simyulation	**simulation**
sinalagmetic contract	

Incorrect	Correct
	synallagmatic contract
sinchronism	**synchronism**
sindacate	**syndicate**
sindic	**syndic**
sindicalism	**syndicalism**
sindicate	**syndicate**
sindrome	**syndrome**
sined	**signed**
sinergism	**synergism**
singel	**single**
singking fund	**sinking fund**
singraph	**syngraph**
singuler	**singular****
sinicure	**sinecure**
sinndicating	**syndicating**
sinne	**sine****
sinnister	**sinister**
sinnod	**synod**
sinnonamus	**synonymous**
sinntax	**sin tax**
sinod	**synod**
sinonimous	**synonymous**
sinopsis	**synopsis**
sinse	**since**
sintax	**syntax****
sinthesise	**synthesize**
sintila	**scintilla**
sion	**scion**
siot	**soit**
siperior court	**superior court**
siphilis	**syphilis**
si pray	**cy-pres**
siprious	**si prius**
siquester	**sequester**
sircharge	**surcharge**
sircumstantial evidence	
	circumstantial evidence
sircumvention	**circumvention**
sire facius	**scire facias**
sire fecci	**scire feci**
sirenderee	**surrenderee**
sireptitious	**surreptitious**
sirigate	**surrogate**
sirious	**serious****
sirname	**surname**
sirogate	**surrogate**
sirological	**serological**
sirounding	**surrounding**
sirtax	**surtax**
sirvayor	**surveyor**

Incorrect	Correct	Incorrect	Correct
sirvility	servility	skream	scream
sirvitium	servitium	skriba	scriba
sirvitude	servitude	skribe	scribe
sirviver	survivor	skript	script**
sirvus	servus	skriptim	scriptum
sism	schism	skrivener	scrivener
sispended	suspended	skroll	scroll
sisstematise	systematize	skruple	scruple
sisster	sister	skrutinize	scrutinize
sistem	system	skurge	scourge
sistemmic	systemic	skurilus	scurrilous
siteing	siting	slaines	slains
sittuation	situation	slaker	slacker
sittus	situs	slanderrer	slanderer
sivel	civil	slandurus	slanderous
siveneer	souvenir	slannder	slander
sivil liability	civil liability	slav	slave
sivil liberties	civil liberties	slavvery	slavery
sivilian	civilian	slawter	slaughter
skab	scab	slayte	slate
skant	scant	sley	slay**
skapegoat	scapegoat	slic	slick
skar	scar**	slideing scale	sliding scale
skarper	scarper	slipp	slip
skarsity	scarcity	slise	slice
skatological	scatological	slite	slight
skavanger	scavenger	slo-down	slowdown**
skedule	schedule	sloppe	slope
skematic	schematic	slottmachine	slot machine
skeme	scheme	sluchfund	slush fund
skepptical	skeptical	slueth	sleuth
skeptisism	skepticism	sluff	slough
skijack	skyjack	slumlawrd	slumlord
skil	skill	slumm	slum
skilfull	skillful	slurr	slur
skimmpy	skimpy	smal	small
skipptracing	skiptracing	smatering	smattering
skite	scite	smeer	smear
skizophrenia	schizophrenia	smellting	smelting
skofflaw	scofflaw	smere	smear
skolar	scholar	smithakt	Smith Act
skold	scold	smugling	smuggling
skonce	sconce	smutt	smut
skool	school	snair	snare
skope	scope	snatsher	snatcher
skore	score	snattch	snatch
skorn	scorn	sneekthief	sneak thief
skot	scot	snyper	sniper
skoundrel	scoundrel	sobber	sober
skrambling	scrambling	sobbriket	sobriquet

Incorrect	Correct	Incorrect	Correct
soberiety	**sobriety**	sootable	**suitable**
sobre	**sober**	sooter	**suitor**
so cauled	**so-called**	sootors	**suitors**
soccager	**socager**	sooveneer	**souvenir**
sociapath	**sociopath**	soparific	**soporific**
sociatay	**société****	sophamor	**sophomore**
socilism	**socialism**	sophisstacation	**sophistication**
soddomite	**sodomite**	sopporific	**soporific**
sodimy	**sodomy**	sord	**sword**
sofcore	**softcore**	soredid	**sordid**
sofestry	**sophistry**	sorrdid	**sordid**
sofist	**sophist**	sorrogate	**surrogate**
softwhere	**software**	sorroraside	**sororicide**
sogerning	**sojourning**	sorse	**sors****
sokage	**soakage**	soshal security	**Social Security**
soladum	**solidum**	soshial	**social**
solem	**solemn**	sosiopath	**sociopath**
solemmity	**solemnity**	sossiety	**society****
solen	**solon**	sothern	**southern**
soler	**solar**	soundding	**sounding**
soletude	**solitude**	sounness	**soundness**
soliccitus	**solicitous**	sourse	**source****
solice	**solace**	soverenty	**sovereignty**
solicitter	**solicitor**	sovvren	**sovereign**
soliddity	**solidity****	sovyet	**soviet**
solisitation	**solicitation**	sownd	**sound**
solitery	**solitary**	soyl	**soil**
soljer	**soldier**	spacial	**spatial**
soll	**sole****	Spainish	**Spanish**
sollace	**solace**	sparate	**sperate****
sollar	**solar**	spareingly	**sparingly**
sollatuim	**solatium**	sparre	**spare**
sollder	**soldier**	spashious	**spacious**
solled	**sold**	spassmodic	**spasmodic**
sollemn	**solemn**	spatt	**spat**
sollicit	**solicit**	spaun	**spawn**
sollid	**solid**	spazm	**spasm**
sollidarity	**solidarity****	speach	**speech**
sollisiter	**solicitor**	speady	**speedy**
sollitary	**solitary****	speakking	**speaking**
sollvency	**solvency**	specalty	**specialty**
sollvit	**solvit**	speccialist	**specialist**
solvint	**solvent**	speccter	**specter**
sommanbulisim	**somnambulism**	specculate	**speculate**
somnalence	**somnolence**	speccullim	**speculum**
soo	**sue****	spece	**specie****
sooi	**sui**	speceficcation	**specification**
soone	**soon**	specemen	**specimen**
soopra	**supra**	speces	**species****
soos	**sous****	specifficly	**specifically**

Incorrect	Correct	Incorrect	Correct
specifyable	**specifiable**	spowse	**spouse**
speckter	**specter** or **spectre**	spoyl	**spoil**
spectograph	**spectrograph**	sprane	**sprain**
spector	**specter** or **spectre**	spraul	**sprawl**
specullative	**speculative**	sprea	**spree**
specyalation	**speculation**	spred	**spread**
speek	**speak**	spredsheet	**spreadsheet**
speeker	**speaker**	springling trust	**sprinkling trust**
speeker of the house		spue	**spew**
	Speaker of the House	spurm	**sperm**
spektacular	**spectacular**	spurrious	**spurious**
spelbound	**spellbound**	spye	**spy**
speling	**spelling**	squaller	**squalor**
spennd	**spend**	squallid	**squalid**
spenthrift	**spendthrift**	squater	**squatter**
spern	**spurn**	squeazeout	**squeeze-out**
speshalise	**specialize**	squier	**squire**
speshial	**special**	squirarchy	**squirearchy**
speshialist	**specialist**	sqware	**square**
spesific	**specific**	sqwatters rights	**squatter's rights**
spesific proformence		stabalize	**stabilize**
	specific performance	stabb	**stab**
spesimen	**specimen**	stabbility	**stability**
spessify	**specify**	stabble	**stable**
spilage	**spillage**	stach	**stash**
spilige	**spillage**	stachatory rape	**statutory rape**
spinil	**spinal**	staggflation	**stagflation**
spinless	**spineless**	staggnate	**stagnate**
spinnoff	**spin-off**	stagnim	**stagnum**
spinnster	**spinster**	stagnint	**stagnant**
spirritual	**spiritual**	stakholder	**stakeholder**
spittal	**spital** or **spittle**	stakke	**stake****
splitof	**split-off**	stakout	**stakeout**
splitt	**split****	stalage	**stallage**
spoillable	**spoilable**	stalle	**stale**
spokespurson	**spokesperson**	stallwart	**stalwart**
spokessman	**spokesman**	stammp	**stamp**
spokeswomman	**spokeswoman**	stan	**stand**
spoliater	**spoliator**	standallone	**stand-alone**
spolliation	**spoliation**	standerd	**standard**
spondio	**spondeo**	Standerd and Pours	
sponnsor	**sponsor**		**Standard and Poor's**
sponntanious	**spontaneous**	stanndartise	**standardize**
sponsership	**sponsorship**	stannding	**standing**
sponteneity	**spontaneity**	stanse	**stance**
spontions	**sponsions**	stapple	**staple**
sporious	**spurious**	starchamber	**star-chamber**
sporradic	**sporadic**	starrboard	**starboard**
spott	**spot**	starredisesis	**stare decisis**
spouzals	**spousals**	starrk	**stark**

Incorrect	Correct
starrvation	**starvation**
starry desisis	**stare decisis**
stashion	**station**
statedipartment	**State Department**
stateing	**stating**
stateist	**statist****
statemint	**statement**
statessman	**statesman**
statewoman	**stateswoman**
stathood	**statehood**
stathouse	**statehouse**
stationnary	**stationary****
stationnery	**stationery****
statitim	**statutum**
statment	**statement**
statte	**state**
statted	**stated**
statter	**stature****
statting	**stating**
stattis	**status****
stattistics	**statistics**
stattute	**statute****
statue law	**statute law**
statue of limitations	
	statute of limitations
statute of wils	**Statute of Wills**
statwide	**statewide**
statyutory	**statutory**
stavve	**stave**
stawnch	**staunch**
steale	**steal****
stearage	**steerage**
stearer	**steerer**
stedfast	**steadfast**
stedy	**steady**
steemship	**steamship**
stelar	**stellar**
stelth	**stealth**
stennographer	**stenographer**
stenoggrafy	**stenography**
steparent	**step-parent**
stepchile	**stepchild**
stepdawter	**stepdaughter**
stepfathr	**stepfather**
stepingstone	**steppingstone**
stepmuther	**stepmother**
steppbrother	**stepbrother**
steppdown	**step-down**
stepsisster	**stepsister**
stepsun	**stepson**

Incorrect	Correct
stereing committee	
	steering committee
stereotipe	**stereotype**
stergeon	**sturgeon**
sterillize	**sterilize**
sterpes	**stirpes**
sterrilization	**sterilization**
sterriotype	**stereotype**
sterroid	**steroid**
stettprosessus	**stet processus**
stevdor	**stevedore**
stewwardess	**stewardess**
stey	**stay**
sticler	**stickler**
stiffle	**stifle**
stiflling a prosecution	
	stifling a prosecution
stiggma	**stigma**
stigmitise	**stigmatize**
stikker	**sticker**
stil	**still**
stillborne	**stillborn**
stille	**style**
stilleto	**stiletto**
stimie	**stymie**
stimmulant	**stimulant**
stimyalate	**stimulate****
stinng	**sting**
stinnt	**stint**
stipelation	**stipulation**
stipendeary	**stipendiary**
stipilation	**stipulation**
stippes	**stipes**
stipppulate	**stipulate**
stipullated	**stipulated**
stirility	**sterility**
stoage	**stowage**
stockolder	**stockholder**
stock sertificate	**stock certificate**
stogy	**stodgy**
stok	**stock**
stokastic	**stochastic**
stokholders	**stockholders**
stollen	**stolen**
stonned	**stoned**
stonwall	**stonewall**
stopage	**stoppage**
stopgapp	**stopgap**
stopige	**stoppage**
stopless order	**stop-loss order**

Incorrect	Correct
stoplimmit order	**stop-limit order**
stopp	**stop**
storeage	**storage**
storhouse	**storehouse**
storkeeper	**storekeeper**
storme	**storm**
storoom	**storeroom**
storr	**store**
stow	**stowe**
stowwaway	**stowaway**
stox	**stocks**
straddel	**straddle**
stradles	**straddles**
stragetic	**strategic**
straght	**straight****
stragler	**straggler**
straightjacket	**straitjacket**
straitforward	**straightforward**
straitline	**straight-line**
strammineous homo	
	stramineus homo
stran	**strand**
straned	**strained**
strangel	**strangle**
strangullation	**strangulation**
strangyulate	**strangulate**
stranjer	**stranger**
strannding	**stranding**
stratagy	**strategy**
strategem	**stratagem**
strateggic	**strategic**
stratelaced	**straight-laced**
or **strait-laced**	
stratim	**stratum**
strattegic	**strategic**
strattify	**stratify**
strattocricy	**stratocracy**
strattum	**stratum**
strawer	**straw**
straye	**stray**
streat	**street**
streattwaker	**streetwalker**
strecher	**stretcher**
streem	**stream**
streetwyse	**streetwise**
streif	**strife**
stremeline	**streamline**
strengthin	**strengthen**
strennuous	**strenuous**
strenous	**strenuous**

Incorrect	Correct
strenth	**strength**
striccture	**stricture****
strichinine	**strychnine**
strick	**strict**
strickt construction	
	strict construction
stricktly	**strictly**
stricktus simijurus	**strictissimi juris**
strikbreaker	**strikebreaker**
strikeing	**striking**
strikke	**strike**
strikken	**stricken**
striksher	**stricture****
striktejurus	**stricti juris**
striktojury	**stricto jure**
striktumjus	**strictum jus**
stringint	**stringent**
stripp	**strip**
strippmining	**strip-mining**
strokke	**stroke**
strongam	**strong-arm**
strongg	**strong**
strongmindid	**strong-minded**
stronhold	**stronghold**
struccteral	**structural**
struckter	**structure**
strugle	**struggle**
struk	**struck**
strummpet	**strumpet**
strunngout	**strung-out**
strydent	**strident**
stryknin	**strychnine**
stryve	**strive**
stuard	**steward**
stubbren	**stubborn**
stuborn	**stubborn**
studdied	**studied****
studeous	**studious**
stulltify	**stultify**
stultefy	**stultify**
stumbel	**stumble**
stumbleing bloc	**stumbling block**
stummble	**stumble**
stumpige	**stumpage**
stumpp	**stump**
stupafaction	**stupefaction**
stupendis	**stupendous**
stuper	**stupor**
stupify	**stupefy**
stuppefasint	**stupefacient**

Incorrect	Correct	Incorrect	Correct
stuppor	**stupor**	subcurie	**sub curia**
stupprum	**stuprum**	subdavision	**subdivision**
sturling	**sterling**	subdivvide	**subdivide**
stymee	**stymie**	subdoo	**subdue**
stypend	**stipend**	subduck	**subduct**
su	**sue****	suberban	**suburban**
suage	**sewage**	subernation	**subornation**
subajent	**subagent**	subgective	**subjective**
suballtern	**subaltern**	subgudice	**sub judice**
subawn	**suborn**	subirigate	**subirrigate**
subawner	**suborner**	subjagate	**subjugate**
subb	**sub**	subjeck	**subject**
subbconscious	**subconscious**	subjecktion	**subjection**
subbdue	**subdue**	subkontrack	**subcontract**
subbject	**subject**	subkultur	**subculture**
subb judice	**sub judice**	sublamate	**sublimate**
subbjugate	**subjugate**	subleese	**sublease**
subblime	**sublime**	sublesee	**sublessee**
subbmit	**submit**	subleser	**sublessor**
subbnormal	**subnormal**	subleting	**subletting**
subbordinate	**subordinate**	sublisense	**sublicense**
subborn	**suborn**	submerjence	**submergence**
subbpoena	**subpoena**	subminnimim wage	
subbpottestate	**sub potestate**		**subminimum wage**
subbrogation	**subrogation**	submision	**submission**
sub broza	**sub rosa**	submitle	**submittal**
subbscribed	**subscribed**	submitt	**submit**
subbseqquent	**subsequent**	submoddo	**sub modo**
subbserveint	**subservient**	submorgage	**submortgage**
subbsidiery	**subsidiary**	submurge	**submerge**
subbsist	**subsist**	subnominn	**sub nomine**
subbsoil	**subsoil**	subnormel	**subnormal**
subbstance	**substance**	subnottations	**subnotations**
subbstantially	**substantially**	subnum	**sub nom**
subbstituted	**substituted**	subodinated	**subordinated**
subbsume	**subsume**	subopptimal	**suboptimal**
subburb	**suburb****	suborne	**suborn**
subbversive	**subversive**	suborrdination	**subordination**
subchaptre S	**Subchapter S**	subregation	**subrogation**
subcide	**subside****	subroger	**subrogor**
subcidize	**subsidize**	subroggee	**subrogee**
subcidy	**subsidy****	subrossa	**sub rosa**
subcollor juris	**sub colore juris**	subsadize	**subsidize**
subcomision	**subcommission**	subscribor	**subscriber**
subcomittee	**subcommittee**	subscrippption	**subscription**
subcommitee	**subcommittee**	subsekwent	**subsequent**
subconcious	**subconscious**	subsiddy	**subsidy****
subconntract	**subcontract**	subsillenteo	**sub silentio**
subcontrakter	**subcontractor**	subsiquent	**subsequent**

Incorrect	Correct	Incorrect	Correct
subsistance	subsistence	sufisient	sufficient
subsoom	subsume	sufocate	suffocate
subsscribe	subscribe	sufrage	suffrage
substanchial	substantial	sugest	suggest
substanderd	substandard	sugjestive	suggestive
substanntiate	substantiate	suiccide	suicide
substanse	substance	suisidal	suicidal
substatute	substitute	suiter	suitor
substatutionery	substitutionary	suitible	suitable
substince	substance	sujjestion	suggestion
substintive	substantive	sulen	sullen
substittution	substitution	sullin	sullen
substitutionel	substitutional	sulltry	sultry
substracktion	substraction	sumarily	summarily
subtafuge	subterfuge	sumarry court-martial	
subtenent	subtenant		summary court-martial
subteranean	subterranean	sumation	summation
subterrfuge	subterfuge	sumery	summary
subtracktion	subtraction	suming up	summing up
subverrsive	subversive	suminns	summons
subvursion	subversion	sumit	summit
succeser	successor	summ	sum**
succesive	successive	summens	summons
succint	succinct	summerize	summarize
succondittioni	sub conditione	sumon	summon
suceptable	susceptible	sumtuous	sumptuous
sucharge	surcharge	sumumjus	summum jus
suchure	suture	sundey	Sunday
sucksession	succession	sundrees	sundries
sucsinct	succinct	sundrey	sundry
sucumb	succumb	sun-in-laws	sons-in-law
sucurity	security	sunnder	sunder
suddinly	suddenly	sunnset law	sunset law
suden	sudden	sunnshine law	sunshine law
sudonim	pseudonym	sunnstroke	sunstroke
sueable	suable	suoe	suo**
suecide	suicide	supartner	subpartner
sueet	suite**	supasilious	supercilious
suesponti	sua sponte	supasition	supposition
suey	sui	supavise	supervise
sufacate	suffocate	supeena	subpoena
sufer	suffer	supera	supra
suference	sufferance	superanuate	superannuate
suff	sough	supercede	supersede
suffishensy	sufficiency	supercedeas	supersedeas
suffrable	sufferable	superceeding	superseding
suffrige	suffrage	supercession	supersession
suffring	suffering	superfisial	superficial
sufice	suffice	superflous	superfluous

Incorrect	Correct	Incorrect	Correct
superier	**superior**	supress	**suppress**
superimmpose	**superimpose**	supriem judishial court	
superinntend	**superintend**		**Supreme Judicial Court**
superkargo	**supercargo**	supurvize	**supervise**
superlitive	**superlative**	suragate's court	**surrogate's court**
supernattural	**supernatural**	surajoinder	**surrejoinder**
supernoomerary	**supernumerary**	surch	**search**
supernummereries		surchage	**surcharge**
	supernumeraries	surebutal	**surrebuttal**
superrintendant	**superintendent**	surebutter	**surrebutter**
superrsedees	**supersedeas**	surejoinder	**surrejoinder**
superrvision	**supervision**	surender	**surrender**
supersnyority	**superseniority**	surenderee	**surrenderee**
superveening	**supervening**	surenndorer	**surrenderor**
supevisery	**supervisory**	sureptitious	**surreptitious**
supistitious	**superstitious**	surfice	**surface**
suplamental	**supplemental**	surfit	**surfeit**
suplant	**supplant**	surily	**surely****
suplement	**supplement**	surity	**surety**
suplicant	**supplicant**	surjery	**surgery**
suplimentary	**supplementary**	surment	**serment**
suplise	**supplies**	surmize	**surmise**
suplucate	**supplicate**	surogacy	**surrogacy**
suply	**supply**	suround	**surround**
suport	**support**	surpluss	**surplus**
supose	**suppose**	surppas	**surpass**
supperable	**superable**	surpress	**suppress**
supperannuate	**superannuate**	surprize	**surprise**
supperfluous	**superfluous**	surrety	**surety**
supperiority	**superiority**	surrgical	**surgical**
suppersede	**supersede**	surrplus	**surplus**
supperstition	**superstition**	surrtax	**surtax**
suppervizer	**supervisor**	surrvailance	**surveillance**
supplementery	**supplementary**	surrviving	**surviving**
supplyer	**supplier**	survailence	**surveillance**
supportible	**supportable**	survale	**surveil**
supportiv	**supportive**	survay	**survey**
suppozed	**supposed**	survess	**service**
suppra	**supra**	survitas	**servitus**
suppremacy	**supremacy**	survivil	**survival**
suppreme	**supreme**	survivillist	**survivalist**
suppresion	**suppression**	survivvership	**survivorship**
supprise	**surprise**	suseranty	**suzerainty**
supravention	**supervention**	suspeck	**suspect**
supraviser	**supervisor**	suspennsive	**suspensive**
supream court	**Supreme Court**	suspensery	**suspensory**
supreem	**supreme**	suspention	**suspension**
supremisist	**supremacist**	suspishus	**suspicious**
supremmacy	**supremacy**	susseptible	**susceptible**

Incorrect	Correct
susspect	suspect
susspense	suspense
susspicion	suspicion
susstain	sustain
sustane	sustain
sustinence	sustenance
sute	suit**
sutle	subtle
suttle	subtle
sutyer	suture
suwage	sewage
swa	soit
swair	swear
swalow	swallow
swammp	swamp
sware	swear
swareing	swearing
swarn	sworn
swasion	suasion
swathe	swath
sweaping	sweeping
sweathart contract	sweetheart contract
sweatting	sweating
sweepsteaks	sweepstakes
sweetners	sweeteners
swel	swell
swellter	swelter
swet equity	sweat equity
swetshop	sweatshop
swey	sway
swich	switch
swichblade	switchblade
swil	swill

Incorrect	Correct
swindel	swindle
swindlor	swindler
swinndling	swindling
switshyard doctrine	switchyard doctrine
swoone	swoon
swurve	swerve
syche	psyche
sychiatrist	psychiatrist
sychic	psychic**
sychological	psychological
sychopath	psychopath
syenter	scienter
syfilis	syphilis
sykonurosis	psychoneurosis
sylogism	syllogism
symboll	symbol
symetry	symmetry
sympithise	sympathize
symtomatic	symptomatic
synchronnazation	synchronization
syncronise	synchronize
syndiccate	syndicate
synical	cynical
synndrome	syndrome
synnopsis	synopsis
synonnamous	synonymous
synthettic	synthetic
syoot	suit**
syphillis	syphilis
sysstem	system
systimatic	systematic
syte	sight**

T

Incorrect	Correct
tabacco	tobacco
tabbetic dementa	tabetic dementia
tabblet	tablet
tabbloid	tabloid
tabbula	tabula
tabel	table
tablo	tableau
tabu	taboo
tabuler	tabular
tabulla	tabula
tabullate	tabulate

Incorrect	Correct
taburnacle	tabernacle
tabyular	tabular
taccing	tacking
tacctic	tactic
tacitt	tacit**
tacity	tacite
tacless	tactless
tactles	tactless
taft harley act	Taft-Hartley Act
taill	tail**
tailsman	talesman

Incorrect	Correct	Incorrect	Correct
taim	**tame**	taskseter	**tasksetter**
tak	**tack**	taskwerk	**taskwork**
takdown	**takedown**	tasmaster	**taskmaster**
takeing	**taking**	tassit	**tacit****
takerr	**taker**	tassk	**task**
takhome pay	**take-home pay**	tastfull	**tasteful**
takover	**takeover****	tastless	**tasteless**
taks	**tax****	tatoo	**tattoo**
taksation	**taxation**	taudry	**tawdry**
taksing	**taxing**	tautolijy	**tautology**
taktic	**tactic**	tauttologous	**tautologous**
talage	**tallage** or **tailage**	tavurn	**tavern**
taljium	**tallagium**	tavverner	**taverner**
talles	**tales****	tawdree	**tawdry**
talley	**tally**	tawnt	**taunt**
tallmud	**Talmud**	tawtollogy	**tautology**
tallweg	**talweg**	tax-brake	**tax break**
talsman	**talisman**	tax-dodj	**tax dodge**
taly	**tally**	tax-evation	**tax evasion**
tammper	**tamper****	taxexemp	**tax exempt**
tammpon	**tampon**	tax-heaven	**tax haven**
tammquam	**tam quam**	taxible	**taxable**
tamperring	**tampering**	taxible income	**taxable income**
tandim	**tandem**	taxiccab	**taxicab**
tangeible	**tangible**	tax-lean	**tax lien**
tangk	**tank**	taxles	**taxless**
tanjent	**tangent**	taxpayor	**taxpayer**
tanjible	**tangible**	taxx	**tax****
tankige	**tankage**	taxxes	**taxes****
tanndem	**tandem**	taxxi	**taxi**
tanngent	**tangent**	tayke	**take**
tanntrum	**tantrum**	tea-bill	**T-bill**
tantallize	**tantalize**	tea-bond	**T-bond**
tantammount	**tantamount**	teame	**team****
tante	**taint**	teammster	**teamster**
tantimount	**tantamount**	teanager	**teenager**
tantrumm	**tantrum**	tea note	**T-note**
tappe	**tape**	teatotaller	**teetotaler**
taprecorder	**tape recorder**	techer	**teacher**
targett	**target**	technecality	**technicality**
targit	**target**	techneek	**technique**
tarif	**tariff**	techniccaly	**technically**
tarnich	**tarnish**	tecknician	**technician**
tarpulin	**tarpaulin**	tedjum	**tedium**
tarrdy	**tardy**	tee-bill	**T-bill**
tarre	**tare****	tee-bond	**T-bond**
tarrget	**target**	teech	**teach**
tarrif	**tariff**	teedium	**tedium**
tarrnish	**tarnish**	teejus	**tedious**
tasaturn	**taciturn**	teemerity	**temerity**

Incorrect	Correct
teemwork	**teamwork**
tee-note	**T-note**
teer	**tier****
teergas	**tear gas**
teering of will	**tearing of will**
teir	**tier****
teknical	**technical**
teknique	**technique**
tekst	**text**
telacommunications	**telecommunications**
telagraph	**telegraph**
teleccast	**telecast**
telecomunications	**telecommunications**
telefone	**telephone**
telejenic	**telegenic**
teleppathy	**telepathy**
teler	**teller**
teletipe	**Teletype**
teligram	**telegram**
telivision	**television**
tellecast	**telecast**
tellegram	**telegram**
tellethon	**telethon**
telletypewriter	**teletypewriter**
tellevision	**television**
tellex	**telex**
teltale	**telltale**
temarious	**temerarious**
temmerareous	**temerarious**
temmerity	**temerity**
temmperamental	**temperamental**
temmplate	**template**
temmporise	**temporize**
temmporray	**temporary**
temmpus	**tempus**
tempel	**temple**
temperal lords	**temporal lords**
temperary emerjency court of appeals	**Temporary Emergency Court of Appeals**
tempererily	**temporarily**
temperery restraining order	**temporary restraining order**
temperize	**temporize**
temperranse	**temperance**
tempesed	**tempest**
tempesstuous	**tempestuous**
tempis	**tempus**

Incorrect	Correct
templers	**Templars**
templet	**template**
temporallity	**temporality**
tempori	**tempore**
temporralis	**temporalis**
temprament	**temperament**
temprance	**temperance**
tempreture	**temperature**
temt	**tempt**
temtation	**temptation**
tenament	**tenement**
tenasity	**tenacity**
tenative	**tentative**
tendancy	**tendency**
tendenntious	**tendentious**
tendir offer	**tender offer**
teneager	**teenager**
teneer	**tenere****
tenency	**tenancy**
tener	**tenor****
tenett	**tenet****
tenible	**tenable**
tenints	**tenants**
tenit	**tenet****
teniut	**tenuit**
tennable	**tenable**
tennacious	**tenacious**
tennanship	**tenantship**
tennant	**tenant****
tenncon	**tencon**
tennder	**tender**
tenned	**tend**
tennement	**tenement**
tennent	**tenant****
tennor	**tenor****
tennsion	**tension**
tenntative	**tentative**
tennuity	**tenuity**
tennura	**tenura**
tenpersenter	**ten-percenter**
tensel	**tensile**
tentetive	**tentative**
tention	**tension**
tenurre	**tenure****
tenyered faculty	**tenured faculty**
tenyure	**tenure****
tera	**terra****
terbid	**turbid**
terbulent	**turbulent**
tereble	**terrible**

Incorrect	Correct
tererist	**terrorist**
teretoriality	**territoriality**
terettory	**territory**
terf and twigg	**turf and twig**
tergid	**turgid**
terible	**terrible**
terific	**terrific**
terify	**terrify**
teritorial	**territorial**
termanal	**terminal**
termanation	**termination**
termegent	**termagant**
termenable	**terminable**
terminnal	**terminal**
terminner	**terminer**
terminni	**termini**
terminnus	**terminus**
terminolagy	**terminology**
termles	**termless**
terms dela lay	**Termes de la Ley**
terncote	**turncoat**
tern down	**turn down**
ternover	**turnover****
teror	**terror****
terpetude	**turpitude**
terpis	**turpis**
terrefy	**terrify**
terrer	**terra****
terreristic	**terroristic**
terrmer	**termor****
terrminnology	**terminology**
terrtenant	**terre-tenant**
ters	**terse**
tershiary	**tertiary**
tessed	**test**
tesstament	**testament**
tesstate	**testate**
tesstemonial	**testimonial**
tesste of a rit	**teste of a writ**
tesstes	**testes****
tesstify	**testify**
tesstis	**testis****
testamment	**testament**
testamoney	**testimony**
testasion	**testation**
testaytim	**testatum**
testees	**testes****
testefy	**testify**
testemoneum	**testimonium**
testetricks	**testatrix**

Incorrect	Correct
testible	**testable**
testickle	**testicle**
testicy	**testacy**
testimentery	**testamentary**
testimint	**testament**
testimoney	**testimony**
testiss	**testis****
testiter	**testator**
testube	**test-tube**
tetta tett	**tête-à-tête**
tettrarck	**tetrarch**
tex	**text**
texbook	**textbook**
texter	**texture**
texteral	**textual**
thain	**thane**
thankfull	**thankful**
thankles	**thankless**
thanlands	**thanelands**
thanship	**thaneship**
thawtful	**thoughtful**
thealogy	**theology**
theef	**thief**
theem	**theme**
theeretical	**theoretical**
theerize	**theorize**
theesis	**thesis****
theeter	**theater** or **theatre**
theevery	**thievery**
thefft	**theft**
theif	**thief**
theirfor	**therefor****
theirs'	**theirs****
their's	**theirs****
thencforth	**thenceforth**
thense	**thence**
thensefoward	**thenceforward**
theokrasy	**theocracy**
theorettical	**theoretical**
theorry	**theory**
therabout	**thereabout**
therafter	**thereafter**
theramong	**thereamong**
therappist	**therapist**
therat	**thereat**
therby	**thereby**
therd	**third**
thereoff	**thereof**
thereputic abortion	**therapeutic abortion**

Incorrect	Correct	Incorrect	Correct
theretoofor	**theretofore**	thugg	**thug**
therfor	**therefor****	thumprint	**thumbprint**
therfrom	**therefrom**	thunnder	**thunder**
therin	**therein**	thuss	**thus**
therinafter	**thereinafter**	tickit	**ticket**
therinbefore	**thereinbefore**	tideal	**tidal**
therof	**thereof**	tideous	**tedious**
theron	**thereon**	tidey	**tidy**
therrepy	**therapy**	tidland	**tideland**
therrfore	**therefore****	tidwater	**tidewater**
therto	**thereto**	tiell	**tiel**
therunder	**thereunder**	tik	**tick**
theruntil	**thereuntil**	tiket	**ticket**
therunto	**thereunto**	tikker tape	**ticker tape**
therupon	**thereupon**	tilage	**tillage**
therwith	**therewith**	tillible	**tillable**
thesaurris	**thesaurus**	timberrload	**timberlode**
thesees	**theses****	timbreland	**timberland**
thessaurus	**thesaurus**	timkeeper	**timekeeper**
thessis	**thesis****	timly	**timely**
theyery	**theory**	timmber	**timber****
thiev	**thieve**	timme	**time**
thinggs	**things**	timmid	**timid**
thingk	**think**	timprice diferential	
thinkible	**thinkable**		**time-price differential**
thinn	**thin**	timserver	**timeserver**
thinskind	**thin-skinned**	timshare	**timeshare**
thirdpaty	**third party**	timtable	**timetable**
thirdz	**thirds**	timwork	**timework**
thirtenth amendment		tinacity	**tenacity**
	Thirteenth Amendment	tinnpeny	**tinpenny**
thoghttles	**thoughtless**	tipecast	**typecast**
thorney	**thorny**	tiper	**tipper****
thorogh	**thorough****	tipewriter	**typewriter**
thorogoing	**thoroughgoing**	tiphoid fever	**typhoid fever**
thorowfare	**thoroughfare**	tipical	**typical**
thorrily	**thoroughly**	tipler	**tippler****
thouht	**thought**	tipology	**typology**
threatning	**threatening**	tippoff	**tip-off**
threatt	**threat****	tippster	**tipster**
thred	**thread****	tippsy	**tipsy**
threemile limit	**three-mile limit**	tirannical	**tyrannical**
threshol	**threshold**	tirent	**tyrant**
thret	**threat**	tiresum	**tiresome**
threwout	**throughout**	tirless	**tireless**
throwback rule	**Throwback Rule**	tirrade	**tirade**
throwout	**throw out**	tite	**tight**
thru	**through****	titel	**title**
thrusst	**thrust**	titheing	**tithing**
thruway	**throughway**	tithfree	**tithe-free**

Incorrect	Correct
tiths	**tithes**
tittanic	**titanic**
tittilate	**titillate**
tittlholder	**titleholder**
tittular	**titular**
tituller	**titular**
toard	**toward**
tobacanist	**tobacconist**
tobacoe	**tobacco**
tobbaco	**tobacco**
toggether	**together**
togsemia	**toxemia**
tokin	**token**
toksemia	**toxemia**
toksin	**toxin**
tolarate	**tolerate**
tolarent	**tolerant**
tolbooth	**tollbooth**
tole	**toll**
toler	**toller**
tolgate	**tollgate**
tollerance	**tolerance**
tolleration	**toleration**
tols	**tolls**
tomain	**ptomaine**
tommorow	**tomorrow**
tomstone	**tombstone**
tonage	**tonnage**
tonn	**ton****
tonshure	**tonsure**
tonteen	**tontine**
toofaced	**two-faced**
toogether	**together**
too issue rule	**two-issue rule**
tooition	**tuition**
toole	**tool****
toom	**tomb**
too quoque argument	
	tu quoque argument
toorde force	**tour de force**
tophevy	**top-heavy**
tople	**topple**
toppsecret	**top-secret**
to quoque argument	
	tu quoque argument
tora	**Torah**
torcher	**torture**
torchuous	**tortuous****
torement	**torment**

Incorrect	Correct
Torens title sistem	
	Torrens title system
torepedoe doctrine	**torpedo doctrine**
tornament	**tournament**
torper	**torpor**
torshious	**tortious****
tortfeaser	**tort-feasor**
tortous	**tortuous****
torturus	**torturous****
tory	**Tory**
totallitarien	**totalitarian**
totel	**total**
toten trust	**Totten Trust**
totilise	**totalize**
tottality	**totality**
touff	**tough**
toun	**town**
toutt	**tout**
toweable	**towable**
towerd	**toward**
tower dechel	**tour d'echelle**
towern	**tourn**
towige	**towage**
towitt	**to wit**
townshipp	**township**
towwer	**tower**
toxacal	**toxical**
toxagennic	**toxigenic**
toxefy	**toxify**
toxiccate	**toxicate**
toxiccity	**toxicity**
toxicommania	**toxicomania**
toxikosis	**toxicosis**
toxxemia	**toxemia**
toxxic	**toxic**
toxxin	**toxin**
toxxisity	**toxicity**
toxxoyd	**toxoid**
toxycology	**toxicology**
toylsome	**toilsome**
traceing	**tracing**
trachee	**trachea**
tracktion	**traction**
tracter	**tractor**
tractible	**tractable**
traddition	**tradition**
tradduce	**traduce**
tradegy	**tragedy**
tradeing	**trading**

Incorrect	Correct	Incorrect	Correct
trademmark	trademark	transexual	transsexual
tradin	trade-in	transferance	transference
tradisionery evidence		transferer	transferor
	traditionary evidence	transferible	transferable
traditeo	traditio	transfermation	transformation
traditionnal	traditional	transferree	transferee
tradmark	trademark	transfigger	transfigure
tradoff	trade-off	transfixx	transfix
tradoos	traduce	transfrance	transference
trador	trader**	transgresion	transgression
tradsman	tradesman	transgresser	transgressor
traducktion	traduction	transhent	transient
trafaking	trafficking	transhipment	transshipment
trafic	traffic	transiever	transceiver
traficker	trafficker	transir	transire
tragady	tragedy	transittory	transitory
tragectory	trajectory	translait	translate
traggic	tragic	translater	translator
traid	trade	translattion	translation
traiter	traitor**	transloosent	translucent
trajic	tragic	transmittle	transmittal
trakea	trachea	transmision	transmission
traks	tracks	transmyutation	transmutation
traksion	traction	transparrent	transparent
trakt	tract**	transpawrt	transport
traleblazer	trailblazer	transpier	transpire
traler	trailer	transportattion	transportation
tramatic	traumatic	transpossition	transposition
tramel	trammel	transpotation	transportation
tramer	trammer	transpoze	transpose
trammway	tramway	transsaction	transaction
trampel	trample	transscribe	transcribe
tranceform	transform	transscript	transcript
trancendant	transcendent	transsplant	transplant
trane	train	transvesstite	transvestite
tranee	trainee	transvurse	transverse
tranlode	trainload	trantient	transient
trannsatlantic	transatlantic	tranzact	transact
trannscript	transcript	tranzition	transition
trannsfer	transfer	trapp	trap
trannsit	transit	trapse	traipse
trannsvestite	transvestite	trasans	trassans
tranquilliser	tranquilizer	trasatis	trassatus
transaktional	transactional	traser	tracer
transative	transitive	trasing	tracing
transatory	transitory	trate	trait
transcrip	transcript	traummatise	traumatize
transe	trance	travale	travail**
transend	transcend	travell	travel**

111

Incorrect	Correct
travelling	**traveling**
traverce jury	**traverse jury**
travler's check	**traveler's check**
travurser	**traverser**
travveled	**traveled** or **travelled**
travverse	**traverse**
travvesty	**travesty**
trawmatism	**traumatism**
trax	**tracks**
treachory	**treachery**
treaserer of the United States	**Treasurer of the United States**
treasher trove	**treasure-trove**
treatice	**treatise****
treatmint	**treatment**
treazon	**treason**
treazury	**treasury**
trebble	**treble**
trecherous	**treacherous**
tredmill	**treadmill**
treedweel	**treadwheel**
treeson	**treason**
treetise	**treatise****
treetment	**treatment**
treety	**treaty**
tremalous	**tremulous**
tremenjous	**tremendous**
tremmble	**tremble**
tremmendous	**tremendous**
tremmer	**tremor****
trenchent	**trenchant**
trendey	**trendy**
trendseter	**trendsetter**
trennchant	**trenchant**
trennd	**trend**
trepadation	**trepidation**
treppidation	**trepidation**
trespasor	**trespasser**
tresspass	**trespass**
tresure	**treasure**
trew bill	**true bill**
triaje	**triage**
triall	**trial****
triangullate	**triangulate**
triangyalated	**triangulated**
tribbadism	**tribadism**
tribbal	**tribal**
tribbulation	**tribulation**
tribbune	**tribune**

Incorrect	Correct
tribbutery	**tributary**
trible	**tribal**
tribunnel	**tribunal**
tributte	**tribute**
tribyalation	**tribulation**
tribyute	**tribute**
trickel-down	**trickle-down**
tricster	**trickster**
trieble	**triable**
triel jury	**trial jury**
triffle	**trifle**
triger	**trigger**
trik	**trick**
trikery	**trickery**
trikinossis	**trichinosis**
trikle	**trickle**
Trinnity term	**Trinity Term**
trinnkets	**trinkets**
triplacate	**triplicate**
tripple tax exempt	**triple tax-exempt**
tripple wishing hour	**triple witching hour**
tripplicate	**triplicate**
triumfant	**triumphant**
triumvarate	**triumvirate**
triveal	**trivial**
trivvial	**trivial**
trofy	**trophy**
trogglodite	**troglodyte**
trojin horse	**Trojan horse**
troley	**trolley**
tronnage	**tronage**
troo	**true**
troopps	**troops**
trooth	**truth**
troubelmaker	**troublemaker**
troublesum	**troublesome**
troublshooter	**troubleshooter**
trouma	**trauma**
trovver	**trover**
trowma	**trauma**
troye weight	**troy weight**
tru	**true**
truble	**trouble**
trucculent	**truculent**
trucklode	**truckload**
truckor	**trucker**
trucullince	**truculence**

Incorrect	Correct
truent	**truant**
truimphant	**triumphant**
truincy	**truancy**
truk	**truck**
trukulence	**truculence**
trummpery	**trumpery**
trumpdup	**trumped-up**
trumvirate	**triumvirate**
trunkate	**truncate**
trunncate	**truncate**
trunsheon	**truncheon**
trusbusting	**trust-busting**
truse	**truce**
trusst	**trust****
trussty	**trusty****
truster	**trustor**
trustey	**trustee****
trust inndentur act	**Trust Indenture Act**
trustyship	**trusteeship**
trusworthy	**trustworthy**
truthe in lending act	**Truth-in-Lending Act**
truthfull	**truthful**
tryable	**triable**
tryad	**triad****
tryage	**triage**
tryal	**trial****
tryarky	**triarchy**
tryaxial	**triaxial**
trybe	**tribe**
trybunal	**tribunal**
trye	**try**
tryed	**tried****
tryer of fact	**trier of fact**
tryfling	**trifling**
tryible	**triable**
tryors	**triors**
trypartite	**tripartite**
trypod	**tripod**
tubb	**tub**
tubbular	**tubular**
tuch and go	**touch-and-go**
tuchstone	**touchstone**
tuder	**Tudor**
tuker act	**Tucker Act**
tumer	**tumor**
tumessence	**tumescence**
tumestone	**tombstone**

Incorrect	Correct
tummesense	**tumescence**
tummid	**tumid**
tummor	**tumor**
tummultous	**tumultuous**
tuneing	**tuning**
tunel	**tunnel**
tunige	**tunnage**
tunn	**ton****
tunne	**tun****
tunnil	**tunnel**
turbery	**turbary**
turbullent	**turbulent**
turjid	**turgid**
turm	**term**
turminate	**terminate**
turms	**terms**
turne	**turn****
turnky	**turnkey**
turnnout	**turnout****
turnovver	**turnover****
turnpyke	**turnpike**
turntabble	**turntable**
turrpitude	**turpitude**
turse	**terse**
turtiary	**tertiary**
turtiumquid	**tertium quid**
tuter	**tutor****
tutilery	**tutelary**
tution	**tuition**
tutorrship	**tutorship**
tuttelage	**tutelage**
tuttor	**tutor****
tuttrix	**tutrix**
twenypercent rool	**twenty-percent rule**
twich	**twitch**
twinje	**twinge**
twisst	**twist**
two quoque argument	**tu quoque argument**
tyde	**tide****
tye	**tie****
tye in arrangement	**tie-in arrangement**
tyeing	**tying**
tyfoid fever	**typhoid fever**
typafy	**typify**
typriter	**typewriter**
tyrade	**tirade**

Incorrect	Correct	Incorrect	Correct
tyranacal	**tyrannical**	tytheing	**tything**
tyriny	**tyrany**	tyther	**tither**
tyth	**tythe**	tytin	**titan****

U

Incorrect	Correct	Incorrect	Correct
ubbiquitous	**ubiquitous**	unalateral	**unilateral**
ubbiquity	**ubiquity**	unalienable	**inalienable**
ucher	**usher**	unalowed	**unallowed**
uelogy	**eulogy****	unaltarable	**unalterable**
ugenics	**eugenics**	unambigguous	**unambiguous**
ugglify	**uglify**	unamed	**unnamed**
uggly	**ugly**	unameracan	**un-American**
ugsurious	**uxorious**	unamertized	**unamortized**
ulage	**ullage**	unammancipated	**unemancipated**
ullteemes hearez	**ultimus haeres**	unammbiguous	**unambiguous**
ullterior	**ulterior**	unamotional	**unemotional**
ulltra	**ultra**	unanamus	**unanimous**
ultimma ration	**ultima ratio**	unanimis verdict	
ultireor	**ulterior**		**unanimous verdict**
ultrism	**ultraism**	unanserable	**unanswerable**
umberage	**umbrage**	unanticapated	**unanticipated**
umbillical	**umbilical**	unanticcipated	**unanticipated**
umbragge	**umbrage**	unapealable	**unappealable**
umbrela	**umbrella**	unapeelible	**unappealable**
umbudesman	**ombudsman**	unapropriated	**unappropriated**
ummpire	**umpire**	unarguble	**unarguable**
umperage	**umpirage**	unarmd	**unarmed**
unabbated	**unabated**	unartikulated	**unarticulated**
unabel	**unable**	unasailable	**unassailable**
unacceptible	**unacceptable**	unasigned	**unassigned****
unaccountible	**unaccountable**	unasisted	**unassisted**
unaceptable	**unacceptable**	unassalible	**unassailable**
unackceptable	**unacceptable**	unassertained	**unascertained**
unacnoledged	**unacknowledged**	unassined	**unassigned****
unacompanied	**unaccompanied**	unassumming	**unassuming**
unacountable	**unaccountable**	unasuming	**unassuming**
unacrued	**unaccrued**	unatached	**unattached**
unacused	**unaccused**	unatashed	**unattached**
unaddulterated	**unadulterated**	unatested	**unattested**
unadjussted	**unadjusted**	unatural	**unnatural**
unadornd	**unadorned**	unauddited	**unaudited**
unadultarated	**unadulterated**	unauditted	**unaudited**
unadvized	**unadvised**	unautherized	**unauthorized**
unafied	**unified**	unavalable	**unavailable**
unafiliated	**unaffiliated**	unaversel	**universal**
unajusted	**unadjusted**	unaversity	**university**

Incorrect	Correct	Incorrect	Correct
una voice	**una voce**	uncompennsated	**uncompensated**
unavoidible	**unavoidable**	uncomplacated	**uncomplicated**
unavoydable	**unavoidable**	uncomprimising	**uncompromising**
unavvailable	**unavailable**	unconceeled	**unconcealed**
unawair	**unaware****	uncondisional	**unconditional**
unawthorized	**unauthorized**	unconfortable	**uncomfortable**
unawware	**unaware****	unconnditional	**unconditional**
unbalansed	**unbalanced**	unconnscious	**unconscious**
unballanced	**unbalanced**	unconnstitutional	**unconstitutional**
unbarable	**unbearable**	unconntrovertable	**uncontrovertible**
unbawrn	**unborn**	unconnventional	**unconventional**
unbeecoming	**unbecoming**	unconsealed	**unconcealed**
unbeleivable	**unbelievable**	unconserned	**unconcerned**
unbenown	**unbeknown**	unconshonable	**unconscionable**
unberrable	**unbearable**	unconshonible	**unconscionable**
unbicoming	**unbecoming**	unconsionible	**unconscionable**
unbiesed	**unbiased**	unconsios	**unconscious**
unbilical	**umbilical**	unconstittutionel	**unconstitutional**
unbilievable	**unbelievable**	unconstraned	**unconstrained**
unborne	**unborn**	unconsumated	**unconsummated**
unbownded	**unbounded**	uncontamminated	**uncontaminated**
unbrakible	**unbreakable**	uncontessted	**uncontested**
unbrideled	**unbridled**	uncontraddicted	**uncontradicted**
unbrokken	**unbroken**	uncontraverted	**uncontroverted**
unbyased	**unbiased**	uncontrodicted	**uncontradicted**
uncalld for	**uncalled-for**	uncontrolable	**uncontrollable**
uncany	**uncanny**	uncoopperative	**uncooperative**
uncel	**uncle**	uncooth	**uncouth**
uncensered	**uncensored**	uncoroborated	**uncorroborated**
uncertinty	**uncertainty**	uncovver	**uncover**
unchalenged	**unchallenged**	unctous	**unctuous**
unchanjed	**unchanged**	uncumfortable	**uncomfortable**
uncharatible	**uncharitable**	uncuthe	**uncouth**
uncharrted	**uncharted**	undacheive	**underachieve**
unchased	**unchaste**	undamajed	**undamaged**
uncivalized	**uncivilized**	undammaged	**undamaged**
unclamed	**unclaimed**	undastand	**understand**
unclasified	**unclassified**	undatted	**undated**
uncleen	**unclean**	undawnted	**undaunted**
uncleer	**unclear**	undaworld	**underworld**
uncloth	**unclothe**	undeffended	**undefended**
uncolectable	**uncollectible**	undelying	**underlying**
uncolected	**uncollected**	undenyible	**undeniable**
uncomftable	**uncomfortable**	underacheeve	**underachieve**
uncommplicated	**uncomplicated**	underaje	**underage**
uncommplying	**uncomplying**	underasesment	**underassessment**
uncommpromizing		underbos	**underboss**
	uncompromising	undercappitalized	**undercapitalized**
uncompeled	**uncompelled**	undercovver	**undercover**

Incorrect	Correct	Incorrect	Correct
undercutt	**undercut**	undesided	**undecided**
underdevveloped	**underdeveloped**	undesserved	**undeserved**
underdraun	**underdrawn**	undessirable	**undesirable**
underemmployment		undestributed	**undistributed**
	underemployment	undeterrmined	**undetermined**
underrepresented	**underrepresented**	undetterminable	**undeterminable**
underesstimate	**underestimate**	undevveloped	**undeveloped**
undergoe	**undergo**	undew	**undue****
undergradduate	**undergraduate**	undewriter	**underwriter**
undergroth	**undergrowth**	undianosed	**undiagnosed**
undergrownd	**underground**	undicided	**undecided**
underhandded	**underhanded**	undignafied	**undignified**
underimployed	**underemployed**	undiniable	**undeniable**
underinnsured	**underinsured**	undinied	**undenied**
underite	**underwrite**	undirrected	**undirected**
underleese	**under-lease**	undisbersed	**undisbursed**
underlett	**underlet**	undisipplined	**undisciplined**
underlyeing	**underlying**	undisirable	**undesirable**
undermyne	**undermine**	undisklosed	**undisclosed**
underneeth	**underneath**	undisputted	**undisputed**
undernorished	**undernourished**	undisscharged	**undischarged**
underpade	**underpaid**	undissclosed	**undisclosed**
underpining	**underpinning**	undissiplined	**undisciplined**
underprised	**underpriced**	undissposed	**undisposed**
underrage	**underage**	undissputed	**undisputed**
underrestimate	**underestimate**	undistribbuted	**undistributed**
underright	**underwrite**	undivvided	**undivided**
underriter	**underwriter**	undoccumented	**undocumented**
underscor	**underscore**	undully	**unduly**
undersecratery	**undersecretary**	undyagnosed	**undiagnosed**
undersel	**undersell**	undyeing	**undying**
undersexxed	**undersexed**	unearned	**unearned**
undersherrif	**under-sheriff**	uneate	**Uniat** or **Uniate**
undersined	**undersigned**	uneazy	**uneasy**
undersised	**undersized**	unecessary	**unnecessary**
understan	**understand**	uneddited	**unedited**
understannding	**understanding**	unedducated	**uneducated**
understat	**understate**	uneeded	**unneeded**
understatment	**understatement**	uneek	**unique****
undersubbscribed	**undersubscribed**	uneequivocal	**unequivocal**
undertak	**undertake**	uneering	**unerring**
undertakeing	**undertaking**	uneesy	**uneasy**
undertakker	**undertaker**	uneform	**uniform**
undertenent	**under-tenant**	uneggsecuted	**unexecuted**
under the tabble	**under-the-table**	unegotiable	**unnegotiable**
underton	**undertone**	unekseptionable	**unexceptionable****
undertoock	**undertook**	uneksercised	**unexercised**
undervalluation	**undervaluation**	unemmotional	**unemotional**
underwerld	**underworld**	unemmployed	**unemployed**
underwey	**underway**	unenclozed	**unenclosed**

Incorrect	Correct	Incorrect	Correct
unenforsable	**unenforceable**	ungovvernable	**ungovernable**
unenncumbered	**unencumbered**	ungradded	**ungraded**
unenntered	**unentered**	ungratful	**ungrateful**
unenntitled	**unentitled**	ungtion	**unction**
unenterred	**unentered**	ungtuous	**unctuous**
unequivvocal	**unequivocal**	ungust	**unjust**
uneqwal	**unequal**	unguvernable	**ungovernable**
unering	**unerring**	unhapy	**unhappy**
unerned	**unearned**	unharmd	**unharmed**
unerth	**unearth**	unheallthy	**unhealthy**
unesential	**unessential**	unhelthy	**unhealthy**
unet	**unit****	unhibited	**uninhibited**
unethecal	**unethical**	unhinndered	**unhindered**
unethickel	**unethical**	unholesome	**unwholesome**
unevenful	**uneventful**	unidentefiable	**unidentifiable**
uneventfull	**uneventful**	unifacterel	**unifactoral**
unexpekted	**unexpected**	unifform	**uniform**
unexpiered	**unexpired**	unifformity	**uniformity**
unexplaned	**unexplained**	uniffy	**unify**
unexxercised	**unexercised**	unillateral	**unilateral**
unexxpended	**unexpended**	unimpared	**unimpaired**
unexxpressed	**unexpressed**	unimpeachible	**unimpeachable**
unfaithfull	**unfaithful**	unimpeechable	**unimpeachable**
unfammiliar	**unfamiliar**	unimployment	**unemployment**
unfare	**unfair**	unimployment compensation	
unfashunible	**unfashionable**	...**unemployment compensation**	
unfathful	**unfaithful**	unimprooved land	
unfathimible	**unfathomable**	**unimproved land**	
unfaverible	**unfavorable**	unincombered	**unencumbered**
unfimiler	**unfamiliar**	unincorperated	**unincorporated**
unfinnished	**unfinished**	uninfeckted	**uninfected**
unfitt	**unfit**	uninhabbitable	**uninhabitable**
unflapable	**unflappable**	uninhibbited	**uninhibited**
unflatering	**unflattering**	uninimmity	**unanimity**
unfoccused	**unfocused**	uninnformative	**uninformative**
unforchunately	**unfortunately**	uninnhabitable	**uninhabitable**
unforeseible	**unforeseeable**	uninnsured	**uninsured**
unforgettable	**unforgetable**	uninshurable	**uninsurable**
unforgivvable	**unforgivable**	uninspeckted	**uninspected**
unforrtunate	**unfortunate**	uninspiered	**uninspired**
unforseable	**unforeseeable**	uninsurrable	**uninsurable**
unforsene	**unforeseen**	unintarupted	**uninterrupted**
unforttunnate	**unfortunate**	uninteligible	**unintelligible**
unfownded	**unfounded**	unintennded	**unintended**
unfrendly	**unfriendly**	unintenntional	**unintentional**
unfullfiled	**unfulfilled**	uninterrested	**uninterested**
unfunnded	**unfunded**	uninterupted	**uninterrupted**
unganely	**ungainly**	unintrested	**uninterested**
ungarded	**unguarded**	unionazation	**unionization**
ungoddly	**ungodly**	unionise	**unionize**

Incorrect	Correct
unionn	**union**
unishued	**unissued**
unitery	**unitary**
unitt	**unit****
unitted nations	**United Nations**
unittization	**unitization**
univversity	**university**
unjusst	**unjust**
unjustafiable	**unjustifiable**
unjust inrichment	**unjust enrichment**
unkemp	**unkempt**
unklassified	**unclassified**
unknone	**unknown**
unkonscious	**unconscious**
unkooperative	**uncooperative**
unlawfily	**unlawfully**
unlawfull	**unlawful**
unleesh	**unleash**
unles	**unless**
unlikkely	**unlikely**
unliklihood	**unlikelihood**
unlimmited	**unlimited**
unliqwidated	**unliquidated**
unlisensed	**unlicensed**
unlissted	**unlisted**
unliveable	**unlivable**
unlode	**unload**
unloding	**unloading**
unlukky	**unlucky**
unmanigible	**unmanageable**
unmareed	**unmarried**
unmarrketable	**unmarketable**
unmenntionable	**unmentionable**
unmisstakible	**unmistakable**
unmistakeable	**unmistakable**
unmittegated	**unmitigated**
unmurciful	**unmerciful**
unnabashed	**unabashed**
unnable	**unable**
unnanimity	**unanimity**
unnarmed	**unarmed**
unnateral	**unnatural**
unncomplicated	**uncomplicated**
unndated	**undated**
unnder	**under**
unnderstanding	**understanding**
unndue	**undue**
unnearned	**unearned**
unnedited	**unedited**

Incorrect	Correct
unneducated	**uneducated**
unnemployed	**unemployed**
unnerage	**underage**
unnesesery	**unnecessary**
unngraded	**ungraded**
unniform comercial code	**Uniform Commercial Code**
unnify	**unify**
unnion	**union**
unnissued	**unissued**
unnite	**unite**
Unnited States	**United States**
unnitize	**unitize**
unniversal	**universal**
unnown	**unknown**
unnsafe	**unsafe**
unntil	**until**
unntrue	**untrue**
unnulaterel	**unilateral**
unocupied	**unoccupied**
unoficial	**unofficial**
unorginized	**unorganized**
unorthadox	**unorthodox**
unoticed	**unnoticed**
unowingly	**unknowingly**
unpade	**unpaid**
unpallatable	**unpalatable**
unpattented	**unpatented**
unpire	**umpire**
unprafesional	**unprofessional**
unpreccedented	**unprecedented**
unpreedictable	**unpredictable**
unpreemeditated	**unpremeditated**
unprejediced	**unprejudiced**
unpresedented	**unprecedented**
unprettentious	**unpretentious**
unprinsipled	**unprincipled**
unprodductive	**unproductive**
unprofatable	**unprofitable**
unproffesional	**unprofessional**
unproffitable	**unprofitable**
unprooven	**unproven**
unprovvoked	**unprovoked**
unpunnished	**unpunished**
unqualefide	**unqualified**
unquessionable	**unquestionable**
unquess	**unques**
unquestinable	**unquestionable**
unreasonible	**unreasonable**
unrecovvered	**unrecovered**

Incorrect	Correct
unreecorded	**unrecorded**
unreedresed	**unredressed**
unreesonable	**unreasonable**
unreggulated	**unregulated**
unritten	**unwritten**
unrellated	**unrelated**
unrellenting	**unrelenting**
unreppresented	**unrepresented**
unressponsive	**unresponsive**
unresstrained	**unrestrained**
unrilated	**unrelated**
unristricted	**unrestricted**
unriteful	**unrightful**
unritten	**unwritten**
unruley	**unruly**
unsanatery	**unsanitary**
unsatissfactery	**unsatisfactory**
unsavery	**unsavory**
unschedduled	**unscheduled**
unscruppulous	**unscrupulous**
unscrupullus	**unscrupulous**
unseamly	**unseemly**
unseccured	**unsecured**
unseeled	**unsealed**
unsellfish	**unselfish**
unsensored	**uncensored**
unsertainty	**uncertainty**
unsetled	**unsettled**
unsicured	**unsecured**
unsined	**unsigned**
unsitely	**unsightly**
unskathed	**unscathed**
unskeduled	**unscheduled**
unskiled	**unskilled**
unsofisticated	**unsophisticated**
unsownd	**unsound**
unspeekable	**unspeakable**
unstopable	**unstoppable**
unstuddied	**unstudied**
unsucksesful	**unsuccessful**
unsuppervised	**unsupervised**
unsurable	**uninsurable**
unsusspecting	**unsuspecting**
unsuteable	**unsuitable**
unswarn	**unsworn**
untaxxed	**untaxed**
untennable	**untenable**
unthingking	**unthinking**
unthinkible	**unthinkable**
untill	**until**

Incorrect	Correct
untimly	**untimely**
untord	**untoward**
untride	**untried**
untroo	**untrue**
untruthfull	**untruthful**
untuchable	**untouchable**
unubridged	**unabridged**
unumbered	**unnumbered**
unumployed	**unemployed**
unumproved land	**unimproved land**
unurned	**unearned**
unuseable	**unusable**
unussisted	**unassisted**
unusuel	**unusual**
unverefied	**unverified**
unvoyced	**unvoiced**
unwaranted	**unwarranted**
unwerthy	**unworthy**
unwery	**unwary**
unwiling	**unwilling**
unwiting	**unwitting**
unwriten	**unwritten**
unyeilding	**unyielding**
unyun jack	**Union Jack**
upbeet	**upbeat**
upheeval	**upheaval**
uphemism	**euphemism****
upkepe	**upkeep**
uplifft	**uplift**
upold	**uphold**
uppeat	**upbeat**
upp to date	**up-to-date**
upringing	**upbringing**
uprore	**uproar**
upshott	**upshot**
upsset price	**upset price**
uptern	**upturn**
urbann	**urban****
urinanalysis	**urinalysis**
urned	**earned**
uro currency	**Eurocurrency**
urodollars	**Eurodollars**
urrgent	**urgent**
urrinalysis	**urinalysis**
usafrucht	**usufruct**
useage	**usage**
useance	**usance**
useble	**usable** or **useable**
usefull	**useful**
useing	**using**

Incorrect	Correct	Incorrect	Correct
userer	usurer**	utilise	utilize
userp	usurp	utillity	utility
usery	usury**	utillize	utilize
useto	used to	utterine	uterine
usful	useful	utterus	uterus
ushurious	usurious	uttility	utility
uskew	usque	uttily	utterly
usless	useless	uttmost	utmost
ussual	usual	uttopia	utopia
ussufruck	usufruct	uttrance	utterance
ussure	usura**	uturus	uterus
ussurer	usurer**	uxer	uxor
usuall	usual	uxxoricide	uxoricide
usurpper	usurper	uzable	usable or useable
usurrpation	usurpation	uze	use
uter	utter	uzee	usee
uterly	utterly	uzer	user
uthanasia	euthanasia	uzery	usury
uther	other	uzual	usual
utilazation	utilization	uzurer	usurer**

V

Incorrect	Correct	Incorrect	Correct
vacasion	vacation**	valey	valley
vacater	vacatur	validdity	validity
vaccant	vacant	valient	valiant
vaccilate	vacillate	valition	volition
vacincy	vacancy	valledate	validate
vacous	vacuous	vallentia	valentia
vacsine	vaccine	vallerous	valorous
vacum	vacuum	vallet	valet**
vacuty	vacuity	valleur	valuer
vadeum	vadium	valliant	valiant
vage	vague	vallid	valid**
vagery	vagary	valluate	valuate
vaggabond	vagabond	vallue	value
vaggina	vagina	valorrize	valorize
vaggrant	vagrant	valuble	valuable
vagrincy	vagrancy	valueation	valuation
vailings	veilings	valued aded tax	value added tax
vajina	vagina	valuless	valueless
vakant	vacant	valyable	valuable**
vakate	vacate	vandallism	vandalism
vaksination	vaccination	vandelism	vandalism
valadate	validate	vandil	vandal
valadiction	valediction	vandilise	vandalize
valatudinery	valetudinary	vaneglory	vainglory
valer	valor	vangard	vanguard

Incorrect	Correct
vankwish	**vanquish**
vanndal	**vandal**
vannish	**vanish**
vantige	**vantage**
vareable	**variable**
vareant	**variant**
varius	**various**
varriable	**variable**
varriety	**variety**
varyance	**variance**
varyation	**variation**
vasal	**vassal**
vasectimy	**vasectomy**
vasscular	**vascular**
vassectomy	**vasectomy**
vasstum	**vastum**
vavaser	**vavasor** or **vavasour**
vawdeville	**vaudeville**
vea	**via**
vecayture	**vacatur**
veehement	**vehement**
veehiculer	**vehicular**
veeicle	**vehicle**
veenal	**venal****
veeni	**visne****
veesa	**visa****
veeto	**veto**
veez a vee	**vis-à-vis**
veggetative	**vegetative**
vegtable	**vegetable**
veid	**vide**
veilane	**villein**
veilaneage	**villeinage**
veis	**veies****
veks	**vex**
vekter	**vector**
vellocity	**velocity**
vement	**vehement**
venall	**venial****
venarria	**venaria**
vendable	**vendible**
vender	**vendor**
vendetricks	**venditrix**
vendision	**vendition**
venditer	**venditor**
vendo	**vende**
vendy	**vendee**
venea	**venia****
veneal	**venial****
veneer facias	**venire facias**

Incorrect	Correct
veneerman	**venireman**
venel	**venal****
venereman	**venireman**
venerration	**veneration**
vengful	**vengeful**
venimous	**venemous**
venirial disease	**venereal disease**
venjance	**vengeance**
vennality	**venality**
vennatio	**venatio**
venndeta	**vendetta**
venned	**vend**
vennerable	**venerable**
vennereal disease	**venereal disease**
vennery	**venery**
vennew	**venue**
vennit	**venit**
vennture	**venture**
ventalation	**ventilation**
venter	**venture**
ventillate	**ventilate**
ventor	**venter**
venu	**venue**
venyal	**venial****
venyue	**venue**
verbage	**verbiage**
verball	**verbal**
verbeage	**verbiage**
verderrer	**verderer** or **verderor**
verdick	**verdict**
verdictum	**veredictum**
vereffy	**verify**
vereficatioin	**verification**
vergata	**virgata**
vergin	**virgin**
vergo intact	**virgo intacta****
verility	**virility**
verracity	**veracity**
verranda	**veranda** or **verandah**
verray	**veray**
verrbatum	**verbatim**
verrdikt	**verdict**
verrified	**verified**
verrify	**verify**
verrity	**verity**
verrtego	**vertigo**
verrus	**verus**
verry	**very**
versimiltude	**verisimilitude**
versitile	**versatile**

Incorrect	Correct	Incorrect	Correct
verssus	versus	viggor	vigor
vertual	virtual	vigill	vigil
vessted	vested	vigillantizm	vigilanteism
vesstige	vestige		or vigilantism
vesstry	vestry	vihiculer	vehicular
vestera	vestura	vijilance	vigilance
vestid	vested	vikinage	vicinage
vestigum	vestigium	viktim	victim
vestijial	vestigial	vilable	violable
vestyer	vesture	vilefy	vilify
veterrastatute	vetera statuta	vilence	violence
vetoe	veto	vilenus judgment	
vetos	vetoes		.... villenous judgment
vetren	veteran	vilige	village
vetrinarien	veterinarian	villent	violent
vetteran	veteran	villify	vilify
vexare	vexari	vinajum	vinagium
vexasious	vexatious	vindacated	vindicated
vexatta question	vexata quaestio	vindecate	vindicate
vexxation	vexation	vindicar	vindicare
viabbility	viability	vindiccater	vindicator
vialation	violation	vindicktiv	vindictive
vicarrial	vicarial	vindikatery	vindicatory
viccarious	vicarious	vinette	vignette
viccisitude	vicissitude	vinndication	vindication
vicer	vicar	vinnous	vinous
vicerel	visceral	vintige	vintage
vicinnity	vicinity	violenntly	violently
vicktory	victory	violense	violence
vicktus	victus	vior deer	voir dire
viconteel	vicontiel	viragoe	virago**
vicous	vicious	virall	viral
victery	victory	virchue	virtue
victimise	victimize	virdict	verdict
victimm	victim	virel	viral
victimmless	victimless	virgat	virgate
victry	victory	virginnity	virginity
viddelecit	videlicet	virill	virile
viddeocassete	videocassette	viris	virus
viddeotape	videotape	virjin	virgin
vidio	video	virr	vir**
viduct	viaduct	virrago	virago**
viduety	viduity	virral	viral
vie et armus	vi et armis	virres	vires
vieing	vying	virricide	viricide
vielative	violative	virrile	virile
vien	vein**	virrulence	virulence
viger	vigor	virrus	virus**
viggilant	vigilant	virtous	virtuous

Incorrect	Correct	Incorrect	Correct
virtut	**virtute**	voideable	**voidable**
virullent	**virulent**	voidince	**voidance**
viruss	**virus****	voir dier	**voir dire**
visable	**visible**	voise	**voice**
viscus	**viscous**	vokabulery	**vocabulary**
viseral	**visceral**	vokation	**vocation****
viseroy	**viceroy**	volentery	**voluntary**
viseversa	**vice versa**	volinteer	**volunteer**
vishiate	**vitiate**	volisionel	**volitional**
vishous	**vicious**	volitile	**volatile**
visinity	**vicinity**	volitility	**volatility**
visisitude	**vicissitude**	vollatile	**volatile**
visitter	**visitor**	vollens	**volens**
viss	**vis****	vollition	**volition**
vissitation	**visitation**	volluble	**voluble**
vissne	**visne****	vollume	**volume**
vissual	**visual**	vollumenous	**voluminous**
vitel	**vital**	vollunterily	**voluntarily**
vitimin	**vitamin**	volluptous	**voluptuous**
vitlagate	**vitiligate**	volsted act	**Volstead Act**
vitner	**vintner**	voluntere	**volunteer**
vitreol	**vitriol**	volyable	**voluble****
vitrious	**vitreous**	volyume	**volume**
vittal	**vital**	vommit	**vomit**
vittamin	**vitamin**	vorashous	**voracious**
vittle	**victual**	vosiferous	**vociferous**
vittuperative	**vituperative**	voteing	**voting**
vitual	**victual**	votor	**voter**
vitupperate	**vituperate**	vouchor	**voucher**
vivarum	**vivarium**	vouchy	**vouchee**
vive vocka	**viva voce**	voushsafe	**vouchsafe**
vividdly	**vividly**	voutch	**vouch**
vivvary	**vivary**	vowch	**vouch**
vivvid	**vivid**	vowching	**vouching**
vivvim vakum	**vivum vadium**	voxx populi	**vox populi**
viza	**visa****	voyd	**void**
vizable	**visible**	voyerism	**voyeurism**
viz a viz	**vis-à-vis**	voyige	**voyage**
vize	**vise****	voyure	**voyeur**
vizhonary	**visionary**	vue	**view**
vizible	**visible**	vulger	**vulgar**
vizit	**visit**	vullgaraty	**vulgarity**
vizual	**visual**	vullnrable	**vulnerable**
vizz	**viz****	vullva	**vulva**
voccabular artes	**vocabula artis**	vulnorible	**vulnerable**
vocoe	**voco**	vulvae	**vulva**
vog	**vogue**	vurba	**verba**
voge	**vogue**	vurbal	**verbal**
voicprint	**voiceprint**	vurbatim	**verbatim**

Incorrect	Correct	Incorrect	Correct
vurdant	**verdant**	vurtigo	**vertigo**
vurdict	**verdict**	vuwers	**viewers**
vurge	**verge****	vwar deer	**voir dire**
vurgin	**virgin**	vwar dire	**voir dire**
vuriety	**variety**	vyalater	**violator**
vurje	**virge****	vyce	**vice****
vurnacular	**vernacular**	vycount	**viscount**
vurses	**versus**	vye	**vie****
vurtical	**vertical**	vyeing	**vying**
vurtiginous	**vertiginous**	vyible	**viable**

W

Incorrect	Correct	Incorrect	Correct
wable	**wobble**	wantoness	**wantonness**
wach	**wash**	warant	**warrant**
wachdog	**watchdog**	warantees	**warranties**
wachman	**watchman**	wardda	**warda**
wachout	**washout****	wardin	**warden**
wack	**whack**	wardz	**wards**
wacrer	**wacreour**	ware and tare	**wear and tear**
waddia	**wadia**	wareby	**whereby**
wadge	**wage**	waren	**warren**
wadger	**wager**	warentible	**warrantable**
wafe	**waif****	warf	**wharf**
wafle	**waffle**	warfair	**warfare**
wagerring	**wagering**	warhouse	**warehouse**
wagger	**wager**	warhouseman's lien	
waggon	**wagon**		**warehousemen's lien**
wagless	**wageless**	waring apparel	**wearing apparel**
wagnor act	**Wagner Act**	warintee	**warranty****
waight	**weight****	warinty	**warrantee****
waile	**whale****	warr	**war**
waity	**weighty**	warrd	**ward****
waivver	**waiver****	warrden	**warden**
wajes	**wages**	warrenter	**warrantor****
wakout	**walkout****	warrmonger	**warmonger**
waksen	**waxen**	warrning	**warning**
wakup	**walkup****	warry	**wary****
walch healy act	**Walsh-Healey Act**	warton rule	**Wharton Rule**
walow	**wallow**	wasaw convention	
wampom	**wampum**		**Warsaw Convention**
wanable	**wainable**	washd sale	**wash sale**
wangel	**wangle****	wasstrel	**wastrel**
wanige	**wainage**	wasteing	**wasting**
wannder	**wander****	wastfull	**wasteful**
wannton	**wanton****	wastige	**wastage**
wantin	**wanton****	watafront	**waterfront**

Incorrect	Correct	Incorrect	Correct
wataway	waterway	welldun	well-done
waterborn	waterborne	wellfare	welfare
waterd stock	watered stock	wellfownded	well-founded
waterrshed	watershed	wellgrownded	well-grounded
watertite	watertight	wellmeening	well-meaning
watever	whatever	wellsh	welsh
wateworks	waterworks	wellspocken	well-spoken
watorgate	Watergate	welltadoe	well-to-do
watshword	watchword	wellthy	wealthy
watter	water	wellwicher	well-wisher
watterloged	waterlogged	welm	whelm
wavor	waver**	welps	whelps
wavvering	wavering	welth	wealth
wawder	warder	wenn	when**
wayr	ware**	wepon	weapon
wayst	waist**	werd processing	word processing
wayve	waive**	werefor	wherefore
wayver	waiver**	werewithall	wherewithal
wayword	wayward	werk	work
wayylay	waylay	werker	worker
wayz and meens	ways and means	werker's compensation	
weadlock	wedlock		workers' compensation
weakday	weekday	werkshopp	workshop
weaknis	weakness	werld	world
wealer deeler	wheeler-dealer	werthles	worthless**
wearabouts	whereabouts	werthy	worthy
wearas	whereas	wetbak	wetback
wearhouseman	warehouseman	wethering	weathering
wearon	whereon	wethor	wether**
wear with all	wherewithal	wettland	wetland
web pomorene act		weybill	way-bill
	Webb-Pomerene Act	whalor	whaler
wedd	wed	wharewith	wherewith
weding	wedding	wharfige	wharfage
weeken	weaken	whatch	watch
weekminded	weak-minded	whatsover	whatsoever
weel	weal**	whealright	wheelright
weerysome	wearisome	whearoff	whereof
weif	wife	wheather	whether**
wein	wine**	wheell	wheel
weke	weak**	whenevver	whenever
wekend	weekend	whenisued	when issued
wekly	weekly	wherafter	whereafter
welapointed	well-appointed	wheras	whereas
welbein	well-being	whereever	wherever
welcher	welsher	wherfore	wherefor
weldispozed	well-disposed	wherfrom	wherefrom
welfair	welfare	wherin	wherein
welhed	wellhead	whersover	wheresoever

Incorrect	Correct	Incorrect	Correct
wherto	**whereto**	winstorm	**windstorm**
wherunder	**whereunder**	wiplash	**whiplash**
wherupon	**whereupon**	wipout	**wipe-out****
whigg	**Whig**	wipplash	**whiplash**
whiping	**whipping**	wippsaw	**whipsaw**
whiretapping	**wiretapping**	wiretapp	**wiretap**
whissky	**whiskey**	wirth	**worth**
whitchever	**whichever**	wisened	**wizened**
white night	**white knight**	wishfull	**wishful**
whithholding	**withholding**	wisky	**whiskey**
witholding tax	**withholding tax**	wisper	**whisper**
whittingly	**wittingly**	wissdom	**wisdom**
wholl	**whole****	wissedful	**wistful**
whollsailor	**wholesaler**	witchsover	**whichsoever**
wholsale	**wholesale**	wite	**white**
wholy	**wholly****	witecolar crime	**white-collar crime**
whomsover	**whomsoever****	wite coller	**white-collar**
whooever	**whoever**	wite nite	**white knight**
whoor	**whore****	witewash	**whitewash**
whorhouse	**whorehouse**	withall	**withal**
whosover	**whosoever****	withdrawe	**withdraw**
whyle	**while****	withdrawl	**withdrawal**
wich	**which****	withdrawwing	**withdrawing**
widdow	**widow**	witherr	**whither**
widjet	**widget**	withinn	**within**
widoer	**widower**	withold	**withhold**
widohood	**widowhood**	withoutt	**without**
wier	**weir****	witim	**witam**
wierd	**weird**	witing	**witting**
wiertap	**wiretap**	witnes	**witness**
wiget	**widget**	witnising part	**witnessing part**
wil	**will**	witstand	**withstand**
wilcatter	**wildcatter**	witt	**whit****
wildcase	**Wild's Case**	wittnes	**witness**
wildeing	**wilding**	wittness	**witness**
wiled	**wild**	wizdom	**wisdom**
wilfull	**willful**	wobegon	**woebegone**
wilingly	**willingly**	wochfull	**watchful**
wim	**whim**	woirkout	**workout****
wimen	**women****	wommens rights	**women's rights**
wimper	**whimper**	wondaful	**wonderful**
wimsy	**whimsy**	wonndrous	**wondrous**
windfal	**windfall**	woodbe	**would-be**
windoe	**window**	woodwerker	**woodworker**
winer	**winner**	woold	**would****
winfall	**windfall**	woond	**wound**
winnter	**winter**	woosted	**worsted**
winsom	**winsome**	wordly	**worldly**

worent .... **warrant**
worenty .... **warranty****
woreship .... **worship**
workeing .... **working**
worklode .... **workload**
workmin .... **workman**
worled cort .... **World Court**
worlwind .... **whirlwind**
worp .... **warp**
worpath .... **warpath**
worthwile .... **worthwhile**
worysome .... **worrisome**
wouldwork .... **woodwork**
woundid feelings ... **wounded feelings**
wrathfull .... **wrathful**
wreckige .... **wreckage**
wreckless indangerment ....
.... **reckless endangerment**
wrek .... **wreck****
wreker .... **wrecker**
wresst .... **wrest****
wrestitution .... **restitution**

wringleader .... **ringleader**
wrissdrop .... **wristdrop**
writeful .... **rightful**
writehanded .... **right-handed**
writeing .... **writing**
writen .... **written**
write-to-work .... **right to work**
writoff .... **write-off****
writ of sertiori .... **writ of certiorari**
writt .... **writ**
writup .... **write-up****
wrongdooer .... **wrongdoer**
wrongfily .... **wrongfully**
wrongfull .... **wrongful**
wunst .... **once**
wurds .... **words**
wurkday .... **workday**
wurkmans compensation ....
.... **workmens' compensation**
or **workers' compensation**
wyves .... **wives**

Y

yae and nae .... **yea and nay**
yardmasster .... **yardmaster**
yarrd .... **yard**
yat .... **yacht**
yays and nays .... **yeas and nays**
yaysayer .... **yea-sayer**
yearz .... **years**
yeeld .... **yield**
yeeld-to-maturity .... **yield to maturity**
yeer .... **year**
yeer-end .... **yearend**
yeest .... **yeast**
yeild .... **yield**
yelow dog contract ....
.... **yellow-dog contract**
yenn-denominated ....
.... **yen-denominated**
yere to yere .... **year to year**
yesteday .... **yesterday**

yesterrday .... **yesterday**
yidish .... **Yiddish**
Yik woe doctrine .... **Yick Wo doctrine**
yoeman .... **yeoman**
yooth .... **youth**
yot .... **yacht**
youman .... **human**
younique .... **unique****
your's .... **yours**
yours' .... **yours**
yubi juss, ibbi remedium ....
.... **ubi jus, ibi remedium**
yubiquitous .... **ubiquitous**
yungster .... **youngster**
yunion .... **union**
yure .... **ure**
yuse .... **use**
yuss .... **jus**
yuthfool .... **youthful**

Z

Incorrect	Correct	Incorrect	Correct
zaney	**zany**	zerography	**xerography**
zeallot	**zealot**	ziggzaged	**zigzagged**
zeenith	**zenith**	zoneing	**zoning**
zeles	**zealous**	zonning	**zoning**
zellotry	**zealotry**	zown	**zone**
zenomania	**xenomania**	zyegot	**zygote**
zenophobia	**xenophobia**	zygot	**zygote**
zeroe coopon bond	**zero coupon bond**		

Words Commonly Confused Because They Look Alike or Sound Alike

A

abbreviate (to shorten; to substitute for longer word) • breviate (brief; short statement)

abject (lacking resources or pride) • object (to oppose)

abjure (to recant under oath) • adjure (to command; to beg)

aboriginal (native; indigenous) • Ab origine (from the source)

Ab origine—see aboriginal

above (over) • ab ovo (from the beginning)

ab ovo—see above

abrogate (to abolish) • arrogate (to claim without justification)

absentee (one who is not present) • absentia (in the absence of: in absentia)

absentia—see absentee

absorb (to take in; to understand) • adsorb (to adhere to a surface)

abstract (to condense) • obstruct (to interfere)

abstruse (complex; profound) • obtuse (lacking understanding)

academia (higher education) • academy (special school)

academy—see academia

acceed (to agree; to approve) • exceed (to be more than)

accent (distinctive pronunciation) • ascend (to climb) • ascent (an upward climb) • assent (to agree)

accept (to agree or receive) • except (to exclude; to omit) • excerpt (brief extract or selection)

access (entry, availability) • assess (to value; to set damages) • excess (too much, a surplus)

accessible (easy to reach) • assessable (can be taxed)

acclamation (strong praise) • acclimation (adaptation to change)

acclimation—see acclamation

accomplice (partner in crime) • accomplish (to perform)

accomplish—see accomplice

acidulous (caustic, acid) • assiduous (hard-working)

action (movement or deed) • auction (sale via bidding)

activate (to motivate to act) • actuate (to cause to operate)

actuate—see activate

ad (advertisement) • add (to increase; to find a sum arithmetically)

adapt (adjust) • adept (able) • adopt (to accept; to take into one's family)

add—see ad

addable (can be increased) • edible (can be eaten)

addict (to habituate; one dependent on a controlled substance) • attic (room beneath roof) • edict (an official order)

ad diem (at the day) • adeem (to revoke)

addition (extra; the act of adding) • edition (an issue or form of publication)

additur (increased award for damages) • auditor (examiner of financial records) • auditory (relating to hearing) • editor (person who controls publication contents)

adduce (to provide an example) • educe (to bring forth; to elicit)

adeem—see ad diem

adept—see adapt

adit (a mine entrance) • audit (examination of financial books)

aditus (a way or a public way) • audits (pl. of audit)

adjoin (to be close to) • adjoint (a math operation) • adjourn (to end; to postpone)

adjoint—*see* adjoin

adjourn—*see* adjoin

adjournment (postponement) • **ajournment** (document to start suit)

adjure—*see* abjure

adjuster (one who settles claims) • **agister** or **agistor** (one who pastures animals for a fee)

adjutant (aide to officer) • **adjuvant** (a drug enhancement)

adjuvant—*see* adjutant

adolescence (stage before adulthood) • **adolescents** (people at that stage)

adolescents—*see* adolescence

adopt—*see* adapt

adsorb—*see* absorb

adulteress (woman who commits adultery) • **adulterous** (pertaining to sexual relations between a married person and a person to whom he or she is not married)

adulterous—*see* adulteress

adverse (unfavorable) • **adverts** (refers) • **averse** (opposed or reluctant)

advert (to refer) • **aver** (to assert) • **avert** (to avoid; to evade) • **evert** (to overturn, to reverse)

adverts—*see* adverse

advice (opinion, counsel) • **advise** (to suggest; to recommend)

advise—*see* advice

aegis (sponsorship, support) • **ages** (a long time; epochs)

affair (matter; business; issue) • **affaire** (a love relationship)

affaire—*see* affair

affect (to influence or shape) • **effect** (to bring about; a result)

affluent (wealthy) • **effluent** (sewage or other substances that flow out of various sources)

afflux (the act of flowing to) • **efflux** (expiration, as of a lease)

afterward (later) • **afterword** (short end of a literary work)

afterword—*see* afterward

ageist (prejudiced toward the elderly) • **agist** (taking in and feeding cattle for compensation)

ager (land, a field) • **agger** (a dam or bank, per civil law)

ages—*see* aegis

agger—*see* ager

aggression (unjustified attack) • **egression** (emergence)

agist—*see* ageist

agister or **agistor**—*see* adjuster

ague (malarial fever, bad shivers) • **argue** (to dispute; to disagree)

aid (one who helps; to help) • **aide** (assistant)

aide—*see* aid

aides—*see* AIDS

AIDS (acquired immune deficiency syndrome) • **aides** (pl. of *aide*)

ailment (sickness) • **alimenta** (help or means of support)

air (what we breathe; one's manner) • **e'er** (before) • **err** (to do wrong) • **heir** (inheritor)

aisle (narrow passage) • **I'll** (contr. for *I will*)

ajournment—*see* adjournment

alea (game of chance) • **alia** (other things, especially *inter alia*)

alia—*see* alea

alimenta—*see* ailment

alimentary (relating to food or the digestive system) • **elementary** (simple; on a lower level)

aliter (otherwise, held otherwise) • **altar** (center structure in religious services) • **alter** (to change)

allay (to calm; to curb fears) • **alley** (slim passage between buildings)

allegation (a charge; an accusation) • **alligation** (state of being attached)

allergenic (causing an allergy) • **allergic** (having a negative physical reaction, as to medication) • **allogeneic** (genetically different)

allergic—*see* allergenic

alley—*see* allay

alligation—*see* allegation

allision (two vessels colliding) • **allusion** (reference to something) • **elision** (skipping letters in word pronunciation) • **elusion** (evasion) • **illusion** (false appearance)

alliterate (to repeat consonants in written or spoken words) • **illiterate** (unable to read)

allocation (allotment or share) • **allocution** (query to defendant about charges; formal speech) • **elocution** (style of speech)

allocator (one who allots) • **allocatur** (it is allowed, as in a writ)

allocatur—*see* allocator

allocution—*see* allocation

allogeneic—*see* allergenic

allowed (permitted) • **aloud** (using one's voice)

alloy (mixed metals) • **ally** (strong supporter)

allude (refer or imply) • **elude** (to escape; to evade) • **elute** (to extract a material) • **illud** (that)

allusion—*see* allision

alluvion (water flowing against a shore) • **alluvium** (matter deposited by water) • **eluvium** (matter deposited by wind)

alluvium—*see* alluvion

ally—*see* alloy

alms (donations to the needy) • **arms** (upper limbs; instruments of war)

alogical (beyond logical reasoning) • **illogical** (not making sense)

aloud—*see* allowed

altar—*see* aliter

alter—*see* aliter

alteration (change) • **altercation** (loud quarrel) • **alternation** (following in turn)

altercation—*see* alteration

alternation—*see* alteration

altitude (height above sea level) • **attitude** (feeling or idea about person or thing)

alumna (female graduate) • **alumnae** (pl. of *alumna*) • **alumni** (pl. of *alumnus*) • **alumnus** (male graduate)

alumnae—*see* alumna

alumni—*see* alumna

alumnus—*see* alumna

amend (to correct or revise) • **emend** (to correct text)

amerce (to fine or penalize) • **immerse** (to submerge; to get deeply involved)

amiable (friendly) • **amicable** (peaceable)

amicable—*see* amiable

amoral (neither moral nor immoral) • **immoral** (acting contrary to standards of right and wrong) • **unmoral** (having no relation to morality)

amotio (removal) • **amotion** (dispossession of land or removal from office) • **emotion** (intense feelings)

amotion—*see* amotio

amour (illicit love affair) • **armoire** (wardrobe) • **armor** (protective clothing, military hardware)

amputation (removal of a limb) • **imputation** (implied accusation)

anal (pertaining to the anus or to rigid behavior) • **anneal** (to temper glass or metal) • **annual** (occurring every year)

analog or **analogue** (relating to the conversion of data to physical quantities; item that partially resembles another item) • **analogy** (similarity between two items; comparison)

analogue—*see* analog

analogy—*see* analog

analyses (pl. of *analysis*) • **analysis** (breaking whole into parts; a psychological method) • **analyze** (to break whole into parts)

analysis—*see* analyses

analyst (one who studies a subject carefully; psychiatrist or psychotherapist) • **annalist** (keeper of historical records)

analyze—*see* analyses

androgenous (fostering male traits) • **androgynous** (having male and female characteristics)

androgynous—*see* androgenous

anecdote (brief, amusing tale) • **antedate** (to give a document an earlier date) • **antidote** (anti-poison substance)

angaria (involuntary contribution of vessel for public service) • **angary** (belligerent's right to use neutral property for military purposes) • **angry** (raging, wrathful)

angary—*see* angaria

angel (heavenly being; lovely person) • **angle** (an improper method; a corner)

angle—*see* angel

angry—*see* angaria

annalist—*see* analyst

annals (historical records) • **annuals** (yearly publications)

anneal—*see* anal

annual—*see* anal

annuals—*see* annals

annunciate (to announce) • **enunciate** (to speak clearly)

ante (before; a business share) • **anti** (against)

antecedence (priority, precedence) • **antecedents** (earlier events; words referred to by pronouns)

antecedents—*see* antecedence

antedate—*see* anecdote

anti—*see* ante

antidote—*see* anecdote

anus (bodily opening for waste) • **heinous** (extremely wicked)

anyone (any person in general) • **any one** (any of several or of a group)

any one—*see* anyone

anything (any thing or happening) • **any thing** (any of several things)

any thing—*see* anything

anytime (at any time, when one chooses) • **any time** (any one of several times)

any time—*see* anytime

anyway (nevertheless, at any rate) • **any way** (any means or method)

any way—*see* anyway

apace (swiftly) • **a pais** (at issue)

a pais—*see* apace

aphagia (inability to swallow) • **aphasia** (inability to speak or understand language)

aphasia—*see* aphagia

apologia (defense of one's ideas or behavior) • **apologue** (story with a moral) • **apology** (expression of regret)

apologue—*see* apologia

apology—*see* apologia

apostille or **appostile** (an added or marginal note) • **apostle** (preacher of the gospel)

apostle—*see* apostille or appostile

apposite (appropriate) • **opposite** (completely different)

appostile—*see* apostille

appraise (to evaluate) • **apprise** (to inform) • **apprize** (to appreciate)

appressed (lying flat) • **oppressed** (ruled cruelly; weighed down)

apprise—*see* appraise

apprize—*see* appraise

arbiter (judge) • **orbiter** (object that circles a planet or moon) arc (curve) • arch (curved structure in building) • ark (ship; cabinet)

arch—*see* arc

area (surface) • arere (behind, back) • arrears (lateness in paying)

arere—*see* area

argue—*see* ague

ark—*see* arc

armoire—*see* amour

armor—*see* amour

arms—*see* alms

arraign (to bring criminal to court to answer indictment) • arrange (to organize; to prepare)

arrange—*see* arraign

arrant (extremely) • errand (brief trip) • errant (mistaken; moving aimlessly)

array (display; large group) • arret (court decree)

arrears—*see* area

arret—*see* array

arrogate—*see* abrogate

artistic (relating to art) • autistic (abnormally withdrawn)

ascend—*see* accent

ascendance (domination) • ascendants or ascendents (states of dominant power)

ascendants—*see* ascendance

ascent—*see* accent

ashore (on or approaching land) • assure (to guarantee)

assay (to evaluate) • essay (to attempt; a short composition)

assent—*see* accent

assess—*see* access

assessable—*see* accessible

assiduous—*see* acidulous

assistance (help or aid) • assistants (helpers)

assistants—*see* assistance

assurance (pledge; instrument for conveying real property;

insurance) • insurance (guarantee against loss)

assure—*see* ashore

attach (to fasten or join; to seize property) • attaché (embassy specialist) • attack (to strike, to criticize)

attaché—*see* attach

attack—*see* attach

attendance (number of people present) • attendants (people who serve others)

attendants—*see* attendance

attic—*see* addict

attitude—*see* altitude

auction—*see* action

audit—*see* adit

auditor—*see* additur

auditory—*see* additur

audits—*see* aditus

aught (zero) • ought (should)

aural (relating to sound or to the ear) • oral (relating to speech or to the mouth)

auricle (part of the heart or ear) • oracle (prophet; prophecy)

autarchy (dictatorial rule) • autarky (economic self-sufficiency)

autarky—*see* autarchy

auteur (film director) • author (writer) • autre (another) • hauteur (arrogance)

author—*see* auteur

autistic—*see* artistic

automation (machines replacing workers) • automaton (robot)

automaton—*see* automation

autre—*see* auteur

aver—*see* advert

averse—*see* adverse

aversion (strong dislike) • eversion (turning inside out)

avert—*see* advert

avocation (hobby, extra interest) • evocation (calling forth)

avoid (to evade; to refrain from) • ovoid (egg-shaped)

awe (fearful wonder or respect) • oar (paddle) • o'er (over) • or (indicates an alternative) • ore (a mineral)

aweful (inspiring worship) • awful (terrible) • offal (waste)

awful—see aweful

axial (related to an axis) • axle (the bar on which wheels turn) • exile (one who must leave country)

axle—see axial

aye (yes) • I (first person, oneself) • eye (organ of sight)

B

backup (substitute, replacement) • back up (to support)

back up—see backup

bail (security for court appearance) • bale (big package tied with twine)

bailee (holder of property for another) • Bailey (type of steel bridge)

Bailey—see bailee

bait (decoy, lure) • bate (to restrain, reduce)

bale—see bail

balm (soothing substance or act) • bomb (explosive weapon)

ban (to forbid, bar) • bane (cause of one's troubles)

banc (court's regular site) • bank (money center)

band (musical ensemble, ring) • banned (forbade, barred)

bands (pl. of band) • banns (marriage notice) • bans (prohibits)

bane—see ban

bank—see banc

banned—see band

banns—see bands

bans—see bands

bare (to uncover; to expose) • bear (to carry; to withstand)

base (foundation) • bass (low vocal range)

based (founded or located) • baste (to thrash; to moisten, to sew loosely)

bases (foundations; military installations) • basis (taxpayer's cost; basic principle)

basis—see bases

bass—see base

baste—see based

bate—see bait

bathetic (maudlin) • pathetic (pitiful; terribly inadequate)

bathos (triteness) • pathos (capability to evoke pity)

battel (trial by combat) • battle (fight or contest)

battle—see battel

baud (unit of data transmission) • bawd (madam; prostitute)

bawd—see baud

bazaar or bazar (charity sale; Middle Eastern market) • bizarre (strange; unconventional)

bear—see bare

beat (to hit repeatedly; usual route) • bit (small amount)

been (past participle of be; was) • biens (most property in English law) • bin (compartment)

begat (produced a child) • beget (to produce children) • bigot (prejudiced person)

beget—see begat

belie (contradict; give a false impression) • **belly** (stomach)

belief (trust; idea) • **believe** (to have strong conviction)

believe—*see* belief

bellow (loud, deep shout) • **below** (under)

belly—*see* belie

below—*see* bellow

berth (sleeping place) • **birth** (origin; process of bring born)

beseech (to beg) • **besiege** (to surround, in war)

beside (at the side of) • **besides** (moreover, in addition to)

besides—*see* beside

besiege—*see* beseech

better (higher quality, more useful) • **bettor** (gambler)

bettor—*see* better

biannual (twice a year) • **biennial** (every two years)

bidding (offer to buy; command) • **biding** (waiting)

biding—*see* bidding

biennial—*see* biannual

biens—*see* been

bigot—*see* begat

billed (charged) • **build** (to construct)

billion (a thousand million) • **bouillon** (broth) • **bullion** (gold or silver by quantity)

bin—*see* been

birth—*see* berth

bit—*see* beat

bite (to cut with teeth) • **byte** (unit of computer memory)

bizarre—*see* bazaar

black bag (a bag that is black) • **black-bag** (consisting of illegal entry by government)

bland (dull, tasteless) • **blend** (join together, combine)

blasé (bored, not interested) • **blaze** (bright flame)

blaze—*see* blasé

bleat (plaintive or sad sound; to complain) • **bleed** (to lose blood)

bleed—*see* bleat

blend—*see* bland

blew (expelled air or breath) • **blue** (color)

bloc (united group) • **block** (obstruction)

block—*see* bloc

blue—*see* blew

blue chip (a chip that is blue) • **blue-chip** (safe for investment)

blue collar (a shirt collar that is blue) • **blue-collar** (pertaining to workers, usu. manual laborers)

board (organized body of directors; plank; to pay for meals and lodging) • **bored** (lost interest; punched holes through; drilled)

boarder (one who pays for meals and lodging) • **border** (edge or frontier)

boast (to claim great accomplishments) • **boost** (to shoplift; to lift, raise)

bodies (pl. of *body*) • **body's** (belonging to a body)

body's—*see* bodies

bolder (more daring) • **boulder** (large stone or rock)

bomb—*see* balm

bona (goods or possessions) • **bone** (component of skeleton)

bona fide (honestly, in good faith) • **bona fides** (credentials)

bona fides—*see* bona fide

bondman (slave) • **bondsman** (bail provider)

bondsman—*see* bondman

bone—*see* bona

boost—-see boast

border—*see* boarder

bored—*see* board

born (came into life) • **borne** (carried)

borne—*see* born

borough (part of a town) • borrow (get a loan) • bureau (department or office; chest of drawers) • burro (donkey)

borrow—*see* borough

Borse (German stock exchange) • bourse (a stock exchange) • Bourse (French stock exchange)

bought (did buy) • brought (did bring)

bouillon—*see* billion

boulder—*see* bolder

bourse—*see* Borse

Bourse—*see* Borse

boy (male child) • buoy (ship danger signal; to support)

brake (part that slows or stops a vehicle) • break (rupture, tear)

brands (product types) • brans (outer part of grains)

brans—*see* brands

brave (courageous) • breve (writ) • brief (attorney's summary)

breach (violation) • breech (part of a weapon)

bread (food) • bred (cultivated or raised)

breadth (width) • breath (inhalation or exhalation) • breathe (to inhale or exhale)

break—*see* brake

breakdown (failure; collapse) • break down (to stop working; to simplify)

break even (to balance profits and losses) • break-even (marked by equal income and expenses)

breath—*see* breadth

breathe—*see* breadth

bred—*see* bread

breech—*see* breach

breve—*see* brave

breviate—*see* abbreviate

brews (makes tea or beer) • bruise (mark caused by injury)

bridal (relating to marriage) • bridle (to get angry; harness)

bridle—*see* bridal

brief—*see* brave

broach (to start to discuss) • brooch (decorative pin)

brocage (broker's commission) • brokerage (broker's business or commission)

brokerage—*see* brocage

brooch—*see* broach

brought—*see* bought

brows (foreheads; eyebrows) • browse (to examine casually)

browse—*see* brows

bruise—*see* brews

build—*see* billed

buildup (accumulation) • build up (to develop)

bullion—*see* billion

buoy—*see* boy

bureau—*see* borough

burnout (exhaustion) • burn out (to stop, as of a fire or match)

burn out—*see* burnout

burro—*see* borough

burrow—*see* borough

burry (full of burrs, prickly) • bury (cover with earth)

bursa (bodily sac) • bursar (treasurer)

bursar—*see* bursa

bury—*see* burry

but (only; except) • butt (object of ridicule) • butte (small mountain)

butt—*see* but

butte—*see* but

buy (to purchase) • by (near) • bye (less important issue)

by—*see* buy

bye—*see* buy

byte—*see* bite

137

C

cabal (secret plot or plotters) • cable (strong wire rope; television transmission system)

cable—see cabal

cache (hiding place) • cachet (distinctive quality) • cash (money)

cachet—see cache

cadet (police or military trainee) • cadit (falls or fails)

cadit—see cadet

calendar (day and month indicator) • calender (machine that makes paper or cloth smooth)

calender—see calendar

calibrate (to check accuracy by comparing to a standard) • celebrate (to mark a special occasion) • celibate (sexual abstainer; one who is unmarried) • cerebrate (to think)

call (right to buy stock at set price; to request payment) • caul (fetal membrane)

callous (cold, insensitive) • callus (thickened skin)

callus—see callous

calm (peaceful, quiet) • cam (part of wheel or shaft)

calvary (ordeal) • Calvary (site of Jesus' crucifixion) • cavalry (mobile soldiers)

Calvary—see calvary

cam—see calm

cancer (disease) • canker (sore) • chancer (to adjust by principles of equity) • chancery (court of equity) • chancre (venereal ulcer)

canker—see cancer

cannon (heavy weapon) • canon (set of broad principles in law or religion) • canyon (gorge)

canon—see cannon

cant (moralizing or hypocritical speech) • can't (cannot; unable to)

can't—see cant

canvas (fabric used by painters and sail makers) • canvass (to solicit business or votes)

canvass—see canvas

canyon—see canon

caper (illegal action) • capper (swindler)

capita (head or person) • capital (wealth, investment) • capitol (state legislature's home) • Capitol (Congress's home)

capital—see capita

capitation tax (poll tax) • captation (control of another person) • caption (brief title of illustration)

capitol—see capita

Capitol—see capita

capper—see caper

captation—see capitation

caption—see capitation

caput (head of a political entity) • kaput (slang for *finished, ruined*)

carat or karat (measure of precious stones) • caret (mark for insert on copy)

card (small piece of cardboard) • cart (carriage)

career (livelihood) • carrier (transport company)

caret—see carat

caries (tooth decay) • carries (transports, moves)

carnal (pertaining to sexual desire) • charnel (home for dead bodies)

carnaliter (pertaining to rape) • carnality (having strong sexual feelings)

carnality—see carnaliter

carousal (drunken revelry) • carousel (merry-go-round)

carousel—see carousal

carrier—*see* career

carries—*see* caries

carryback (tax deduction applied to earlier year) • **carry back** (to apply tax deduction to earlier year)

carryforward (tax credit applied to later year) • **carry forward** (to apply tax credit to later year)

carryover (applying operating losses to later years) • **carry over** (to defer tax deductions)

cart—*see* card

carta (charter or deed) • **carte blanche** (unlimited authority)

carte blanche—*see* carta

cash—*see* cache

cast (performers; stiff dressing for an injury) • **caste** (rigid social group)

caste—*see* cast

casual (informal) • **causal** (acting as a cause)

casualty (injury; death) • **causality** (situation that produces an effect)

cataclasm (breakdown) • **cataclysm** (disaster, war) • **catechism** (collection of religious beliefs)

cataclysm—*see* cataclasm

catechism—*see* cataclasm

catholic (broad, universal) • **Catholic** (member of Roman Catholic Church)

caul—*see* call

causa (reason; motive; condition; cause) • **cause** (reason; to effect)

causal—*see* casual

causality—*see* casualty

cause—*see* causa

cavalry—*see* calvary

cave in (to collapse; surrender) • **cave-in** (collapse or submission)

cease (stop) • **seas** (large bodies of water) • **sees** (views, perceives) • **seize** (to grab, possess by force)

cede (yield) • **seed** (plant)

ceiling (top of room) • **sealing** (closing tightly)

celebrate—*see* calibrate

celibate—*see* calibrate

cell (building block of organisms; prison room) • **sell** (to exchange goods or services for money)

cellar (house basement) • **seller** (one who sells)

censor (one who suppresses ideas) • **censure** (formal rebuke) • **sensor** (detection device)

censure—*see* censor

census (population count) • **senses** (faculties of taste, sight, sound, smell, and touch) • **sensus** (meaning; significance)

cent (penny) • **scent** (odor) • **sent** (conveyed)

cents (pennies) • **scents** (odors) • **sense** (meaning; awareness)

cereal (breakfast food; grain) • **serial** (sequential; released in installments)

cerebrate—*see* calibrate

cessation (end) • **cession** (yielding of property) • **session** (one of a number of meetings)

cession—*see* cessation

chacer (to drive, oblige) • **chaser** (pursuer; informal)

chance (luck, accident) • **chants** (rhythmic protests; repetitive speech or song)

chancer—*see* cancer

chancery—*see* cancer

chancre—*see* cancer

chants—*see* chance

charnel—*see* carnal

charred (burned) • **chart** (map; graphic display)

chart—*see* charred

charta (deed; sealed instrument) • **charter** (rights or privileges)

charter—*see* charta

chased (pursued) • **chaste** (celibate, pure)

chaser—*see* chacer

chaste—*see* chased

checkup (medical exam) • **check up** (to review one's work)

chef (head cook) • **chief** (top person)

chews (grinds or cuts food with the teeth; considers) • **choose** (to select) • **chose** (did select)

chief—*see* chef

choler (angry) • **cholera** (gastrointestinal illness) • **collar** (clothing near neck; to arrest) • **color** (hue) • **cooler** (more cool; slang for *prison cell*)

cholera—*see* choler

choose—*see* chews

chose—*see* chews

christen (to name baby or object, baptize) • **Christian** (religious faith)

Christian—*see* christen

chronic or **chronical** (repeated, persistent) • **chronicle** (detailed historical record)

chronicle—*see* chronic

chute (steep incline) • **shoot** (to fire, propel, wound, or kill)

cingular (ring-shaped, often of bodily features) • **singular** (unusual)

cite (refer to case or other source of material) • **sight** (vision) • **site** (location)

clan (social group; family) • **Klan** (Ku Klux Klan, racist group)

clause (part of legal document; grammatical term for part of sentence) • **claws** (sharp nails)

claws—*see* clause

clench (to close or grasp tightly) • **clinch** (to complete, as a deal)

clew (to provide information) • **clue** (information useful in solving crime or puzzle)

click (light, sharp sound) • **clique** (snobbish group)

clinch—*see* clench

clinic (medical center) • **clink** (to make ringing sound; slang for *jail*)

clink—*see* clinic

clique—*see* click

cloak (loose garment; concealment) • **clock** (instrument that measures time)

clock—*see* cloak

clone (replica) • **clown** (joker, circus performer)

close (to shut; end of time period or event) • **clothes** (garments)

close up (to move near; to shut down) • **close-up** (detailed camera shot)

closure (act of closing) • **cloture** (vote to end legislative debate)

clothes—*see* close

cloture—*see* closure

clown—*see* clone

clue—*see* clew

coarse (rough, crude) • **course** (direction, class) • **curse** (call for harm to someone; profanity)

code (set of symbols; set of rules) • **Code, the** (IRS Code) • **coed** (coeducational)

coed—*see* code

cognatio (relationship, particularly from female side) • **cognation** (blood or family ties)

cognation—*see* cognatio

colds (viral infections) • **colts** (young male horses) • **cults** (sects; people with powerful attachment to belief or person)

coliseum (big stadium) • **Colosseum** (historic Roman ampitheater)

collage (artistic work formed by pasting objects on a surface) • **college** (post-secondary school)

collar—*see* choler

collared (wearing collar; arrested) • **colored** (having color)

collatio (pooling inherited money) • **collation** (comparison; division of inherited moneys)

collation—*see* collatio

college—*see* collage

colonel (military officer) • **kernel** (grain core)

color—*see* choler

colored—*see* collared

Colosseum—*see* coliseum

colts—*see* colds

coma (unconscious state) • **comma** (punctuation mark) • **karma** (destiny)

comedy (humorous performance) • **comity** (diplomatic courtesy) • **committee** (person legally responsible for another; group working together)

comet (shooting star) • **commit** (to pledge; to perform)

comitas (courtesy, particularly between nations) • **comites** (retinue of high officers)

comites—*see* comitas

comity—*see* comedy

comma—*see* coma

command (to order) • **commend** (to praise) • **comment** (to remark)

commend—*see* command

comment—*see* command

commit—*see* comet

committee—*see* comedy

common (shared, known to many) • **commune** (group that shares living arrangements and resources)

commune—*see* common

communis (common, as in common law or opinion) • **communist** (believer in property held in common)

communist—*see* communis

complacence (self-satisfaction) • **complaisance** (desire to please)

complaisance—*see* complacence

complement (amount or item needed to complete or fulfill) • **compliment** (praise)

compliment—*see* complement

composed (calm; put together) • **composite** (combination of separate elements) • **compost** (mix of decaying matter)

composite—*see* composed

compost—*see* composed

comptroller (fiscal officer) • **controller** (one who controls)

concave (curved inward) • **conclave** (private meeting)

concede (give in) • **conceit** (self-pride)

conceit—*see* concede

concessus (grantee) • **consensus** (agreement)

conclave—*see* concave

concord (harmony; agreement) • **conquered** (overcame)

concur (to agree) • **conquer** (to overcome)

condemn (to convict) • **condom** (protective sheath) • **contemn** (to despise) • **contempt** (disdain)

condictio (obligation) • **conditio** (condition) • **condition** (requirement; potential obligation)

conditio—*see* condictio

condition—*see* condictio

condom—*see* condemn

confess (to acknowledge guilt) • **confessio** or **confession** (acknowledgment of guilt) • **confesso** (order upon failure of defendant to respond) • **confessor** (cleric who receives religious confessions)

confessio or **confession**—*see* confess

confesso—*see* confess

141

confessor—*see* confess

confidant (one who shares secrets) • confident (sure)

confident—*see* confidant

confirmatio (validation of a voidable estate) • confirmation (verification) • conformation (form; synthetical shape)

confirmation—*see* confirmatio

conformation—*see* confirmatio

conquer—*see* concur

conquered—*see* concord

consensus—*see* concessus

consign (to transfer goods to another) • consignee (one who receives goods)

consignee—*see* consign

constant (faithful; continuing) • constat (it is clear or evident) • constate (to ordain or establish)

constat—*see* constant

constate—*see* constant

consul (foreign nation's representative) • council (advisory or decision-making group) • counsel (legal representation; advice)

contemn—*see* condemn

contempt—*see* condemn

contest (competition) • context (conditions surrounding an event; related words that clarify meaning)

context—*see* contest

continual (recurring in steady succesion) • continuance (adjournment or postponement) • continuing (going farther; happening without stopping) • continuous (going on without halting) • continuum (uninterrupted sequence or series of actions)

continuance—*see* continual

continuing—*see* continuance

continuous—*see* continuance

continuum—*see* continuance

controller—*see* comptroller

convey (to transfer title; to communicate; to transport) • convoy (to protect or escort)

convoy—*see* convey

cooler—*see* choler

coop (enclosure; slang for prison) • co-op (cooperative; user-owned business; group home in which duties are shared) • coup (sudden action to assume power or achieve objective) • coupe (car)

co-op—*see* coop

core (center, heart) • corps (army unit or specialized group) • corpse (dead body)

co-respondent (third party in divorce action) • correspondent (writer for the media; letter writer)

corner (intersection of two lines or streets) • coroner (examiner of corpses)

coroner—*see* corner

corporal (army lower rank) • corporeal (bodily, not spiritual)

corporeal—*see* corporal

corps—*see* core

corpse (dead body) • corpus (the main body or aggregate)

corpus—*see* corpse

correspondence (communication) • correspondents (people who write or report for the media; letter writers)

correspondent—*see* co-respondent

correspondents—*see* correspondence

cosign (to sign jointly) • cosine (mathematical ratio)

cosine—*see* cosign

costume (style of dressing) • custom (usual manner or expectation)

council—*see* consul

councilor (member of a council) • counselor or counsellor (legal advisor)

counsel—*see* consul

counsellor—*see* councilor

counselor—*see* councilor

coup—*see* coop

coupe—*see* coop

courier (messenger) • currier (flatterer)

course—*see* coarse

courtesy (politeness) • curtesy (husband's right to deceased wife's inheritance in land)

cousin (child of aunt or uncle) • cozen (to deceive, cheat)

covered (concealed, protected) • covert (secret) • covet (to strongly desire another's property)

cover up (to conceal or protect) • cover-up (effort to conceal dishonesty or illegality)

covert—*see* covered

cover-up—*see* cover up

covet—*see* covered

coward (one who lacks courage) • cowered (crouched in fear)

cowered—*see* coward

cozen—*see* cousin

craft (manual skills; guile) • kraft (brown wrapping paper)

crap (a losing dice throw) • creep (act of creeping; slang for *disliked person*)

crass (tasteless, stupid) • cross (two intersecting perpendicular lines; religious symbol)

crater (deep hole in ground) • Creator (God) • creator (one who originates or produces) • creature (animal or person)

creator—*see* crater

Creator—*see* crater

creature—*see* crater

credible (believable) • creditable (meriting praise)

creditable—*see* credible

credo (set of beliefs) • creed (basic beliefs)

creed—*see* credo

creep—*see* crap

crewel (thin yarn) • cruel (inflicting pain)

crews (groups of workers) • cruise (boat trip)

crises (dangerous, critical times) • crisis (sing. of *crises*)

crisis—*see* crises

critic (evaluator; fault finder) • critique (evaluation or review)

critique—*see* critic

croak (slang for *to die*; to complain) • crock (disabled, impaired, chronic complainer) • crook (thief)

crock—*see* croak

crook—*see* croak

cross—*see* crass

crotch (place where legs fork) • crouch (to squat, lie low) • crutch (support or prop)

crouch—*see* crotch

cruel—*see* crewel

cruise—*see* crews

crutch—*see* crotch

cue (signal or hint) • queue (waiting line for show)

cults—*see* colds

cure (remedy) • curia (Roman Catholic top offices) • curie (radiation unit)

cure all (to fix all ailments) • cure-all (panacea)

curia—*see* cure

curie—*see* cure

currier—*see* courier

curse—*see* coarse

curser (one who curses) • cursor (computer control) • cursory (hasty; careless)

cursor—*see* curser

cursory—*see* curser

curtesy—*see* courtesy

curtsy—*see* courtesy
custom—*see* costume
cymbal (percussive instrument)

• **symbol** (something that stands for an idea; a sign)

D

daily (every day) • **dally** (to waste time)

dairy (milk products) • **diary** (personal record; date book)

dais (platform for speakers) • **dies** (n. a day or days) • **dyes** (changes color)

dally—*see* daily

dam (barrier, especially for water) • **dame** (titled woman) • **damn** (curse)

dame—*see* dam

damn—*see* dam

Dane (citizen of Denmark) • **deign** (condescend)

days (pl. of *day*; 24-hour periods) • **daze** (bewildered state)

daze—*see* days

dead (no longer alive) • **deed** (an action)

deadbeat (one who reneges on debts) • **dead beat** (very tired)

dean (official in church or school; leader in field) • **dene** (sandy land)

debauch (to corrupt; to seduce) • **debouch** (to march into open area)

debet (legal action relating to debt) • **debit** (amount owed or owing) • **debt** (what is owed)

debit—*see* debet

debouch—*see* debauch

debt—*see* debet

decadent (having low moral standards) • **decedent** (dead person)

decease (to die) • **disease** (illness) • **disseise** (to dispossess or deprive)

decedent—*see* decadent

decent (proper, respectable) • **descend** (to go down) • **descent** (lineage; act of going down) • **dissent** (minority judicial opinion; disagreement)

decree (command) • **degree** (certification accorded graduate of higher education; extent)

deed—*see* dead

defer (to comply) • **differ** (to disagree)

deference (respect) • **difference** (state of being unlike)

deferential (respectful) • **differentia** (the element that shows or defines the difference between classes of items) • **differential** (making a distinction between individuals or classes)

definite (certain) • **definitive** (conclusive)

definitive—*see* definite

defuse (to end a dangerous situation) • **diffuse** (to disseminate)

degree—*see* decree

deign—*see* Dane

delude (to deceive) • **dilate** (to widen) • **dilute** (to weaken)

demesne (held in one's own right) • **domain** (area of control)

demise (conveyance of an estate; death) • **demisi** (leased)

demisi—*see* demise

demote (to reassign to lower-level job) • **denote** (to symbolize; to refer to specifically)

demur (to object) • **demure** (shy, modest)

demure—*see* demur

dene—*see* dean

denote—*see* demote

dense (thick) • dents (depressions caused by blows or pressure)

dents—*see* dense

dependance or dependence (reliance on someone or something) • dependents (people who rely on others for help)

dependents—*see* dependance

depose (to give sworn evidence; to dismiss) • depots (transit stations)

depositary (party holding trust) • depositor (one who makes a deposit) • depository (place where a deposit is held)

deposition (sworn statement taken out of court) • disposition (temperament)

depositor—*see* depositary

depository—*see* depositary

depots—*see* depose

deprecate (to be very critical of) • depreciate (to lose value)

depreciate—*see* deprecate

descend—*see* decent

descent—*see* decent

desperate (in a critical or hopeless situation) • disparate (distinctly different)

deter (to prevent) • detour (temporary deviation from route)

detour—*see* deter

deuces (pair of twos) • duces tecum (writ)

devest or divest (to remove or take away legally) • dives (normal legal costs)

device (mechanism; plan, method) • devise (to plan or invent)

devise—*see* device

devisee (recipient of property) • deviser (inventor, planner; one who wills property) • devisor (one who transmits property through will) • divisor (in mathematics, the number by which another number is divided)

deviser—*see* devisee

devisor—*see* devisee

diagnoses (pl. of *diagnosis*) • diagnosis (analysis of physical condition or other problem)

diagnosis—*see* diagnoses

diagram (drawing of an item and its works) • diaphragm (contraceptive device; bodily membrane that aids in breathing)

dialectal (of speech dialects) • dialectical (relating to a philosophical method)

dialectical—*see* dialectal

diaphragm—*see* diagram

diary—*see* dairy

dictate (to speak for another; to record, transcribe) • diktat (harsh, dictatorial decree)

die (to cease to live; a metal-cutting device) • dye (pigment)

dies—*see* dais

diet (eating habits; reduction or alteration of food intake) • Diet (the Japanese parliament) • dieta (day's work or travel)

Diet—*see* diet

dieta—*see* diet

differ—*see* defer

difference—*see* deference

differentia—*see* deferential

differential—*see* deferential

diffuse—*see* defuse

digest (summary; to absorb food) • digesta (digests of Justinian Codes) • Digests (formal name for digests of Justinian Pandects)

digesta—*see* digest

Digests—*see* digest

diktat—*see* dictate

dilate—*see* delude

dilute—*see* delude

dime (coin worth ten cents) • **dismes** (tithes; tenths)

dinar (Mideast currency) • **dinner** (evening meal)

dinner—*see* dinar

diplomat (tactful person; governmental representative) • **diplomate** (holder of diploma)

diplomate—*see* diplomat

disapprove (to condemn or reject) • **disprove** (to show to be false or wrong)

disburse (to pay out) • **disperse** (to scatter)

discomfit (to disconcert or thwart) • **discomfort** (to make uneasy)

discomfort—*see* discomfit

discreet (tactful; able to keep secrets) • **discrete** (separate or distinct)

discrete—*see* discreet

disease—*see* decease

disillusion (to correct mistaken ideas) • **dissolution** (act of cancelling, annulling, or terminating)

disinter (to dig up a corpse; to revive an old practice) • **dysentery** (intestinal disease)

dismes—*see* dime

disparagatio (marriage beneath oneself) • **disparage** (to belittle)

disparage—*see* disparagatio

disparate—*see* desperate

disperse—*see* disburse

disposition—*see* deposition

disprove—*see* disapprove

disseise—*see* decease

dissent—*see* decent

dissidence (disagreement with authority) • **dissidents** (people who disagree with or fight authority)

dissidents—*see* dissidence

dissolution—*see* disillusion

divers (people who dive; sundry, several) • **diverse** (varied, unalike)

diverse—*see* divers

dives—*see* devest

divest—*see* devest

divisor—*see* devisee

divorce (dissolution of marriage) • **divorcé** (divorced man) • **divorcée** (divorced woman)

divorcé—*see* divorce

divorcée—*see* divorce

do (perform, act, effectuate) • **due** (owing; fair treatment; credit for achievement)

doable (achievable) • **double** (twice as much)

doer (achiever) • **door** (entrance to room or house) • **dour** (harsh) • **dower** (widow's interest in husband's real estate)

does (acts; pl. of *female deer*) • **dose** (amount of medication) • **doze** (to sleep lightly)

dole (a part or share; unemployment compensation; distributions) • **doll** (toy figure) • **dull** (boring)

doll—*see* dole

dollar (bill equal to 100 cents) • **dolor** (state of mournfulness) • **duller** (more dull or boring)

dolor—*see* dollar

domain—*see* demesne

donatio (gift; transfer of property as a gift) • **donation** (contribution)

donation—*see* donatio

done (finished) • **donee** (power of appointment) • **doun** (gift) • **dun** (press repeatedly for late payment)

donee—*see* done

door—*see* doer

dose—*see* does

double—*see* doable

double time (overtime rate of pay) • **double-time** (quick marching tempo)

double-time—*see* double time

doun—*see* done

dour—*see* doer

dower—*see* doer

doze—*see* does

draff (refuse, waste) • **draft** (written order for payment; early version of a document) • **drought** (long dry spell)

draft—*see* draff

driven (compulsive) • **drive in** (to enter or go by car) • **drive-in** (place to order or do business from car)

drive in—*see* driven

drive-in—*see* driven

droop (to hang down) • **drop** (to let fall; tiny amount of falling liquid)

drop—*see* droop

drop off (to leave something) • **drop-off** (steep decline)

dropout (person who quits school) • **drop out** (to withdraw)

drought—*see* draff

dual (of two parts) • **duel** (contest; fight with weapons)

duces tecum—*see* deuces

due—*see* do

duel—*see* dual

dull—*see* dole

duller—*see* dollar

dully (in a boring manner) • **duly** (in proper form)

duly—*see* dully

dum (as long as) • **dumb** (of low intelligence; unable to speak)

dumb—*see* dum

dun—*see* done

dye—*see* die

dyeing (process of coloring things) • **dying** (near death)

dyes—*see* dais

dying—*see* dyeing

dysentery—*see* disinter

E

earn (to be paid for work; to deserve) • **urn** (container for ashes; receptacle for making tea or coffee)

earthly (possible; worldly) • **earthy** (natural; crude)

earthy—*see* earthly

economic (related to management of resources) • **economical** (thrifty)

economical—*see* economic

edible—*see* addable

edict—*see* addict

edition—*see* addition

editor—*see* additur

educe—*see* adduce

e'er—*see* air

effect—*see* affect

effluent—*see* affluent

efflux—*see* afflux

egoism (ethical view of self-interest as motivator) • **egotism** (conceit)

egotism—*see* egoism

egression—*see* aggression

either (one of two) • **ether** (gas)

ejection (expulsion) • **ejectione** (ejection from land)

ejectione—*see* ejection

elapse (passage of time) • **illapse** (influx)

elder (person with authority) • **older** (more old)

elegy (lament) • **eulogy** (praise for deceased at funeral)

elementary—*see* alimentary

elicit (to evoke) • **illicit** (illegal)

elision—*see* allision

elocution—*see* allocation

elude—*see* allude

elusion—*see* allision

elute—*see* allude

elusive or elusory (hard to grasp; evasive) • illusive (misleading)

eluvium—*see* alluvion

emend—*see* amend

emersed (standing above) • immersed (absorbed; under water)

emigrant (one who moves from a country) • immigrant (one who moves to a country)

emigrate (to move from one's country) • immigrate (to move permanently to a new country)

eminent (well-known) • immanent (inherent) • imminent (about to occur)

emit (to issue; to give off) • omit (to leave out)

emollient (mollifying) • emolument (income from work)

emolument—*see* emollient

emotion—*see* amotio

empathize (sympathize) • emphases (pl. of *emphasis*) • emphasis (stress or importance)

emphases—*see* empathize

emphasis—*see* empathize

empire (dominion over territories) • umpire (referee)

enable (to make possible) • unable (not able to)

endorse (to sign or certify; to support) • endorsee (one to whom a document or check is signed over) • endorser (one who signs over a document or check)

endorsee—*see* endorse

endorser—*see* endorse

enervate (to reduce strength) • innervate (to stimulate muscles) • innovate (to invent; initiate)

ensure (to guarantee) • insure (to provide insurance)

enunciate—*see* annunciate

envelop (to surround) • envelope (paper holder for a letter)

envelope—*see* envelop

equable (even tempered; consistent) • equatable (equal to) • equitable (fair)

equatable—*see* equable

equitable—*see* equable

era (an age; a long period of time) • error (mistake)

erasable (can be wiped out) • irascible (ill-tempered)

ergo (hence) • ergot (grain disease; medicine)

ergot—*see* ergo

erotic (arousing sexual feelings) • erratic (uneven; irregular)

err—*see* air

errand—*see* arrant

errant—*see* arrant

erratic—*see* erotic

error—*see* era

eruption (sudden outbreak) • irruption (bursting in; invasion)

esoteric (understood by few) • exoteric (clear; understandable) • exotic (foreign; unusual)

essay—*see* assay

ether—*see* either

ethic (moral principle) • ethnic (pertaining to people with same heritage)

ethnic—*see* ethic

et seq. (and the following) • et sic (and so; therefore)

et sic—*see* et seq.

eulogy—*see* elegy

eunuch (castrated male) • unique (sole; having no equal)

euphemism (substitute for unpleasant language) • euphuism (false elegance in communication)

euphuism—*see* euphemism

evasio (escape from prison) • evasion (avoidance, dodging)

evasion—*see* evasio

eversion—*see* aversion

evert—*see* advert

everyday (common; daily) • every day (each day)

everyone (everybody) • every one (each one)

everything (all that exists) • every thing (each thing separately)

evocation—*see* avocation

ewe (female sheep) • hew (to chop or shape) • hue (tint, color) • you (person(s) being addressed; people in general)

examen (trial; critical study) • examine (to inspect; to investigate)

examine—*see* examen

exceed—*see* acceed

except—*see* accept

exceptio (plea alleging new facts) • exception (exclusion; omission; objection)

exception—*see* exceptio

exceptionable (objectionable) • exceptional (unusual)

exceptional—*see* exceptionable

excerpt—*see* accept

excess—*see* access

exercise (practice; to use) • exorcise (to drive away evil spirits)

exile—*see* axial

exorcise—*see* exercise

exoteric—*see* esoteric

exotic—*see* esoteric

expansive (friendly; able to expand) • expensive (costly)

expensive—*see* expansive

expire (to terminate; to die) • expiry (termination of time fixed by law or contract)

expiry—*see* expire

expose (to display; to bring to light) • exposé (revelation of scandal)

exposé—*see* expose

extant (now in existence) • extend (to prolong; to offer) • extent (degree, amount)

extend—*see* extant

extent—*see* extant

exterritorial (located outside a nation's boundaries) • exterritoriality or extraterritoriality (foreigners' exemption from a nation's laws)

exterritoriality or extraterritoriality—*see* exterritorial

eye—*see* aye

eyed (looked at) • ID (identification, as in ID card) • I'd (I had; I should; I would) • id (the unconscious)

F

faces (pl. of *face*) • feces (excrement)

facet (aspect; side of cut gem) • faucet (spigot)

facial (relating to the face) • facile (easy; glib)

facile—*see* facial

fact (truth) • facta (deeds) • facto (in fact; *ipso facto*: by the act itself)

facta—*see* fact

faction (small, cohesive group within a larger one) • fraction (portion; mathematical expression)

factious (quarrelsome) • factitious (false) • fatuitas (idiocy) • fatuous or fatuus (silly) • fictitious (invented)

factitious—*see* factious

facto—*see* fact

facts (truths) • fax (machine that transmits printed matter)

fain (eager) • feign (to fake)

fair (pleasant; just) • fare (cost of passage; food)

fait (deed) • fate (destiny) • fête (festival) • fiat (command)

fallout (negative effects; debris from an atomic explosion) • fall out (to end relationship because of a quarrel)

fallow (barren) • fellow (associate; member of special society) • follow (to come after; to go along with)

familia (household) • familiar (known; recognizable)

familiar—*see* familia

fare—*see* fair

farther (at greater distance) • father (male parent) • further (additional; beyond; to help someone)

fas (justice) • fast (period of not eating; rapid)

fast—*see* fas

fatal (causing death) • fetal (pertaining to fetus)

fate—*see* fait

fated (destined) • fêted (honored) • fetid (bad-smelling)

father—*see* farther

fatuitas—*see* factious

fatuous—*see* factious

fatuus—*see* factious

faucet—*see* facet

faux (artificial) • foe (enemy)

fax—*see* facts

faze (disturb) • phase (aspect; stage)

feasance (performance) • feasant (causing or doing)

feasant—*see* feasance

feat (accomplishment) • feet (pl. of *foot*; unit of measure)

feces—*see* faces

feet—*see* feat

feign—*see* fain

fellow—*see* fallow

felonice (relating to commission of grave crime; feloniously) • felonies (grave crimes) • felonious (relating to grave crime)

felonies—*see* felonice

felonious—*see* felonice

feoffee (person who receives a fee or grant) • feoffer or feoffor (one who makes a grant)

feoffer—*see* feoffee

ferae (wild, bestial) • feria (holiday)

feria—*see* ferae

ferment (agent; enzyme; to turn into alcohol) • foment (to instigate)

fetal—*see* fatal

fête—*see* fait

fêted—*see* fated

fetid—*see* fated

fiancé (engaged male) • fiancée (engaged female) • finance (to raise money)

fiancée—*see* fiancé

fiat—*see* fait

fiche (sheet of microfilm) • fish (a water animal)

fictitious—*see* factious

fiend (monster) • friend (close acquaintance)

file (court record; place to keep papers) • phial (small bottle)

filing (putting papers in sequence) • filling (completing; satisfying; something that fills a cavity)

Filipina (female native of Philippines • Filipino (male native of same) • Philippines (the nation) • Pilipino (language of Philippines)

Filipino—*see* Filipina

filling—*see* filing

filum (thread, line) • phylum (major division of organisms)

finance—*see* fiancé

find (to locate; a nice discovery) •
fined (penalized)

fined—*see* find

fineness (quality of being good;
delicate, or thin) • **finesse**
(skillfulness) • **finis** (conclusion) •
finish (to end; to complete)

finesse—*see* fineness

finis—*see* fineness

finish—*see* fineness

fiscal (pertaining to government
financial policies) • **physical**
(relating to the body or to matter)

fish—*see* fiche

fisher (fisherman) • **fissure** (crack;
disagreement)

fissure—*see* fisher

fists (closed hands) • **fits** (sudden
outbursts; is right size)

fits—*see* fists

flagrans (in actual process) •
flagrant (outrageous) • **flagrante
delicto** (in act of committing
crime) • **fragrant** (pleasant
smelling)

flagrant—*see* flagrans

flagrante—*see* flagrans

flair (ability; style) • **flare** (bright
light; to become angered
suddenly)

flap (scandal; loose part) • **flop**
(failure; to fall suddenly)

flare—*see* flair

fleece (to rob; sheep's wool) • **flees**
(runs away)

flees—*see* fleece

flew (did fly) • **flu** (influenza) • **flue**
(passageway; shaft)

flop—*see* flap

flounder (to act ineffectually) •
founder (to fail; person who starts
an entity)

flu—*see* flew

flue—*see* flew

foe—*see* faux

follow—*see* fallow

foment—*see* ferment

fondling (caressing) • **foundling**
(deserted infant)

fool (stupid person) • **fuel** (substance
that stores energy) • **full**
(complete; containing as much as
possible)

for (preposition showing purpose,
goal, aim) • **fore** (to the front) •
four (a number)

forbear (refrain from) • **forebear**
(ancestor)

fore—*see* for

forebear—*see* forbear

forego (to go before) • **forgo** (to do
without)

foreword (preface) • **forward** (to
move ahead; ahead; bold) •
froward (unruly)

forgo—*see* forego

forma (proper judicial form) • **formal**
(proper)

formal—*see* forma

formally (properly) • **formerly**
(previously)

formerly—*see* formally

formula (rule; prescription) •
formulary (form or model;
medical book of substances and
mixes)

formulary—*see* formula

fort (stronghold) • **forte** (strong
point) • **forty** (a number) • **fought**
(battled, opposed)

forte—*see* fort

forth (forward) • **fourth** (adjectival
number)

fortior (stronger evidence) • **(a)
fortiori** (with more convincing
information or forcefulness)

fortiori—*see* fortior

forty—*see* fort

forward—*see* foreword

fought—*see* fort
foul (unfair; dirty) • **fowl** (bird)
founder—*see* flounder
foundling—*see* fondling
four—*see* for
fourth—*see* forth
fowl—*see* foul
fraction—*see* faction
fragrant—*see* flagrans
franc (French monetary unit) • **frank** (blunt; direct)
frank—*see* franc
fraud (deception) • **fraught** (charged; associated)
fraught—*see* fraud
frays (battles) • **phrase** (group of words)
freak (abnormal person or object) • **phreak** (phone or computer manipulator)
frees (sets free, liberates) • **freeze** (intense cold; to preserve in cold)

freeze—*see* frees
freight (cargo; cost of moving goods) • **fright** (great terror)
friend—*see* fiend
fright—*see* freight
froward—*see* foreword
fuel—*see* fool
full—*see* fool
funeral (service for dead) • **funereal** (mournful)
funereal—*see* funeral
fungous (like or marked by fungus) • **fungus** (type of plant)
fungus—*see* fungous
further—*see* farther
fuse or **fuze** (protector of electric circuits) • **fuss** (bother) • **fuzz** (fluffy hair; slang for *police*)
fuss—*see* fuse
fuze—*see* fuse
fuzz—*see* fuse

G

gabble (indistinct talk) • **gabel** (an excise or rent)
gabel—*see* gabble
gaff (fishing hook; faux pas) • **gaffe** (faux pas)
gaffe—*see* gaff
gage (pawn, security against a loan) • **gauge** (measuring instrument)
gait (walk) • **gate** (movable barrier)
gamble (to take risks; to play game of chance) • **gambol** (to frolic)
gambol—*see* gamble
gap (missing piece or portion) • **gape** (to stare; to look in astonishment)
gape—*see* gap
gaps (missing parts; openings) • **gasps** (draws in one's breath)
garnish (to embellish) • **garnishee**

(person whose pay is withheld to pay a debt)
garnishee—*see* garnish
garret (attic) • **garotte** or **garrotte** (strangulation)
garotte or **garrotte**—*see* garret
gasps—*see* gaps
gassed (supplied with gas, poisoned) • **gast** (waste)
gast—*see* gassed
gate—*see* gait
gauge—*see* gage
gays (homosexuals) • **gaze** (steady look)
gaze—*see* gays
geld (to castrate a horse) • **jelled** (came together; cohered)
genera (pl. of *genus*; biological

groups) • **general** (prevalent; officer)

general—*see* genera

genital (sexual organ) • **genteel** (polite) • **gentile** (not Jewish or Mormon) • **gentle** (kind, pleasant)

genius (exceptionally bright person) • **genus** (biological class or group)

gens (patrilineal clan) • **gentes** (all people) • **gents** (gentlemen)

genteel—*see* genital

gentes—*see* gens

gentile—*see* genital

gentle—*see* genital

gentlemen (formal address for men) • **gentle men** (kind men)

gents—*see* gens

genus—*see* genius

german (closely related) • **German** (resident of Germany) • **germane** (relevant)

germane—*see* german

get together (to meet) • **get-together** (gathering)

ghastly (frightening) • **ghostly** (resembling a ghost)

ghostly—*see* ghastly

gibe (to insult) • **jibe** (to agree; to shift course suddenly)

gild (to prettify in order to deceive) • **guild** (business or crafts association)

gilt (gold surface) • **guilt** (responsibility for wrongdoing)

giveaway (unintended betrayal; product offering) • **give away** (to disclose; betray)

glance (quick look) • **glands** (bodily organs) • **glans** (tip of male or female sex organ)

glands—*see* glance

glans—*see* glance

gleam (small beam of light) • **glean** (to get information slowly)

glean—*see* gleam

glom (slang for steal) • **gloom** (dejection) • **glum** (in low spirits)

gloom—*see* glom

glos (a husband's sister) • **gloss** (annotation or interpretation)

gloss—*see* glos

glum—*see* glom

gnaw (chew on) • **nor** (also not)

golf (a sport) • **gulf** (gap; waterway)

gorilla (largest type of ape) • **guerrilla** (underground fighter)

grade (angle of inclination; mark; school level) • **grayed** (became gray)

graffiti (pl. of *graffito*; wall drawings) • **graffito** (wall drawing) • **graphite** (carbon compound)

graffito—*see* graffiti

graft (illegal payment; transplant) • **graphed** (diagrammed)

graphed—*see* graft

graphite—*see* graffiti

grate (to annoy) • **great** (very good; remarkable)

grave (tomb; very serious; to carve) • **greve** (word of authority) • **grieve** to mourn)

grayed—*see* grade

great—*see* grate

greve—*see* grave

grieve—*see* grave

grill (to question closely) • **grille** (protective device)

grille—*see* grill

grip (strong grasp or control) • **gripe** (complaint) • **grippe** (flu)

gripe—*see* grip

griper (one who complains) • **gripper** (tool that grips)

grippe—*see* grip

gripper—*see* griper

groan (moan) • **groin** (body part near abdomen) • **grown** (older, bigger)

grocer (seller of food) • **grosser** (big money earner)

groin—*see* groan

groove (channel cut into surface) • **grove** (group of trees)

grope (to feel one's way blindly) • **group** (people with something in common)

gross (flagrant, shameful; twelve dozen; total amount before deductions) • **grouse** (complain)

grosser—*see* grocer

group—*see* grope

grouse—*see* gross

grove—*see* groove

grown—*see* groan

guerrilla—*see* gorilla

guessed (gave approximate answer; thought) • **guest** (invitee; hotel patron)

guest—*see* guessed

Guiana (region on north coast of South America) • **guinea** (former English coin) • **Guinea** (West African nation) • **Guyana** (South American nation)

guild—*see* gild

guilt—*see* gilt

guinea—*see* Guiana

Guinea—*see* Guiana

guise (a pretense) • **guys** (males)

gulf—*see* golf

Guyana—*see* Guiana

guys—*see* guise

H

hack (one who does uninteresting work, especially a writer; slang for *taxi*) • **haec** (agreement)

haec—*see* hack

hail (call or summon; frozen rain) • **hale** (healthy)

hair—*see* air

hairy (frightening; having lots of hair) • **harry** (to annoy; to pressure)

hale—*see* hail

half (one of two equal parts) • **halve** (to divide into two equal parts) • **halves** (pl. of *half*) • **have** (to possess; to be obligated to)

hall (large room used for affairs) • **haul** (to carry; to transport)

hallow (to make holy) • **halo** (circle of light) • **hollow** (empty; a hole)

halo—*see* hallow

halve—*see* half

halves—*see* half

handsale (handshake deal) • **handsel** (first installment)

handsel—*see* handsale

handyman (person who does odd jobs) • **handy man** (person who is skilled with tools)

hang up (to end a phone call; to put on a hanger or hook) • **hang-up** (inhibition)

hard (difficult; durable) • **hart** (male deer) • **heart** (body organ)

harry—*see* hairy

hart—*see* hard

haul—*see* hall

haunch (part of buttocks) • **hunch** (intuition)

hauteur—*see* auteur

have—*see* half

haven (safe place) • **heaven** (paradise; great place)

hays (pl. of *hay*) • **haze** (unclear air; to harass)

haze—*see* hays

head (top of body or of organization) • **he'd** (he had; he would) • **heed** (to obey) headless (without a head) • heedless (reckless)

heal (to recover) • heel (back of foot; back of shoe; rotten person) • hell (the netherworld; bad situation) • he'll (he will)

hear (to receive sounds) • here (this place)

heard (did hear) • herd (group of animals)

heart—see hard

hearth (fireplace floor) • heath (open land)

heath—see hearth

heaven—see haven

he'd—see head

heed—see head

heedless—see headless

heel—see heal

heinous—see anus

heir—see air

hell—see heal

he'll—see heal

hence (therefore; in a future time) • whence (from where)

herd—see heard

here—see hear

heroin (an addictive drug) • heroine (central female character in story; woman or girl who performs a brave deed)

heroine—see heroin

hertz (electrical unit) • hurts (suffers; feels pain)

hew—see ewe

hide (to conceal) • hied (hastened)

hie (to go quickly) • high (above normal level; on drugs)

hied—see hide

high—see hie

higher (above something else) • hire (to employ)

high grade (high mark) • high-grade (top quality)

him (objective of he) • hymn (religious song)

Hindi (language of India) • Hindu (follower of India's main religion)

Hindu—see Hindi

hire—see higher

historical (pertaining to history) • hysterical (uncontrollably emotional)

hoar (frost) • whore (prostitute) • who're (who are)

hoard (well-guarded valuables; to stash) • horde (large crowd) • whored (prostituted)

hoars (frosts) • hoarse (having difficulty speaking) • hors (out of; hors de combat: out of the fight) • horse (kind of animal) • whores (prostitutes)

hoarse—see hoars

hobby (spare-time recreation) • hubby (slang for husband)

hoc (this; ad hoc: for this, for a specific purpose) • hock (to pawn)

hock—see hoc

hockey (an ice sport) • hooky (skipping school)

hold (to keep; to contain) • holed (placed holes in something)

holdup (robbery) • hold up (to raise or keep up; to rob) • holed up (slang for in hiding)

hole (opening, gap) • whole (complete; intact; all)

holed—see hold

holed up—see holdup

holey (full of holes) • holly (type of shrub) • holy (religious) • wholly (completely)

holiday (nonworking day; special celebration) • holy day (religious observance)

hollow—see hallow

holly—*see* holey

holm (inland island) • **home** (residence; to aim for target) • **hone** (to sharpen; to improve)

holy—*see* holey

holy day—*see* holiday

home—*see* holm

homogeneous (at same level, same type) • **homogenous** (similar biological structures)

homogenous—*see* homogeneous

hone—*see* holm

hooky—*see* hockey

horde—*see* hoard

hors—*see* hoars

horse—*see* hoars

hospitable (receptive, friendly) • **hospital** (medical institution)

hospital—*see* hospitable

hostel (cheap lodging) • **hostile** (as an enemy)

hostile—*see* hostel

hour (sixty minutes) • **our** (belonging to us)

houseboat (boat to live on) • **house-bote** (tenant's right to timber)

house-bote—*see* houseboat

however (nevertheless) • **how ever** (how come? why?)

how ever—*see* however

hubby—*see* hobby

hue—*see* ewe

hui (tenants in common) • **huis** (a door)

huis—*see* hui

human (a person; pertaining to qualities of people) • **humane** (compassionate)

humane—*see* human

humerus (bone in upper arm) • **humorous** (funny)

humorous—*see* humerus

hunch—*see* haunch

hunter (one who hunts) • **junta** or **junto** (usurpers of power)

hurdle (to jump over; an obstacle) • **hurtle** (to move quickly or recklessly)

hurtle—*see* hurdle

hurts—*see* hertz

hymn—*see* him

hyperbola (mathematical curve) • **hyperbole** (exaggeration)

hyperbole—*see* hyperbola

hypercritical (very critical, fault-finding) • **hypocritical** (insincere, false)

hypocritical—*see* hypercritical

hysterical—*see* historical

I

I—*see* aye

id—*see* eyed

ID—*see* eyed

I'd—*see* eyed

idea (thought) • **ideal** (perfect)

ideal—*see* idea

idle (unemployed; lazy) • **idol** (one who is worshipped; image that is worshipped)

idol—*see* idle

ikrah (compulsion; control) • **ikrar** (agreement)

ikrar—*see* ikrah

ileum (part of small intestine) • **ilium** (large pelvic bone)

ilium—*see* ileum

I'll—*see* aisle

illapse—*see* elapse

illegible (unreadable) • **ineligible** (unqualified; unentitled) illicit—*see* elicit

illiterate—*see* alliterate

illogical—*see* alogical

illud—*see* allude

illusion—*see* allision

illusive—*see* elusive

imbrue (to stain; to drench in liquid) • imbue (to infuse with feeling)

imbue—*see* imbrue

imitable (able to be imitated) • inimical (hostile) • inimitable (unable to be imitated)

immanent—*see* eminent

immerse—*see* amerce

immersed—*see* emersed

immigrant—*see* emigrant

immigrate—*see* emigrate

imminent—*see* eminent

immoral—*see* amoral

immunity (state of being protected or exempt) • impunity (exemption from punishment)

immure (to bury; to imprison) • inure (to result in a benefit)

impartable (able to be transmitted) • impartible (not divisible)

impartible—*see* impartable

impassable (blocked) • impassible (not subject to pain; unfeeling) • impossible (not possible)

impassible—*see* impassable

important (valuable) • impotent (powerless; unable to have sex)

impossible—*see* impassable

impostor (fraudulent use of another's identity) • imposture (the act of assuming a fraudulent identity)

imposture—*see* imposter

impotent—*see* important

impracticable (not doable, not achievable with methods used) • impractical (unrealistic)

impractical—*see* impracticable

impressed (gained admiration) • imprest (loan)

imprest—*see* impressed

imprudent (unwise) • impudent (disrespectful)

impudent—*see* imprudent

impunity—*see* immunity

imputation—*see* amputation

inane (silly) • insane (mad)

inapt (unsuitable) • inept (incompetent)

incestuosi (offspring of incest) • incestuous (having sexual relations with close relatives)

incestuous—*see* incestuosi

incidence (frequency) • incidents (events; dangerous occurrences)

incidents—*see* incidence

incipient (developing) • insipient (silly)

incite (to stir to action) • in sight (in view) • insight (perception)

inciter (one who stirs someone or something to action) • insider (a privileged member; one with access to secrets)

incompetence (inability) • incompetents (those unable to perform well)

incompetents—*see* incompetence

in corpore (in substance) • incorporeal (pertaining to right based on non-material things; not material)

incorporeal—*see* in corpore

inculcate (to teach by means of repetition) • inculpate (to blame) • inoculate (to provide immunity)

inculpate—*see* inculcate

incurable (impossible to cure) • incurrable (can be brought upon oneself)

incurrable—*see* incurable

indelible (making a lasting impression) • inedible (unsafe to eat) indelicate (tactless) • in delicto (in fault)

in delicto—see indelicate

indict (to bring formal charges by a grand jury) • indite (to write)

indiscreet (careless) • indiscrete (not divisible)

indiscrete—see indiscreet

indite—see indict

inedible—see indelible

ineligible—see illegible

inept—see inapt

inequity (injustice) • iniquity (evil act)

infection (disease) • inflection (change in voice's tone)

infer (to reason; to grasp implication) • infra (below, underneath)

infest (to invade) • invest (to spend money for a future return)

inflect (to vary pitch; to modulate) • inflict (to do damage; to impose)

inflection—see infection

inflict—see inflect

in flight (fleeing) • in-flight (relating to activity on an airplane)

influx (inflow) • in flux (in state of change)

infra—see infer

ingenious (brilliantly original) • ingenuous (innocent, naive)

ingenuous—see ingenious

inhuman (savage; pitiless) • inhumane (lacking compassion)

inhumane—see inhuman

inimical—see imitable

inimitable—see imitable

iniquity—see inequity

injure (to hurt) • in jure (according to law) • injury (damage or harm)

injury—see injure

inmate (prisoner) • innate (inherent)

innate—see inmate

innervate—see enervate

innocence (lack of guilt; naiveté) • innocents (people who are not guilty)

innocents—see innocence

innovate—see enervate

inoculate—see inculcate

insane—see inane

insert (to place inside) • inset (small object put in larger one)

inset—see insert

insider—see inciter

insidious (deceitful) • invidious (negative; envious)

in sight—see incite

insight—see incite

insipient—see incipient

insolate (to expose to sun) • insolent (rude) • insulate (to protect) • isolate (to set apart from others)

insolent—see insolate

instance (example) • instants (short intervals)

instants—see instance

instrument (formal document; tool or means) • instrumenta (evidence not under seal) • instrumental (useful)

instrumenta—see instrument

instrumental—see instrument

insulate—see insolate

insurance—see assurance

insure—see ensure

intense (strong) • intents (aims)

intension (state of being intense) • intention (aim)

intention—see intension

intents—see intense

inter (to bury; between) • intra (within, nearby)

interagency (between agencies) • intra-agency (within an agency)

intercession (intervention) • intersection (meeting of two or more streets) • **intersession** (time between sessions)

interesse (monetary interest; land claim) • **interest** (legal right; claim; share)

interest—*see* interesse

interment (burial) • **internment** (imprisonment)

intermission (break in action) • **intromission** (insertion; letting in)

intern or **interne** (advanced professional student) • **in turn** (in order)

internment—*see* interment

inter pares (between equals) • **inter partes** (between parties)

inter partes—*see* inter pares

interpellate (to address formal question to counsel) • **interpolate** (insert words into document)

interpolate—*see* interpellate

intersection—*see* intercession

intersession—*see* intercession

interstate (between states) • **intestate** (died without having made a will) • **intrastate** (within a state)

intestate—*see* interstate

intra—*see* inter

intra-agency—*see* interagency

intrastate—*see* interstate

intromission—*see* intermission

in turn—*see* intern

inure—*see* immure

invade (to attack) • **inveighed** (complained bitterly)

inveighed—*see* invade

inventor (creator of something new) • **inventory** (stock of goods)

inventory—*see* inventor

invest—*see* infest

invidious—*see* insidious

ion (electrically charged atom) • **iron** (metal)

irascible—*see* erasable

iron—*see* ion

irredeemable (hopeless; unable to be returned) • **irremeable** (unable to return) • **irremediable** (incurable)

irrelevant (inapplicable) • **irreverent** (disrespectful)

irremeable—*see* irredeemable

irremediable—*see* irredeemable

irreverent—*see* irrelevant

irruption—*see* eruption

Islam (the faith of Muslims) • **Moslem** or **Muslim** (adherent to Islamic faith)

isolate—*see* insolate

its (indicates possession) • **it's** (it is)

it's—*see* its

J

jelled—*see* geld

jest—*see* gest

jewel (precious stone) • **joule** (energy measure in physics)

jewelry (ornaments) • **Jewry** (the Jewish people) • **jury** (group of people who decide a case)

Jewry—*see* jewelry

jibe—*see* gibe

joule—*see* jewel

junta—*see* hunter

junto—*see* hunter

jura (laws, rights) • **jure** (by right) • **juror** (one who serves on jury)

jure—*see* jura

juror—*see* jura

jury—*see* jewelry

jus (body of law; rights) • **just** (fair)

just—*see* jus

K

kaput—*see* caput

karat—*see* carat

karma—*see* coma

kernel—*see* colonel

key (lock opener; problem solver) • quay (boat dock)

kill (to end a life) • kiln (oven)

kiln—*see* kill

Klan—*see* clan

knew (did know) • new (not existing before)

know (to be sure; to be aware of) • no (negative response)

known (understood; recognized) • non (prefix meaning *not*) • none (not any) • no one (nobody)

knows (understands) • noes or nos (negative responses) • nose (part of face)

kraft—*see* craft

L

label (way to identify; mailing aid) • labial (pertaining to the lips or female genitalia) • labile (flexible)

labial—*see* label

labile—*see* label

laches (failure to assert right) • latches (door fasteners)

lacks (doesn't have) • lax (careless)

lade (load) • laid (put down)

laid—*see* lade

lain (reclined) • lane (passageway)

lair (den) • layer (a thickness of a substance that lies on top of or between other items)

lam (slang for *to flee from the law*; to beat) • lamb (young sheep)

lamb—*see* lam

lane—*see* lain

laps (thighs when seated; takes in food) • lapse (failure to act in time; error)

lapse—*see* laps

large (big) • lodge (house; fraternal order)

largess or largesse (generosity) • largest (biggest)

largest—*see* largess

latches—*see* laches

Latina (female of Latin descent) • Latino (male of Latin descent)

Latino—*see* Latina

lax—*see* lacks

lay (nonprofessional, nonclerical; to put something down) • lea (pasture) • ley (law)

layer—*see* lair

lea—*see* lay

leach (chemical cleaning) • leech (exploiter)

lead (a metal) • led (did lead)

lean (thin; to rest against) • lien (right to possess another's property until a debt is paid)

leased (paid for use without owning) • least (smallest; lowest amount) • lest (for fear that)

least—*see* leased

led—*see* lead

ledges (narrow shelves) • leges (laws)

leech—*see* leach

legation (diplomatic offices) • ligation (thing that binds)

leges—*see* ledges

lends (loans money or property) • lens (optical glass; part of the eye)

lens—*see* lends

lese majesty (insult to ruler) • **less** (smaller in quantity or degree) • **lessa** (legacy) • **lessee** (holder of lease) • **lesser** (smaller of two items in size or significance) • **lessor** (holder of lease)

less—*see* lese majesty

lessa—*see* lese majesty

lessee—*see* lese

lessen (to reduce) • **lesson** (learning unit, concept)

lesser—*see* lese majesty

lesson—*see* lessen

lessor—*see* lese majesty

lest—*see* leased

levee (dike) • **levy** (tax; fine; to exact)

levy—*see* levee

ley—*see* lay

liable (bound in equity or law; probable) • **libel** (defamation)

libber (slang for *supporter of women's liberation*) • **liber** (accessible; free) • **LIBOR** (London Interbank Offered Rate)

libel—*see* liable

liber—*see* libber

LIBOR—*see* libber

lie (untruth; to tell an untruth) • **lye** (washing solution)

lien—*see* lean

(in) lieu (of) (in place of) • **loo** (bathroom)

life (the time from birth until death; existence) • **live** (rhymes with *five*: alive) • **live** (rhymes with *give*: reside; be alive)

ligation—*see* legation

light (not heavy; illumination) • **lite pendente** (pending law suit)

lightening (easing a burden) • **lightning** (electric flash in sky)

lighter (not as heavy) • **liter or litre** (metric measure, nearly a quart) • **litera** (letter of the law) • **litter** (trash; stretcher)

lightning—*see* lightening

limb (arm or leg; tree branch) • **limn** (to draw; to describe)

limn—*see* limb

linage (number of lines) • **lineage** (ancestry)

lineage—*see* linage

lineup (line of people for police observation) • **line up** (to stand in a row)

line up—*see* line up

lis (controversy) • **list** (series of written items)

list—*see* lis

lite pendente—*see* light

liter—*see* lighter

litera—*see* lighter

literal (strictly interpreted) • **littoral** (pertaining to the seashore)

litre—*see* lighter

litter—*see* lighter

littoral—*see* literal

live—*see* life

loan (money given that is to be repaid) • **lone** (sole)

loath (reluctant) • **loathe** (to despise)

loathe—*see* loath

local (nearby) • **locale** (particular place or area)

locale—*see* local

lockout (refusal to let workers enter) • **lock out** (to refuse entry)

lodge—*see* large

lone—*see* loan

long term (an extended period of time) • **long-term** (existing for a long period of time)

loo—*see* lieu

lookout (guard; crime partner; place for surveillance) • **look out** (to observe; to be careful)

loose (not tight; immoral) • **lose** (to fail to win; to misplace) • **louse** (unpleasant person; insect)

loot (stolen property; to steal) • **lute** (a musical instrument)

lose—*see* loose

loss (excess of cost over revenue) • **lost** (misplaced; disoriented)

lost—*see* loss

loud (at high volume) • **lout** (clumsy, boorish person)

louse—*see* loose

lout—*see* loud

lumbar (in the lower back) • **lumber** (cut timber)

lumber—*see* lumbar

lute—*see* loot

lye—*see* lie

M

magma (molten rock) • **magna** (great)

magna—*see* magma

magnate (powerful person) • **magnet** (person or thing that attracts)

magnet—*see* magnate

mail (post office deliveries; to send by post) • **male** (man or boy)

maim (to wound severely) • **main** (most important)

main—*see* maim

makeup (cosmetics) • **make up** (to reconcile; to compensate)

male—*see* mail

mall (shopping center) • **maul** (to beat; to batter)

manage (to direct, control) • **ménage** (household)

mandatary (person to whom charge is given) • **mandatory** (compulsory)

mandatory—*see* mandatary

mania (madness; enthusiasm) • **maniac** (person who is mad) • **manic** (possessed of a mental disorder)

maniac—*see* mania

manic—*see* mania

manifest (apparent; cargo or passenger list) • **manifesto** (political statement)

manifesto—*see* manifest

manner (method, way) • **manor** (estate)

manor—*see* manner

mar (to damage) • **mare** (the sea; *mare clausum*: the sea is closed)

mare—*see* mar

marital (relating to marriage) • **marshal** (officer who executes court orders; to lead) • **martial** (warlike)

mark (symbol; to indicate, to record) • **marque** (reprisal, as in law of marque, or form of act outside law)

marked (noticeable; identified) • **market** (place for commercial exchanges)

market—*see* marked

marque—*see* mark

marriage (union of husband and wife) • **mirage** (illusion)

marshal—*see* marital

martial—*see* marital

mask (disguise) • **mosque** (Islamic building of worship)

massage (body rub) • **message** (communication) • **messuage** (home)

materia or **material** (things, matter; necessary or important) • **materiel** (military supplies)

materiel—*see* materia

maul—*see* mall

mean (average; intend; cruel) •
mesne (intermediate) • **mien**
(appearance, conduct)

medal (award) • **meddle** (to interfere)
• **metal** (element such as gold or
iron) • **mettle** (character)

meddle—*see* medal

mediation (resolution of a dispute) •
medication (medicine) •
meditation (quiet reflection)

medication—*see* mediation

meditation—*see* mediation

meets (contacts; sees face to face) •
metes and bounds (boundaries) •
metus (terror)

memoir (autobiography) • **memory**
(mental recall)

memory—*see* memoir

ménage—*see* manage

mendacity (lies) • **mendicity**
(begging)

mendicity—*see* mendacity

mens (mind; *mens rea*: guilty mind) •
mensa (necessities; *mensa et
thoro*: bed and board)

mensa—*see* mens

menses (menstrual discharge; plural
of mensis) • **mensis** (month)

mensis—*see* menses

mesne—*see* mean

message—*see* massage

messuage—*see* massage

meta (goal; prefix expressing change)
• **mete** • (to distribute, assign) •
meter (unit of length; instrument
of measure)

metal—*see* medal

mete—*see* meta

meter—*see* meta

metes—*see* meets

mettle—*see* medal

metus—*see* meets

mien—*see* mean

mil (one thousandth of an inch) •

mile (5,280 feet) • **mill** (factory;
building where grain is ground)

mile—*see* mil

mill—*see* mil

miner (one who extracts materials
from the earth) • **minor** (person
below legal age; unimportant)

minion (servile subordinate) •
minyan (quorum)

minor—*see* miner

minute (unit of time; short time) •
minutes (meeting records) •
minutia (trivia or piece of
information)

minutes—*see* minute

minutia—*see* minute

minyan—*see* minion

mirage—*see* marriage

mishap (accident; misfortune) •
misshape (to shape badly)

misshape—*see* mishap

modal (statistical measure) • **model**
(small version of product or
system) • **module** (standard unit or
component; standard submarine
part)

model—*see* modal

module—*see* modal

monetary (relating to money or
personal property) • **monitory**
(warning)

monitory—*see* monetary

moot (debate; debatable; irrelevant) •
mute (unable to speak)

moral (lesson; pertaining to ethics) •
morale (group's confidence or
spirits)

morale—*see* moral

morning (early part of day) •
mourning (grieving)

mortgage (security interest in land or
buildings) • **mortgagee** (one who
gets a mortgage) • **mortgagor**
(one who grants a mortgage)

mortgagee—*see* mortgage

mortgagor—*see* mortgage

Moslem—*see* Islam

mosque—*see* mask

motif (element in artistic work) • motive (reason)

motive—*see* motif

mourning—*see* morning

movant or movent (one who makes motion) • movement (action; group with common aims)

movement—*see* movant

movent—*see* movant

Muslim—*see* Islam

mute—*see* moot

N

nature (essence; external world) • nurture (upbringing; to protect or nourish)

naval (relating to a navy) • navel (abdominal feature)

navel—*see* naval

neurosis (psychological disorder) • neuroses (pl. of *neurosis*)

neuroses—*see* neurosis

new—*see* knew

nisei (second-generation Japanese American) • nisi (unless)

nisi—*see* nisei

no—*see* know

noes—*see* knows

non—*see* known

none—*see* known

no one—*see* known

nor—*see* gnaw

nos—*see* knows

nose—*see* knows

nurture—*see* nature

O

oar—*see* awe

object—*see* abject

oblige (to bind; to constrain) • obligee (recipient of promise or pledge) • obliger (one who obliges) • obligor (writer of surety bonds)

obligee—*see* oblige

obliger—*see* oblige

obligor—*see* oblige

obstriction (obligation) • obstruction (obstacle)

obstruct—*see* abstract

obstruction—*see* obstriction

obtuse—*see* abstruse

o'er—*see* awe

offal—*see* aweful

older—*see* elder

omit—*see* emit

onetime (former) • one time (once) • on time (meeting a schedule)

on time—*see* onetime

opposite—*see* apposite

oppressed—*see* appressed

or—*see* awe

oracle—*see* auricle

oral—*see* aural

orbiter—*see* arbiter

order (state of peace; command) • ordure (excrement)

ordinance (law; regulation) • ordnance (military arms) • ordonnance (arrangement; laws relating to sea)

ordnance—*see* ordinance

ordonnance—*see* ordinance

ordure—*see* order
ore—*see* awe
ought—*see* aught
our—*see* hour
overall (including everything; general) • over all (above, superior to)
overdo (do in excess) • overdue (late)

overdue—*see* overdo
overseas (abroad) • oversees (supervises) • overseers (supervisors)
overseers—*see* overseas
oversees—*see* overseas
ovoid—*see* avoid

P

PAC (political action committee) • pack (to put items in container)
pack—*see* PAC
packed (did pack) • pact (treaty; agreement)
pact—*see* packed
pain (to hurt, suffering) • pane (part of window)
pairs (couples; twos) • pares (peers, as in jury selection) • pars (party to action)
pane—*see* pain
parens (a parent or ancestor) • parents (mothers and fathers)
parents—*see* parens
pares—*see* pairs
parish (unit of church or government) • perish (to die)
parity (equality) • party (political group; social gathering)
parlay (to greatly increase an amount of wealth) • parley (conference)
parley—*see* parlay
parol (by word of mouth) • parole (conditional release) • parolee (person on parole) • payroll (list of employees and the pay they are due)
parole—*see* parol
parolee—*see* parole
pars—*see* pairs
partition (division; to divide) • petition (request)

party—*see* parity
passable (tolerable; allowed to pass) • possible (susceptible to suffering)
passed (did pass or approve) • past (previous time)
passibility (ability to feel) • possibility (potential; likelihood)
passible—*see* passable
past—*see* passed
paten (metal plate) • patent (exclusive right) • pattern (organized method; repetition)
patent—*see* paten
pathetic—*see* bathetic
pathos—*see* bathos
patiens (one who suffers) • patients (medical clients)
patients—*see* patiens
pattern—*see* paten
pause (temporary halt) • paws (animal feet) • pores (tiny skin openings) • pours (causes liquid to flow)
pawn (security for pledge; person used by another; chess piece) • porn (pornography)
paws—*see* pause
payroll—*see* parol
peace (absence of conflict) • piece (portion)
peak (top; highest level) • peek (to glimpse; a sly look) • pique (anger; to arouse)

peculiar (unique, different) • pecunia (property) • pecuniary (relating to money)

pecunia—*see* peculiar

pecuniary—*see* peculiar

pedal (a lever that is pressed with the foot) • peddle (to travel and sell)

peddle—*see* pedal

peek—*see* peak

peer (equal; to look closely) • pier (dock)

penal (relating to punishment) • penile (relating to the penis)

penance (punishment; absolution) • pennants (nautical flags; flags awarded for winning championships)

pend (to await; to be undecided) • penned (confined; wrote) • pent (kept in; held in)

pendant (attached to a necklace) • pendent (pending) • pendente lite (pending a suit)

pendants (necklace ornaments) • pendens (pending suit)

pendens—*see* pendants

pendent—*see* pendant

pendente lite—*see* pendant

penile—*see* penal

pennants—*see* penance

penned—*see* pend

pent—*see* pend

per (for each) • pur (by and for) • pure (spotless; unmitigated) • purr (soft, vibrating sound)

peremptory (absolute, final) • preemptory (prior claim, right, or heading off)

perfect (flawless; right) • prefect (administrative official)

perish—*see* parish

perquisite (perk; extra benefit) • prerequisite (precondition)

persecute (to maltreat; to harass) • prosecute (to present government's court case)

persona (outward manner) • personal (individual; private) • personnel (employees)

personal—*see* persona

personality (distinctive qualities of character; celebrity) • personalty (personal property in law)

personalty—*see* personality

personnel—*see* persona

perspective (point of view) • prospective (future; likely to happen; possible)

perspicacious (shrewd, discerning) • perspicuous (precise, clearly presented)

perspicuous—*see* perspicacious

perverse (contradicting evidence, stubborn; incorrect) • perverts (people who are corrupt or sexually aberrant) • preserve (to maintain)

perverts—*see* perverse

petit (minor, as in *petit jur*y) • petite (small) • petty (trifling; spiteful; minor)

petite—*see* petit

petition—*see* partition

petty—*see* petit

phase—*see* faze

phial—*see* file

Philippines—*see* Filipina

phrase—*see* frays

phreak—*see* freak

phylum—*see* filum

physic (medicinal purge) • physique (bodily build) • psychic (one who claims special mental powers)

physical—*see* fiscal

physique—*see* physic

pica (measurement used in typography) • piker (slang for *cheapskate*)

picture (visual representation) • pitcher (container for beverages)

piece—*see* peace

pier—*see* peer

piker—*see* pica

pileup (multicar collision) • **pile up** (to amass; to cause a crash)

Pilipino—*see* Filipina

pique—*see* peek

pistil (part of plant) • **pistol** (a type of gun) • **pistole** (old gold coin)

pistol—*see* pistil

pistole—*see* pistil

pitcher—*see* picture

plaid (cloth or pattern with overlapping hotizontal and vertical stripes) • **played** (participated in an amusement; performed upon; competed)

plain (simple; prairie) • **plane** (airplane; flat area; carpenter's tool)

plaint (complaint) • **planned** (designed, arranged) • **plant** (slang for *secret witness* or *evidence*; botanical organism)

plaintiff (one who sues, charges) • **plaintive** (sad)

plaintive—*see* plaintiff

plane—*see* plain

planned—*see* plaint

plant—*see* plaint

plat (map; piece of land) • **plate** (dish; metal cover)

plate—*see* plat

played—*see* plaid

plead (to advocate; to answer for defense) • **pleat** (cloth fold)

pleas (appeals; replies by the defense) • **please** (word used in a polite request; to give pleasure)

please—*see* pleas

pleat—*see* plead

pledgee (one to whom goods are promised or delivered) • **pledger** or **pledgor** (one who promises to deliver)

pledger—*see* pledgee

pleural (pertaining to lung membranes) • **plural** (indicating more than one)

plural—*see* pleural

pole (an opposite; end of axis) • **poll** (survey)

policy (contract; course of action) • **polity** (form of government or organization)

polity—*see* policy

poll—*see* pole

pool (to combine resources; swimming area) • **pull** (influence; to draw something toward)

poor (lacking money; low-quality) • **pore** (skin opening) • **pour** (to cause to flow)

populace (masses) • **populist** (politician who appeals to common folk) • **populous** (with many people)

populist—*see* populace

populous—*see* populace

pore—*see* poor

pores—*see* pause

porn—*see* pawn

portend (to foreshadow) • **portent** (foreshadowing) • **potent** (powerful) • **pretend** (to feign)

portent—*see* portend

portion (child's share of estate; part of a whole) • **potion** (medicine)

possibility—*see* passibility

potent—*see* portend

potion—*see* portion

pour—*see* poor

pours—*see* pause

practicable (possible to be done) • **practical** (realistic; suitable)

practical—*see* practicable

practice (profession; usual procedure; to rehearse) • **praxis** (application or performance of a skill)

praise (compliments) • **prays** (entreats a deity) • **preys** (victimizes)

167

praxis—*see* practice

prayer (religious entreaty; one who prays) • preyer (one who victimizes)

prays—*see* praise

precede (to go before) • proceed (to continue; to advance)

precedence (priority, order) • precedents (earlier legal decisions used as guides) • presidents (heads of governments or other organizations)

precedents—*see* precedence

preceding (going before) • proceeding (conduct of court business)

précis (short summary) • precise (exact)

precise—*see* précis

predicate (to claim as true) • predict (to forecast)

predict—*see* predicate

preemptory—*see* peremptory

prefect—*see* perfect

prefer (to make legal claim; to value more) • proffer (to offer)

premier (most important; head of government) • premiere (first public showing of play or movie)

premiere—*see* premier

premises (land and appurtenances; reasons for legal action; logical basis) • promises (agrees to do)

preposition (combining word, such as by, into, with, at, on, under) • proposition (proposal; formal statement)

prerequisite—*see* perquisite

prescribe (to assert a right; to advise; to order) • proscribe (to forbid)

presence (state of being in a certain place) • presents (grand jury finds; gifts; offers; introduces)

presentiment (foreboding) • presentment (grand jury notice in writing; representation)

presentment—*see* presentiment

presents—*see* presence

preserve—*see* perverse

presidents—*see* precedence

pretend—*see* portend

pretest (preliminary test) • pretext (apparent motive) • protest (objection)

pretext—*see* pretest

preview (early showing) • purvey (to supply provisions) • purview (enactment portion of a statute; range of control)

preyer—*see* prayer

preys—*see* praise

pride (self-respect; excessively high opinion of self) • pried (probed unfairly; opened)

pried—*see* pride

prima facie (first appearance) • prime (basic or best; high quality)

prime—*see* prima

principal (capital amount; chief; lead criminal or abettor) • principle (basic law or idea; high moral conduct)

principle—*see* principal

probatio (direct proof) • probation (controlled criminal release)

probation—*see* probatio

proceed—*see* precede

proceeding—*see* preceding

prodigal (extravagant) • prodigious (enormous; marvelous) • prodigy (child genius) • protegé (person helped by other)

prodigious—*see* prodigal

prodigy—*see* prodigal

proffer—*see* prefer

profit (revenues above costs; gain) • prophet (predictor of future) • (the) Prophet (Muhammad, founder of Islam)

prologue (introduction) • prorogue (to postpone)

promisee (receiver of promise) • **promisor** (maker of promise) • **promissor** (respondent in interrogation) • **promissory** (having the nature of a promise)

promises—*see* premises

promisor—*see* promisee

promissor—*see* promisee

promissory—*see* promisee

proof (reason to accept as true) • **prove** (to provide evidence of truth)

proper (correct) • **propter** (on account of)

prophet—*see* profit

(the) Prophet—*see* profit

propose (suggest; nominate; ask to marry) • **purpose** (aim; determination)

proposition—*see* preposition

propter—*see* proper

pro rata (in proportion) • **prorate** (to divide proportionately)

prorate—*see* pro rata

prorogue—*see* prologue

proscribe—*see* prescribe

pro se (for oneself, in person) • **prose** (connected sentences that are not poetry)

prose—*see* pro se

prosecute—*see* persecute

prospective—*see* perspective

prostate (male gland) • **prostrate** (to show submission)

prostrate—*see* prostate

protegé—*see* prodigal

protest—*see* pretest

prove—*see* proof

psychic—*see* physic

psychoses—*see* psychosis

psychosis (serious mental illness) • **psychoses** (pl. of *psychosis*)

pubic (relating to pelvic area) • **public** (overall population; relating to the people)

public—*see* pubic

puisne (subordinate, inferior) • **puny** (weak)

pull—*see* pool

puny—*see* puisne

pur—*see* per

pure—*see* per

purpart (share) • **purport** (legal substance, meaning; to intend; to profess)

purport—*see* purpart

purpose—*see* propose

purr—*see* per

purvey—*see* preview

purview—*see* preview

put (offer to sell stock at later date at fixed price; to place) • **putt** (golf stroke)

putt—*see* put

Q

qua (in the role or capacity of) • **quae** (thing, things)

quadriplegia (paralysis of both arms and legs) • **quadriplegic** (person who is so paralyzed)

quadriplegic—*see* quadriplegia

quae—*see* qua

quaere (a question; a doubt) • **quare** (wherefore) • **quarry** (victim who is hunted) • **queer** (strange, odd) • **query** (question)

quare—*see* quaere

quarrel (argument) • **querela** (action in court)

quarry—*see* quaere

quay—*see* key

queer—*see* quaere

querela—*see* quarrel

query—*see* quaere

queue—*see* cue

quiet (still) • quit (to resign; to cease) • quite (largely, to a great extent)

quit—*see* quiet

quite—*see* quiet

quota (share, fixed limit) • quote (to give price; to repeat someone else's words)

quote—*see* quota

R

racked (inflicted or filled with pain) • racket (crooked scheme; commotion)

racket—*see* racked

rain (downpour; series of losses) • reign (rule) • rein (to restrain)

raise (to lift; to bring up) • raze (to demolish)

ranch (animal-breeding farm) • raunch (vulgarity)

rap (to criticize; to talk; to knock) • rape (to molest sexually) • wrap (to cover; to enfold)

rape—*see* rap

rational (capable of reasoning) • rationale (reason)

rationale—*see* rational

raunch—*see* ranch

ravage (to plunder; to damage badly) • ravish (to rape)

ravish—*see* ravage

raze—*see* raise

reacquire (to get back) • require (to demand; to insist)

read (rhymes with need: to understand written words; to show computer files) • reed (tall grass; musical instruments)

read (pron. like *dead*: did read) • red (a color)

reak (with an allusion to) • reek (to emit a strong odor) • wreak (to give expression; to inflict)

real (related to property like land; true, actual) • reel (cylinder with wound matter)

reality (what exists) • realty (real estate)

realize (to get gains from investment or sale; to understand) • relies (depends)

Realtor (person officially authorized as real-estate operator) • relator (informer or complainer who causes legal action)

realty—*see* reality

reassign (to change a job or assignment) • resign (pron. reeZINE: to quit) • re-sign (pron. reeSINE: to sign again or extend a contract)

rebait (to put bait on hook again) • rebate (special discount; reduction in interest rate)

rebate—*see* rebait

rebound (to recover, regain prior state) • redound (to reflect on; to affect)

recite (to write about facts or reasons for statement; to repeat) • resight (to see again)

reck (to take heed) • wreck (to destroy; to damage; to ruin)

recluse (one who lives alone or avoids meeting others) • recuse (to request disqualification of judge or juror)

recover (to get again, obtain return) • recoveree (loser in a recovery) •

recoverer (winner of recovery) •
recovery (restoration of right)

recoveree—*see* recover

recoverer—*see* recover

recovery—*see* recover

recuse—*see* recluse

red—*see* read

redoubt (to secure retreat) • **redout**
(a blackout)

redound—*see* rebound

redout—*see* redoubt

reed—*see* read

reefer (slang for *marijuana cigarette*)
• **refer** (to send case to referee; to
send to authority; to cite)

reek—*see* reak

reel—*see* real

reevaluation (review) • **revaluation**
(reassessment of value)

refer—*see* reefer

referee (special appointee of court
who takes testimony) • **reverie**
(dreamy state)

reference (agreement to arbitrate;
testimony regarding one's
character; act of citing) •
reverence (respect or awe)

regime (ruling government) •
regimen (prescribed behavior;
diet) • **regiment** (military unit)

regimen—*see* regime

regiment—*see* regime

regula (rule; practice) • **regulae
generales** (general rules) • **regular**
(lawful, conformable to law;
normal, uniform, usual)

regulae generales—*see* regula

regular—*see* regula

reif (robbery) • **reify** (to view abstract
as real)

reify—*see* reif

reign—*see* rain

rein—*see* rain

relator—*see* Realtor

relief (request for redress; remedy;
aid to poor) • **relieve** (to soothe; to
aid) • **relive** (to live again)

relies—*see* realize

relieve—*see* relief

relive—*see* relief

remittee (recipient of money sent by
another) • **remitter** (transference
from defective title to earlier valid
title) • **remittitur** (return of excess
jury award) • **remittor** (one who
sends money)

remitter—*see* remittee

remittitur—*see* remittee

remittor—*see* remittee

require—*see* reacquire

residence (home; business legal
address • **residents** (occupants of a
home)

residents—*see* residence

resight—*see* recite

resign—*see* reassign

rest (remainder; to stop work) • **wrest**
(to obtain by force; to usurp)

resume (to start again) • **résumé** (list
of job qualifications)

résumé—*see* resume

revaluation—*see* reevaluation

reveal (to disclose; to uncover) •
revel (to enjoy)

revel—*see* reveal

reverence—*see* reference

reverie—*see* referee

ribald (vulgarly humorous) • **ribaud**
(very wicked person)

ribaud—*see* ribald

right (entitlement; interest in an item
of property; correct) • **rite** (special
ceremony) • **wright** (one who
builds or fixes something)

rigorous (tough, demanding) •
vigorish (illegally excessive
interest) • **vigorous** (robust,
energetic)

rip off (to tear off; to steal) • **rip-off** (theft, overcharge)

risk (danger of insured property; person or thing so covered) • **risqué** (off-color; daring)

risqué—*see* risk

rite—*see* right

roil (to upset or stir up) • **role** (function of a person or institution; actor's part) • **roll** (wrapped material; small roll)

role—*see* roil

roll—*see* roil

roomer (lodger) • **rumor** (gossip)

root (heart or source; underground part of tree or plant) • **rout** (bad defeat; riot) • **route** (road; way to achieve goal)

rote (mechanical repetition) • **wrote** (did write)

rouse (to wake someone; to incite) • **rows** (quarrels)

rout—*see* root

route—*see* root

rows—*see* rouse

rumor—*see* roomer

S

said (did say) • **sed per curiam** (statement by court)

salvage (to save property from sunken ship; to save part of loss) • **savage** (cruel; uncivilized)

salve (medicinal ointment) • **salvo** (except for; gun salute) • **salvor** (helper of ship in distress) • **save** (to rescue; to keep; except for)

salvo—*see* salve

salvor—*see* salve

satire (literary work that wittily pokes fun at or criticizes something) • **satyr** (lecher; mythological woodland creature)

satyr—*see* satire

savage—*see* salvage

save—*see* salve

saver (one who saves) • **savior** (rescuer) • **Saviour** (Jesus Christ) • **savoir-faire** (know-how) • **savor** (to enjoy; taste)

savior—*see* saver

Saviour—*see* saver

savoir-faire—*see* saver

savor—*see* saver

scar (mark from wound) • **scare** (to frighten)

scarce (in short supply) • **scares** (frightens) • **scars** (marks from wounds)

scare—*see* scar

scares—*see* scarce

scars—*see* scarce

scene (place of happening; fuss; part of play or movie) • **seen** (observed)

scent—*see* cent

scents—*see* cents

scrip (evidence of ownership or right to shares or profits) • **script** (play or movie manuscript)

script—*see* scrip

sea (body of water) • **see** (to perceive; to understand) • **si** (if; *si aliquid sapid*: if he knows anything)

sealing—*see* ceiling

seamen (sailors) • **semen** (male fluid that contains sperm)

seas—*see* cease

S.E.C. (Securities & Exchange Commission) • **seck** (lack of remedy) • **sect** (political or religious group with common beliefs)

seck—*see* S.E.C.

secret (restricted information; special insight or method) • **secrete** (to hide; to release fluid from the body)

secrete—*see* secret

sect—*see* SEC

sects (pl. of *sect*; dissenters) • **sex** (gender; intercourse)

sed—*see* said

see—*see* sea

seed—*see* cede

seen—*see* scene

sees—*see* cease

seisin (possession in fact or law) • **seizing** (taking by force)

seize—*see* cease

seizing—*see* seisin

sell—*see* cell

seller—*see* cellar

semen—*see* seamen

seminal (leading to new developments; of semen) • **seminar** (class; meeting) • **seminary** (school for training clergy)

seminar—*see* seminal

seminary—*see* seminal

sense—*see* cents

senses—*see* census

sensor—*see* censor

sensus—*see* census

sent—*see* cent

separate (not joined; to divide) • **sperate** (hopeful, promising)

serial—*see* cereal

series (related items in order) • **serious** (solemn, thoughtful)

serious—*see* series

session—*see* cessation

setback (loss, delay; series of recessions in tall building) • **set back** (to force delay; to cause loss)

set off (to begin a trip; to cause) • **set-off** (counter demand; mutual rights)

settler (actual resident; new resident) • **settlor** (donor of deed; creator of trust)

settlor—*see* settler

setup (arrangement to make another appear guilty) • **set up** (to arrange; to put in good shape)

sever (to cut off) • **severe** (strict; simple)

severe—*see* sever

sex—*see* sects

shape up (to improve; to get fit) • **shape-up** (worker lineup)

share (undivided interest of one party; to enjoy with others) • **shear** (to cut; cutting tool) • **sheer** (steep; thin; to swerve)

sharif (Islamic noble) • **sheriff** (local law enforcement officer or administrator)

shear—*see* share

sheer—*see* share

sheik—*see* cheek

sheriff—*see* sharif

shirk (to evade responsibility) • **shriek** (cry of terror or surprise)

shone (lit up; excelled) • **shown** (displayed; indicated; taught)

shoot—*see* chute

shown—*see* shone

shriek—*see* shirk

shut in (to confine, restrain) • **shut-in** (forced to remain inside; one who prefers solitude)

si—*see* sea

sic (thus, so) • **sick** (ill)

sick—*see* sic

side (boundary line; edge) • **sighed** (emitted a soulful sound)

sighed—*see* side

sight—*see* cite

sign (to write name as authentication; symbol; gesture) • **sine** (without; mathematical function)

silicon (sand element used in

electronics) • **silicone** (water-repellent chemical compound once used in breast implants)

silicone—*see* silicon

simile (comparison of separate things) • **smile** (facial expression)

simulate (to create a representation of an item or action; to feign) • **stimulate** (to arouse, animate)

sine—*see* sign

singular—*see* cingular

sin tax (tax on cigarettes, liquor, or other items considered unhealthy or dangerous) • **syntax** (order of parts of speech; grammar)

sir (polite address to man) • **sur** (above, over) • **sure** (certain)

sit down (to take a seat) • **sit-down** (strike inside plant or office)

site—*see* cite

sit in (to attend; to take part in) • **sit-in** (peaceful protest at site of grievance)

slay (to kill) • **sleigh** (sled)

sleigh—*see* slay

sleight (deceit; dexterity) • **slight** (small; slender)

slight—*see* sleight

sloped (set at an angle; slanted) • **slopped** (spilled clumsily)

slopped—*see* sloped

slowdown (worker protest) • **slow down** (to go less fast)

smile—*see* simile

so (very; therefore; as a result) • **sow** (to plant seed)

soar (to rise quickly; to fly high) • **sore** (wound; painful)

sociedad (Spanish: partnership) • **société** (French: partnership) • **société anonyme** (joint stock company) • **society** (organization with common purpose; social organization)

société—*see* sociedad

societé anonyme—*see* sociedad

society—*see* sociedad

sodality (fellowship; Catholic lay society) • **solidarity** (unity, close ties) • **solidary** (joint right or interest) • **solidity** (strength; solidness)

sole (only, single) • **soul** (spirit; personification)

solidarity—*see* sodality

solidary—*see* sodality

solidity—*see* sodality

solvent (having sufficient funds) • **solvit** (paid)

solvit—*see* solvent

some (indefinite amount) • **sum** (total, amount)

son (male child) • **sun** (bright star, source of heat)

soot (chimney ash) • **suit** (legal action) • **suite** (attendants to official; set of rooms)

sordid (vile; depressing) • **sorted** (organized, classified)

sore—*see* soar

sores (injuries) • **sors** (money borrowed or loaned) • **source** (originator; origin)

sors—*see* sores

sorted—*see* sordid

sou (French coin) • **sous** (under) • **sue** (to seek legal redress) • **suo** (his)

soul—*see* sole

source—*see* sores

sous—*see* sou

sow—*see* so

spacious (roomy) • **specie** (coin) • **species** (distinct type or class) • **specious** (false)

specie—*see* spacious

species—*see* spacious

specious—*see* spacious

sperate—*see* separate

spilt (accidentally poured or caused to overflow) • **split** (division; difference; rupture) split—*see* spilt

stake (share of interest; stick, post) •
steak (meat)

standby (substitute; traveler lacking
an assigned seat; reliable item) •
stand by (to support; to wait)

stationary (still; not moving) •
stationery (writing supplies)

stationery—*see* stationary

statist (advocate of strong
government) • status (standing,
rank)

statue (carved figure) • stature
(standing; height) • statute (law)

stature—*see* statue

status—*see* statist

statute—*see* statue

steak—*see* stake

steal (to take unlawfully) • steel
(strong metal)

steel—*see* steal

stimulate—*see* simulate

straight (direct, not curved; off drugs
or criminal acts) • strait (narrow
passageway; difficulty)

strait—*see* straight

stricter (more strict, more severe) •
stricture (restriction; criticism) •
structure (building; method of
organization)

stricture—*see* stricter

strong arm (an arm with strength) •
strong-arm (to apply undue
pressure)

structure—*see* stricter

studded (decorated with nailheads) •
studied (carefully contrived;
learned)

studied—*see* studded

subside (to lower, become less) •
subsidy (special aid from
government)

subsidy—*see* subside

suburb (area around city) • superb
(outstanding)

succor (help) • sucker (victim; one
easily cheated)

sucker—*see* succor

sue—*see* sou

suit—*see* soot

suite—*see* soot

sum—*see* some

summa (highest; greatest) • summer
(warm season)

summer—*see* summa

summary (final legal statement; short
legal proceeding; concise precis) •
summery (like summer)

summery—*see* summary

sun—*see* son

suo—*see* sou

superb—*see* suburb

sur—*see* sir

sure—*see* sir

surely (certainly) • surly (ill-
tempered)

surly—*see* surely

symbol—*see* cymbal

syntax—*see* sin tax

syntheses—*see* synthesis

synthesis (combination of parts to
form a whole) • syntheses (pl. of
synthesis) • synthesize (to pull
together parts to make whole)

synthesize—*see* syntheses

T

tacit (implied, understood) • tacked
(added on) • tact (sensitivity)

tacked—*see* tacit

tacks (attaches something; small
fasteners) • tax (monetary charge
levied by government)

tact—*see* tacit

tail (appendage; an end; to follow someone) • **tale** (story)

tails (appendages; follows) • **tales** (people added to make jury complete; stories)

takeoff (departure; airplane ascent) • **take off** (to remove)

takeover (seizure of control) • **take over** (to seize control)

talc (mineral, usually in powder form) • **talk** (to speak; speech)

tale—*see* tail

tales—*see* tails

talk—*see* talc

tall (above average height; large) • **toll** (fee for use of highway or public facility; loss or damage resulting from disaster; to bar or to take away)

tamper (to alter dishonestly) • **temper** (disposition; anger; to moderate)

taping (recording) • **tapping** (secretly listening to phone conversation; lightly hitting)

tapping—*see* taping

tare (deduction of container weight) • **tear** (to rip; to pull something away forcibly)

taught (did teach) • **taut** (tight) • **tort** (a wrong or injury) • **torte** (rich pastry)

taut—*see* taught

tax—*see* tacks

taxes (government levies) • **taxis** (cabs)

taxis—*see* taxes

team (group of people working together; sports players who compete as a group; farm animals that work together) • **teem** (to be excessively full of)

tear—*see* tare

tear (drop of moisture from the eyes) • **tier** (row; layer)

teem—*see* team

teeter (to waver or walk unsteadily; to be at danger point) • **titter** (to laugh nervously)

temper—*see* tamper

tenant (renter; temporary possessor of land) • **tenent** (zoological term for *holding*) • **tenet** (belief; dogma)

tenent—*see* tenant

tenere (to retain possession) • **tenor** (exact wording of legal document; tone of speech; high male voice) • **tenure** (right to job or to a holding such as land)

tenet—*see* tenant

tenor—*see* tenere

tense (strained, tight; verbal form) • **tents** (cloth shelters)

tents—*see* tense

tenure—*see* tenere

termer (person in prison) • **termor** (person entitled to possession for period of time) • **tremor** (shaking, vibration)

termor—*see* termer

tern (bird) • **turn** (change in direction; shift in events; deed affecting another)

terra (earth) • **terror** (fright)

terror—*see* terra

testes (pl. of *testis*) • **testis** (male reproductive gland)

testis—*see* testes

Thai—*see* tie

than (word indicating comparison of quantity or kind) • **then** (at a specific time; next; therefore)

their (belonging to them) • **there** (at that location) • **they're** (they are)

theirs (belonging to them) • **there's** (there is)

then—*see* than

there—*see* their

therefor (in return or in exchange

for) • **therefore** (hence, for that reason)

therefore—*see* therefor

there's—*see* theirs

theses (dissertations; points of view) • **thesis** (sing. of *theses*)

thesis—*see* theses

they're—*see* their

thrash (to beat badly) • **thresh** (to beat grain)

thread (thin fiber; line of thought) • **threat** (statement of intent to harm; potentially harmful person or situation)

threat—*see* thread

thresh—*see* thrash

threw (hurled; lost dishonestly) • **through** (finished; in and out)

throes (pains) • **throws** (hurls)

through—*see* threw

throws—*see* throes

tic (involuntary motion; spasm) • **tick** (clock's sound; slang for *to anger*; movement of a stock)

tick—*see* tic

tide (cyclical rise and fall of the oceans; surge in opinion) • **tied** (attached with cord; even score)

tie (necktie; connection or bond; even score in competition) • **Thai** (native of Thailand)

tied—*see* tide

tie in (to be consistent with; to connect) • **tie-in** (connection, association)

tier—*see* tear

tie up (to delay; to fasten) • **tie-up** (temporary halt)

timber (cut wood) • **timbre** (sound, resonance)

timbre—*see* timber

tipper (one who tips) • **tippler** (one who drinks)

tippler—*see* tipper

titan (giant) • **titian** (orange-brown color)

titian—*see* titan

titillate (to excite; to stimulate sexually) • **titivate** (to dress up)

titivate—*see* titillate

titter—*see* teeter

to (toward) • **too** (also; excessively) • **two** (number after *one*)

tocsin (alarm; warning) • **toxin** (poison)

toed (touched with the toes; toed the line; conformed) • **towed** (pulled)

toiled (worked) • **told** (did tell) • **tolled** (exacted tax; sounded bell)

told—*see* toiled

toll—*see* tall

tolled—*see* toiled

tomb (burial place) • **tome** (heavy book; volume in set)

tome—*see* tomb

ton (unit of weight; heavy) • **tone** (musical sound; style of speech) • **tun** (cask) • **tune** (melody)

tone—*see* ton

tong (type of kitchen utensil; criminal gang) • **tongue** (organ of taste)

tongue—*see* tong

too—*see* to

tool (device for repairs; any aid) • **tulle** (gauzy material)

topography (physical features of area; representation of those features) • **typography** (printing styles)

tort—*see* taught

torte—*see* taught

tortious (wrongful) • **tortuous** (complicated; twisting) • **torturous** (very painful; causing torture)

tortuous—*see* tortious

torturous—*see* tortious

towed—*see* toed

toxicant (a poison) • toxicate (to poison)

toxicate—*see* toxicant

toxin—*see* tocsin

tracked (trailed, followed) • tract (piece of land; propaganda)

tract—*see* tracked

trade in (to buy or sell; to exchange) • trade-in (an exchange)

trade off (to sell; to exchange) • trade-off (an even exchange; a compromise)

trader (one who buys goods to resell) • traitor (betrayer)

trail (narrow path; to follow) • trial (formal court hearing)

traitor—*see* trader

travail (hard work; suffering) • travel (to journey)

travel—*see* travail

treasure (riches, wealth) • treasury (place where money is stored; government financial assets) • Treasury (the Federal department that handles money)

treasury—*see* treasure

Treasury—*see* treasure

treaties (formal agreements between nations) • treatise (formally written argument)

treatise—*see* treaties

tremor—*see* termer

triad (set of three) • tried (attempted; brought case to court)

trial—*see* trail

tried—*see* triad

trivia (minor matters) • trivial (not important)

trivial—*see* trivia

troop (organized group of soldiers or other people who work together) • troupe (theatrical group)

troupe—*see* troop

trussed (tied up; supported with a beam) • trust (credit; reliance; confidence)

trust—*see* trussed

trustee (holder of property; board member) • trusty (prisoner with privileges)

trusty—*see* trustee

tryout (test of ability) • try out (to compete for a position; to test)

tulle—*see* tool

tune—*see* ton

turn—*see* tern

turnout (audience; appearance) • turn out (to switch off; to get rid of; to produce)

turnover (speed of business sales; rate of employee replacement) • turn over (to pass on; to change position)

tuteur (guardian) • tutor (teacher who usually works with one pupil at a time)

tutor—*see* tuteur

two—*see* to

typography—*see* topography

U

umpire—*see* empire

unable—*see* enable

unassigned (not allotted, not designated) • unsigned (lacking a signature)

unaware (not aware) • unawares (suddenly)

unawares—*see* unaware

underlay (to place support under) • underlie (to be basis for action)

underlie—*see* underlay

undo (to reverse) • undue (extreme, excessive)

undue—*see* undo

unexceptionable (irreproachable) •
unexceptional (ordinary, average)

unexceptional—see unexceptionable

unique—see eunuch

unit (single person; part of larger group or thing) • unite (to join together)

unite—see unit

unmoral—see amoral

unsigned—see unassigned

unwanted (not desired) • unwonted (unusual)

unwonted—see unwanted

urban (referring to city) • urbane (sophisticated)

urbane—see urban

urn—see earn

usura (interest) • usurer (one who charges excess interest) • usury (act of overcharging interest)

usurer—see usura

usury—see usura

V

vacation (holiday) • vocation (job, career)

vain (conceited) • vein (blood vessel)

vale (valley) • veil (cloth that conceals face)

valet (servant) • valid (possessing legal strength; sustainable)

valid—see valet

valuable (of great worth) • voluble (talkative)

vary (to change; to alter) • very (extremely)

veer (to turn; to shift) • vir (man or husband)

veies (refusal of replevin or return of goods) • vies (competes)

veil—see vale

vein—see vain

venal (corrupt; unprincipled) • venia (pardon) • venial (pardonable; excusable)

veneer (superficial layer or quality) • venire (writ summoning jury)

venia—see venal

venial—see venal

venire—see veneer

veracity (truthfulness) • voracity (greediness)

verge (border on) • virge (a tenant's holding)

verses (lines of poetry) • versus (opposed to; against)

versus—see verses

very—see vary

via (in this way or by this route) • vie (to compete)

vial (small bottle) • vile (loathsome; repugnant)

vice (immoral or harmful habit; weakness) • vise (device that clamps)

vie—see via

vies—see veies

vigorish—see rigorous

vigorous—see rigorous

vile—see vial

vine (climbing plant) • visne (area from which jury is drawn)

vir—see veer

virago (shrew) • Virgo (zodiac sign) • virgo intacta (virgin)

vires (powers, authority) • virus (contagious agent)

virge—see verge

Virgo—see virago

virgo intacta—see virago

virus—see vires

vis (force or violence) • viz (that is to say; abbreviation of *videlicet*)

visa (permit to enter a country) •
   visor (front of cap)

vise—*see* vice

visne—*see* vine

visor—*see* visa

viz—*see* vis

vocation—*see* vacation

voluble—*see* valuable

voracity—*see* veracity

W

wad (small mass; slang for *a lot of
   money*) • wade (to walk in shallow
   water) • weighed (checked
   heaviness)

wade—*see* wad

waif (goods that are found but
   unclaimed) • waive (to renounce;
   to surrender) • wave (surge of
   water; movement of arms in
   greeting)

wail (cry of grief; high sound) • wale
   (welt; cloth ridge) • whale (large
   sea mammal)

waist (midpart of body) • waste
   (garbage; loss)

wait (to hold off; to postpone) •
   weight (measure of heaviness)

waive—*see* waif

waiver (voluntary surrender of right)
   • waver (to vacillate)

wale—*see* wail

walk in (to enter) • walk-in (place
   that can be entered directly; visit
   without appointment)

walkout (strike) • walk out (to strike;
   to leave)

walk up (to climb stairs or an incline,
   to approach) • walk-up (building
   without elevator)

wall (partition; barrier) • waul (to
   wail)

wand (thin rod) • want (desire; need)
   • wont (habit) • won't (will not)

wander (to ramble; to meander) •
   wonder (to speculate)

wangle (to get by means of trickery)
   • wrangle (to quarrel)

want—*see* wand

wanton (sexually promiscuous;
   reckless, heedless) • wonton (a
   dumpling)

war (armed conflict; attack) • wore
   (did wear, put on)

ward (person under guardian;
   political subdivision) • warred
   (made war on)

ware (merchandise) • wear (to be
   attired in) • where (location,
   place)

warm up (to prepare for
   performance; to reheat) • warm-
   up (preparation for performance or
   contest)

warn (to alert to danger; notice of
   pending legal threat or action) •
   worn (used)

warrantee (person receiving
   warranty) • warrantor (giver of
   warranty) • warranty (assurance
   of facts or performance as
   promised)

warrantor—*see* warrantee

warranty—*see* warrantee

warred—*see* ward

wary (cautious; alert to danger) •
   weary (tired)

washout (failure) • wash out (to
   eliminate as unsatisfactory)

wasp (insect) • WASP (White Anglo-
   Saxon Protestant)

WASP—*see* wasp

waste—*see* waist

watt (electrical unit) • what (word
   expressing inquiry about a thing)

waul—*see* wall

wave—*see* waif

waver—*see* waiver

wax (polishing substance; to grow stronger) • **whacks** (administers blows)

way (method, route) • **weigh** (to gauge heaviness)

weak (lacking strength) • **week** (seven days)

weal (welfare) • **we'll** (we will) • **wheel** (revolving circular frame)

wear—*see* ware

weary—*see* wary

weather (atmospheric conditions; to withstand) • **wether** (sheep) • **whether** (if)

weave (to combine elements; to make fabrics) • **we've** (we have)

wed (to marry) • **we'd** (we had, we would, we should) • **weed** (a plant; slang for *marijuana*)

we'd—*see* wed

weed—*see* wed

week—*see* weak

weigh—*see* way

weighed—*see* wad

weight—*see* wait

weir (low dam; fence) • **we're** (we are)

we'll—*see* weal

wen (cyst) • **when** (at what time; as soon as)

we're—*see* weir

wether—*see* weather

we've—*see* weave

whacks—*see* wax

whale—*see* wail

what—*see* watt

wheel—*see* weal

when—*see* wen

whence—*see* hence

where—*see* ware

whether—*see* weather

which (word used to refer to one of group or to prior word) • **witch** (sorceress; seducer)

while (during; short time) • **wile** (sly trickery)

whine (to complain) • **wine** (alcoholic beverage made from grapes)

whit (little bit) • **wit** (intelligence; humor)

whitewash (to cover up truth) • **white wash** (white laundry)

whole—*see* hole

wholly—*see* holey

whomsoever (to whichever person or party) • **whosesoever** (relating to whom) • **whosoever** (no matter who; any person)

whore—*see* hoar

who're—*see* hoar

whored—*see* hoard

whores—*see* hoars

who's (who is) • **whose** (belonging to whom)

whose—*see* who's

whosesoever—*see* whomsover

whosoever—*see* whomsoever

width (distance from side to side) • **with** (near; alongside; by means of)

wile—*see* while

windup (conclusion) • **wind up** (to conclude)

wine—*see* whine

wipeout (disaster) • **wipe out** (to erase; to abolish)

wit—*see* whit

witch—*see* which

with—*see* width

woman (female adult) • **women** (female adults)

women—*see* woman

wonder—*see* wander

wont—*see* wand

won't—*see* wand

wonton—*see* wanton

wood (substance of trees) • **would** (word expressing indefiniteness)

wore—*see* war

workout (strenuous exercise) • **work out** (to discharge a debt; to exercise; to resolve)

worn—*see* warn

worthless (of no value at all) • **worth less** (has less value than some other thing)

would—*see* wood

wrangle—*see* wangle

wrap—*see* rap

wreak—*see* reak

wreck—*see* reck

wrest—*see* rest

wright—*see* right

write down (to reduce in price; to disparage) • **write-down** (reduction of entered value of asset)

write in (to enter name of unofficial candidate on ballot; to enter words) • **write-in** (candidate not officially on ballot)

write off (to depreciate asset; to forget) • **write-off** (cancellation or reduction of asset's value)

write up (to bring charges) • **write-up** (increase in book value of asset)

wrote—*see* rote

Y

yoke (restraint; crushing burden) • **yolk** (yellow of egg)

yolk—*see* yoke

yore (olden days) • **your** (belonging to you) • **you're** (you are)

you—*see* ewe

your—*see* yore

you're—*see* yore

SECTION 3

Quick List of Correct Spellings

A

abaction
abandon
abandoned
abandonment
ab ante
ab antiquo
abash
abatable
   nuisance
abate
abatement
abator
abbacy
abbreviate**
abbreviation
abbroachment
abdicate
abdication
abditorium
abdomen
abduct
abearance
aberration
abet
abettor
ab extra
abeyance
abhor
abhorrent
abide
ability
ab initio
ab intra
abiogenesis
abject**
abjudication
abjuration
abjure**
ableism
abnegate
abnormal
abode
abolish
abolition
abominable
à bon droit

aboriginal**
ab origine**
abort
abortifacient
abortion
abortionist
abortive
above**
ab ovo**
abridge
abridgment
abroad
abrogate**
abrogation
abrupt
abscond
absconder
absence
absent
absentee**
absente reo
absentia**
absolute
absolutely
absolution
absolve
absorb**
absorption
absque
absque hoc
abstain
abstention
abstinence
abstract**
abstracter
abstraction
abstract of
   record
abstract of title
abstruse**
absurd
abuse
abuse of process
abusive
abusive tax
   shelter

abut
abutment
abuttals
abutter
academia**
academy**
accede**
accelerate
acceleration
acceleration
   clause
accent**
accentuate
accept**
acceptable
acceptance
acceptor
access**
accessibility
accessible**
accession
accessory
accessory before
   the fact
accessory during
   the fact
accident
accidental
accidentally
acclaim
acclamation**
acclimate
acclimation**
accommodate
accommodation
accompaniment
accompany
accomplice**
accomplish**
accord
accordance
accost
accouchement
account
accountability
accountable

accountant
accounting
accounts
   payable
accounts
   receivable
accretion
accrual
accrual method
accumulate
accumulation
accuracy
accurate
accusable
accusal
accusant
accusation
accusatorial
accusatory
accuse
accused
accuser
achieve
acidulous**
acknowledge
a coelo usque ad
   centrum
a contrario
acquaint
acquaintance
acquiesce
acquiescence
acquire
acquit
acquittal
acquitted
acre
acreage
acrimony
across
act
action**
actionable
activate**
actual
actuary

actuate**
actus
actus reus
acumen
ad**
adamant
adapt**
ad culpam
ad curiam
add**
addable**
ad damnum
addenda
addendum
addible
addict**
addicted
ad diem**
addition**
additive
additur**
address
addressee
adduce**
adeem**
ademption
adept**
adequate
adhere
adherent
adhesion
ad hoc
ad hominem
ad infinitum
ad interim
adipocere
adiratus
adit**
aditus**
adjacent
adjective law
adjoin**
adjoint**
adjourn**
adjournment**
adjudge
adjudicate
adjudication
adjudicator

adjudicatory
adjunct
adjuration
adjure**
adjust
adjustable
adjusted basis
adjusted gross
    income
adjuster**
adjustment
adjutant**
adjuvant**
adlegiare
ad lib
ad litem
administer
administration
administrative
administrative
    law
administrator
administratrix
admiralty law
admissibility
admissible
admission
admit
admittance
admonish
admonition
admonitory
ad nauseam
adolescence**
adolescent
adolescents**
adopt**
adoption
adoptive
ad prosequendam
ad quem
ad rectum
ad respondendum
ad seg
adsorb**
adult
adulterate
adulterer
adulteress**

adulterous**
adultery
ad valentiam
ad valorem
ad valorem tax
advance
advantage
adversarial
adversary
adversary
    proceeding
adverse**
advert**
advertise
advertisement
advice**
advise**
advisedly
advisement
advisory
advocacy
advocate
aegis**
affair**
affaire**
affect**
affection
affectus
affeer
affiant
affidavit
affiliate
affiliation
affinity
affirm
affirmation
affirmative
    action
affix
afflict
affluent**
afflux**
afforce
affranchise
affray
affreightment
affront
aforementioned
aforesaid

aforethought
a fortiori
afoul of
African-
    American
after
aftermath
afternoon
afterthought
afterward**
afterword**
against
against the law
agalma
age
ageism
ageist**
agency
agency bond
agenda
agent
ager**
ages**
agger**
aggrandize
aggravated
aggregate
aggregation
aggression**
aggressive
aggressor
aggrieved
aggrieved party
agio
agist**
agister**
agnate
agnomen
agnomination
agotage
agraphia
agree
agreeable
agreed
agreement
agribusiness
ague**
aid**
aid and abet

aide**
aides**
AIDS**
ailment**
air**
airport
airspace
airway
aisle**
ajournment**
akin
alacrity
alarm
albeit
alcohol
alcoholic
alea**
aleatory
alia**
alias
alibi
alien
alienable
alienage
alienate
alienation
alienee
alienism
alienist
alienor
alignment
alimenta**
alimentary**
alimony
aliquot
aliter**
aliunde
alive
allay**
allegation**
allege
alleged
allegiance
allegiare
Allen charge
allergenic**
allergic**
allergy
alleviate
alley**

alliance
alligation**
allision**
alliterate**
allocable
allocate
allocation**
allocator**
allocatur**
allocution**
allodial
allogeneic**
allograph
allonge
allot
allotment
allow an appeal
allowance
allowed**
alloy**
allude**
allusion**
alluvio maris
alluvion**
alluvium**
ally**
almaria
almost
alms**
alogical**
aloud**
altar**
alter**
alteration**
altercation**
alter ego
alternate
alternation**
alternative
    minimum tax
alternative
    pleading
although
altitude**
alumna**
alumnae**
alumni**
alumnus**
amalgam
amalgamation

amanuensis
amass
ambiguity
ambiguous
ambit
ambivalence
amblotic
ambulance
ambulance
    chaser
ambulate
ambulatory
ameliorate
amelioration
amenable
amenable to law
amend**
amended
    complaint
amended return
amendment
amends
amerce**
American
AMEX
ami
amiable**
amicable**
amicably
amicus curiae
amnesty
among
amoral**
amortizable
amortization
amortize
amotio**
amotion**
amount
amour**
amplification
amplify
amputate
amputation**
anabolic steroid
anachronism
anagraph
anal**
analog**
analogous

analogue**
analogy**
analyses**
analysis**
analyst**
analyze**
anaphrodisiac
anarchy
anathema
anatomical
ancestor
ancient
ancillary
androgenous**
androgynous**
anecdotal
anecdote**
anesthesia
anesthesiologist
aneurism
anew
angaria**
angary**
angel**
angiogram
angle**
angrily
angry**
anguish
animosity
animus
annalist**
annals**
anneal**
annex
annexation
anniversary
anno Domini
annotated
annotation
announced
announcement
annoyance
annual**
annuals**
annuitant
annuities
annuity
annul
annulled

annulment	a posteriori	arbitrable	ascribe
annunciate**	apostille**	arbitrage	ashore**
anomalous	apostle**	arbitrageur	asinine
anomaly	appanage	arbitrament	as is
anonymous	apparatus	arbitrary	asked
answer	apparel	arbitration	aspect
answerable	apparent	arbitrator	asperse
antagonize	apparently	arc**	aspersion
ante**	appeal	arch**	asphyxia
antecedence**	appear	archives	assail
antecedent	appearance	area**	assailable
antecedents**	appellant	areaway	assailant
antedate**	appellate	arere**	assailed
ante mortem	appellee	arguable	assault
ante natus	append	argue**	assay**
antenuptial	appendage	arguendo	assemble
ante status quo	appendant	arguing	assembly
anthracosis	appendices	argument	assemblyman
anthropometry	appendix	argumentative	assemblywoman
anti**	appertain	arise	assent**
antibiotic	applicable	ark**	assert
anticipation	applicant	armoire**	assertion
anticipatory	application	armor**	assess**
antidote**	apply	arms**	assessable**
antitakeover	appoint	arm's length	assessed
antithesis	appointee	arraign**	assessment
antitrust	appointment	arraignment	assessment of
annus mirabilis	apportion	arrange**	deficiency
anus**	apportionment	arrangement	assessor
anyone**	apposite**	arrant**	assets
any one**	appostille**	array**	asseveration
anything**	appraisal	arrearage	assiduous**
any thing**	appraise**	arrears**	assign
anytime**	apprehension	arrest	assignee
any time**	appressed**	arret**	assignment
anyway**	apprise**	arrival	assigns
any way**	apprize**	arrogate**	assiser or assisor
apace**	approach	arrogation	assist
a pais**	approbation	arson	assistance**
apanage	appropriate	article	assistant
apartment	appropriation	artifice	assistants**
aphagia**	approval	artificial	assize
aphasia**	approximate	artificial person	associate
aphorism	appurtenance	artistic**	association
apical	apraxia	ascend**	assume
apogean tides	a prendre	ascendance**	assumpsit
apogee	a priori	ascendants**	assumption
apologia**	apropos	ascendents**	assurance**
apologue**	a quo	ascent**	assure**
apology**	arbiter**	ascertain	astipulation

a teneris annis
a terme
atrocious
atrocious assault
attach**
attaché**
attachment
attack**
attacked
attain
attainder
attaint
attendance**
attendant
attendants**
attest
attestation
attestor
attic**
attitude**
attorn
attorney
attorney at law
attorney general

attorney in fact
attribute
attribution
attrition
atypical
au besoin
au contraire
auction**
audit**
audita querela
auditor**
auditory**
audits**
aught**
aural**
auricle**
auspices
autarchy**
autarky**
auteur**
authentic
authenticate
authenticity
author**

authoritative
authority
authorize
autistic**
automatic
automation**
automaton**
automobile
autonomous
autopsy
autoptic
    evidence
autoptic
    proference
autre**
auxiliary
avails
avatar
avenge
aver**
average
average daily
    volume
averment

averse**
aversion**
avert**
a vinculo
    matrimonii
avocation**
avoid**
avoidance
avouch
avow
avowal
avulsion
avuncular
await
award
awe**
aweful**
awesome
awful**
axial**
axiom
axle**
aye**

B

backdating
backing
backlog
back pay award
backup**
back up**
bail**
bailable
bail bond
bailee**
Bailey**
bailiff
bailment
bailor
bait**
bait and switch
balance
balance sheet
bale**
balk
ballistics

balloon payment
ballot
balm**
ban**
banc**
band**
bandit
bands**
bane**
banishment
bank**
banker
bank reconcili-
    ation
bankrupt
bankruptcy
banned**
banns**
bans**
bar
bar association

barbiturate
bare**
bargain
bargainor
barrator
barratrous
barratry
barred
barrier
barrister
barter
base**
based**
baseless
basement
bases**
basis**
bass**
bastard
baste**
bate**

bathetic**
bathos**
battel**
battered
battery
battle**
bauble
baud**
bawd**
bazaar**
bazar**
bear**
bearer
bearer bond
bear false
    witness
bear market
beat**
bed
been**
beeper

befall
befitting
befuddle
begat**
beget**
beggar
begin
beginning
  inventory
begotten
begrudge
beguile
behalf
behavior
behoof
behooves
belabor
beleaguer
belie**
belief**
believe**
bellicose
belligerent
bellow**
bellum
belly**
belong
below**
bench
benefactor
benefice
beneficial
beneficiary
benefit
benevolence
bequeath
bequest
bereft
berserk
berth**
beseech**
beside**
besides**
besiege**
besoin
bestiality
bestow
bestowal
bête noire
betrothed

better**
betterment
bettor**
beverage
beyond
biannual**
bias
bid and asked
bidder
bidding**
biding**
bielbrief
biennial**
biens**
bigamist
bigamy
Big Board
bigot**
bilan
bilateral
bilboes
billable
billed**
billings
billion**
Bill of Rights
bin**
binary
bind
binding
biodegradable
bioethics
biopsy
birth**
birth name
birthright
bis
bisexual
bit**
bite**
bizarre**
black bag**
black-bag**
blacklist
blackmail
blackout
blame
blameless
blame the victim
bland**

blank
blanket
blasé**
blasphemy
blatant
blaze**
bleat**
bleed**
blees
blend**
bleta
blew**
blight
blind trust
bloc**
block**
blockage
bloc voting
blood
bludgeon
blue**
blue chip**
blue-chip**
blue-chip stock
blue collar**
blue-collar**
blue law
blue-ribbon jury
blue-sky
blue sky laws
bluff
blumba
blunder
board**
boarder**
board of
  directors
boast**
boat
bodies**
bodily
body
body's**
bogus
boilary
boilerplate
boiler-room
bolder**
boldface
bomb**

bona**
bona fide**
bona fides**
bond
bondholder
bondman**
bondsman**
bone**
bonification
bonus
boodle
booked
bookie
bookkeeping
boondoggle
boost**
booty
bordello
border**
bored**
born**
borne**
borough**
borrow**
borrower
Borse**
bottom line
bought**
bouillon**
boulder**
bound
boundary
bounds
bourse**
Bourse**
box
boxes
boy**
boycott
bracket
brain
brake**
Brandeis brief
brands**
brans**
brave**
breach**
bread**
breadth**
break**

breakage
breakdown**
break down**
break even**
break-even**
breaking and
   entering
break the law
breath**
breathalyzer
breathe**
bred**
breech**
brethren
breve**
brevet
brevia
breviate**
brevity
brews**
bribe
bribery
bridal**

bridle**
brief**
brilliant
broach**
broadcast
brocage**
brochure
broken
broker
brokerage**
brooch**
brood**
brother
brought**
brows**
browse**
bruise**
brutalize
brutum fulmen
budget
buffer
buggery
build**

building
buildup**
build up**
bulk
bull
bullet
bulletin
bullion**
bunco
bundle
buoy**
burden
bureau**
bureaucracy
burgage
burgess
burglar
burglary
burial
burking
burnout**
burn out**
burro**

burrochium
burrow**
burry**
bursa**
bursar**
bury**
bushel
business
but**
butt**
buttals
butte**
butted
buttress
buy**
buyer
buy off
by**
bye**
by-laws
byproduct
bystander
byte**

C

cabal**
cabinet
cable**
cabotage
cache**
cachet**
cadaver
cadere
cadet**
cadit**
caduca
caducary
caeterorum
cahoots
cajole
calamity
calcify
calculate
calendar**
calender**
calibrate**

call**
callable
calling
callous**
callus**
calm**
calumnia
calumniator
calumny
calvary**
Calvary**
cam**
camber
camera
cameral
camouflage
campaign
campanarium
campanile
canard
cancel

canceled
cancellation
cancelled
cancer**
candor
canker**
cannabis
cannon**
canon**
canonical
cant**
can't**
cantel or cantle
cantred
canvas**
canvass**
canyon**
capability
capable
capacity
capax

caper**
capias
capiatur pro fine
capillary
capita**
capital**
capital crime
capital gain
capitalization
capitation**
capitol**
Capitol**
Capitol Hill
capitula
capper**
capricious
capstone
captation**
caption**
caput**
carat**

carcanum
carcatus
carcinogen
carcinoma
card**
cardiac
cardiogram
cardiology
cardiopulmonary
cardiovascular
career**
careless
caret**
cargo
caries**
carnal**
carnaliter**
carnality**
carousal**
carousel**
carpe diem
carrier**
carries**
carryback**
carry back**
carryforward**
carry forward**
carryover**
carry over**
cart**
carta**
carte blanche**
cartel
carucate
case
case law
caseload
cas fortuit
cash**
cash disburse-
    ment
cashier
cassare
cast**
caste**
casual**
casualties
casualty **
casuistry
casus

cataclasm**
cataclysm**
catals
catastrophe
catechism**
categorical
catheter
catholic**
Catholic**
CAT scan
caucus
caul**
causa**
causal**
causality**
cause**
cause list
cause of action
causes célèbres
causidicus
caution
cavalry**
cave in**
cave-in**
caveat
caveator
cavere
cease**
cease and desist
cede**
ceiling**
celebrate**
celibate**
cell**
cellar**
cemetery
cenegild
censitaire
censive
censor**
censorship
censure**
census**
cent**
cental
centena
cents**
ceorl
cepi
cepit

cera
cereal**
cerebrate**
certain
certifiable
certificate
certified
certified check
certified public
    accountant
certiorari
cessare
cessation**
cession**
cessment
cestui
cestuy
chacer**
chain
chair
chairman
chairperson
chairwoman
challenge
chamber
chamfer
chamotte
champertor
champerty
chance**
chancellor
chancer**
chancery**
chancre**
channel
chants**
chapter
Chapter 11
character
characterize
character
    witness
charge
chargeable
charge-off
charitable
charlatan
charnel**
charred**
chart**

charta**
charter**
chased**
chaser**
chaste**
chastise
chastity
chattel
cheat
check
checkup**
check up**
chef**
chemical
chevage
chews**
Chicana
chicanery
Chicano
chief**
chief executive
chilling
chilling effect
chiropodist
choate lien
choler**
cholera**
choose**
chose**
christen**
Christian**
chromosome
chronic**
chronical**
chronicle**
church
churches
churn
chute**
cicatrix
cingular**
cipher
circa
circuit
circuit court
circuitous
circular
circumscribe
circumspect
circumstances

191

circumstantial
circumstantial
  evidence
circumvention
cirrhosis
cista
citation
cite**
citizen
city
civic
civil
civilian
civilis
civil liability
civil liberties
claim
claimant
clan**
clannish
class
clause**
clausum
claws**
clean
clear
clearance
clearinghouse
clemency
clench**
clerk
clew**
click**
client
clientela
clinch**
clinic**
clink**
clique**
cloak**
clock**
cloere
clone**
close**
closed-end
close up**
close-up**
closing
closure**

clothes**
cloture**
cloud of
  suspicion
cloud on title
clown**
clue**
coadjutor
coalition
coarse**
co-assignee
cocaine
co-conspirator
code**
Code, the**
codex
codicil
codicillary
codification
codify
coed**
coemption
coequal
coerce
coercion
coexecutor
coexist
coffer
cognatio**
cognation**
cognovit
cohabit
co-heir
coherence
coincidence
coinsurance
coitus
cojudices
colds**
colibertus
coliseum**
collaboration
collage**
collapsible
collar**
collared**
collateral
collateral trust
collatio**

collation**
collect
collective
college**
collide
collision
collocate
collusion
colne
colonel**
color**
colored**
Colosseum**
colpices
colts**
column
coma**
combarones
combination
combustible
combustio
comedy**
comes and
  defends
comet**
Comex
comfort
comitas**
comitatus
comites**
comitissa
comitiva
comity**
comma**
command**
commence
commend**
commendation
commensurate
comment**
commerce
commercial
commingle
commingling of
  funds
comminute
commission
commit**
commitment

committal
committee**
committee of the
  whole
committitur
commodatum
commodities
commodity
common**
commonalty
common law
common stock
commorant
commorientes
commorth
commotion
commune**
communibus
  annis
communication
communis**
communist**
communitas
  regni Angliae
community
community
  property
commutate
commutation
comorth
compact
company
comparative
compatible
compel
compendium
compensable
compensate
compensation
compensatory
comperuit ad
  diem
competent
competent party
competition
compilation
complacence**
complainant
complaint

complaisance**
complement**
complete
compliance
complicity
compliment**
comply
composed**
composite**
composition
compos mentis
compos sui
compost**
compound
comprehensive
comprise
compromise
comptroller**
compulsa
compulsion
compulsory
compunction
compurgation
compurgator
computation
computer
computus
concave**
concealed
concealment
concede**
conceit**
conception
concern
concert
concessi
concession
concessit solvere
concessum
concessus**
conciliabulum
conciliation
concilium
conclave**
conclude
conclusive
concoct
concomitant
concord**

concretion
concubeant
concur**
concurrence
concurrent
  jurisdiction
concurrent
  powers
concurrent
  sentences
concurso
concussion
condemn**
condemnatory
condictio**
condign
conditio**
condition**
conditional
condom**
condominium
condonation
condone
conduce
conduct
confabulate
conference
conference
  committee
conferring
confess**
confessio**
confession**
confesso**
confessor**
confidant**
confident**
confidential
configuration
confinement
confirm
confirmatio**
confirmation**
confirmed
confiscate
confiscator
conflict
conflict of
  interest

conformation**
conformed
confrairie
confreres
confrontation
confute
congeable
congenital
conglomerate
congratulate
congregate
congress
Congress
congressman
congresswoman
congruous
conjectio
conjecture
conjoints
conjugal
conjugal rights
conjunction
conjuratio
connate
connect
connivance
connubial
conquer**
conquered**
consanguineous
consanguinity
conscience
conscientious
conscious
consecutive
consensual
consensus**
consensus ad
  idem
consent
consequence
consequential
  damages
conservator
consider
considerable
consideration
consideratur
consign**

consignee**
consignment
consilium
consist
consistory
consolidate
consonant
consortium
conspiracy
constant**
constat**
constate**
constitutional
constraint
construct
construction
constructive
construe
constuprate
consuetudines
consuetudo
consul**
consuls general
consultation
consumer
consummate
contagious
contaminated
contango
contemn**
contemner or
  contemnor
contemplate
contempt**
contentious
contents
conterminous
contest**
context**
contiguous
contingency
contingent
contingent fee
continual**
continually
continuance**
continuando
continuing**
continuous**

193

continuum**
contra
contraband
contract
contractor
contradict
contrafactio
contraligatio
contramandatio
contramandatum
contraplacitum
contraposition
contrariwise
contrary
contravene
contrectatio
contribute
contributory
    negligence
contrite
contrivance
control
controlled
    substance
controller**
controvert
contumacy
contumax
contumely
contusion
conusant
convene
convenient
convention
converge
conversant
conversation
conversion
convertible
convey**
conveyance
convict
convivium
convoluted
convoy**
co-obligor
cook the
    evidence
cooler**
cooling-off

coop**
co-op**
cooperate
coopertio
coopertus
copartner
copesmate
coppa
coprincipal
coprolalia
copula
copulate
copy
copyright
coram judice
coram nobis
core**
co-respondent**
corner**
corodio habendo
corollary
coroner**
corporal**
corporate
corporation
corporeal**
corps**
corpse**
corpus**
corpus delicti
corpus juris
corral
correct
correctional
correlative
correspondence**
correspondent**
correspondents**
corroborate
corrupt
corselet
corse-present
cortis
Cosa Nostra
cosenage
cosign**
cosignatory
cosinage
cosine**
cost accounting

costs
costume**
cotarius
cotenancy
coterminous
cotsetus
cotton
couchant
council**
councilman
councilor**
councilwoman
counsel**
counsellor**
counselor**
counselor-at-law
counterclaim
counterfeit
countermand
counteroffer
counterplea
countersign
countervail
counts
county
coup**
coup d'état
coupe**
coupon
courier**
course**
court
courtesy**
cousin**
covenant
covenantor
covered**
covert**
cover up**
cover-up**
covet**
coward**
cowered**
cozen**
craft**
cranage
cranium
crap**
crass**
crater**

craven
crazy
create
creator**
Creator**
creature**
credence
credentials
credibility
credible**
credit
creditable**
creditor
credo**
creed**
creep**
cremate
crepusculum
crewel**
crews**
cri de pais
crier
crime
crimen
criminal
criminality
criminal liability
criminatory
criminology
crises**
crisis**
criterion
critic**
criticism
criticize
critique**
croate**
crock**
croiteir
crony
crook**
crooked
cross-claim
cross-complaint
cross-examina-
    tion
cross interroga-
    tory
crotch**
crouch**

crown
cruce signati
cruel**
cruelty
cruise**
crutch**
cry de pais
crypta
cuckold
cue**
cui bono
cul de sac
culminate
culpa
culpability
culpable
culprit

cultivate
cults**
cum copula
cum onere
cum testamento
   annexo
cumulative
cunnilingus
curative
curator
curatrix
curb
cure**
cure all**
cure-all**
curia**
curie**

currency
current assets
current
   liabilities
current ratio
currier**
currit quatuor
   pedibus
curse**
curser**
cursor**
cursory**
curtail
curtain
curtesy**
curtillium
curtis

CUSIP number
custodial
custodian
custody
custom**
customary
custom duties
custos
custuma
cutaneous
cyclical
cymbol**
cynebote**
cynical
cy-pres
cyst

D

daily**
dairy**
dais**
dalliance
dally**
dam**
damage
damages
dame**
damn**
Dane**
dapifer
darrein
data
datum
daughter
daughters-in-law
days**
daze**
dead**
deadbeat**
dead beat**
deadline
deadlock
deadly weapon
deaf
deal
dean**

death
de banco
debasing
debatable
debauch**
de bene esse
debenture
debet**
de biens le mort
debilitate
debit**
debitor
debitum
de bonis non
   administratis
de bono et malo
debouch**
debriefing
debt**
debt ceiling
debtor
debt service
decadent**
decanatus
decease**
deceased
decedent**
deceit

deceive
decenna
decent**
decentralization
deception
deceptive
decide
decimal
decision
declarant
declaration
declaratory
declare
declination
decline
decomposed
de corpore
   comitatus
decorum
decoy
decrease
decree**
decree nisi
decretal
decriminalize
decry
de cursu
dedi

dedicate
de die in diem
dedition
de dolo malo
deduce
deductible
deduction
deed**
deem
deface
de facto
defalcate
defalcation
defalcator
defamation
defaming
default
default-
   judgment
defeasance
defeasible
defeat
defect
defective
defend
defenestration
defense
defensible

defenso
defer**
deference**
deferential**
deferral
deferred
deferring
defiance
deficiency
deficient
deficit
defile
define
definite**
definitio
definitive**
deflation
deflect
defloration
deformity
defraud
defray
defunct
defuse**
degenerate
degrade
degree**
dehors
dehydrate
deify
deign**
de incremento
déjà vu
de jure
de latere
delay
del credere
delegate
delegated
  powers
delete
deleterious
deliberate
deliberations
delict
delictum
delimit
delinquency
delirious
delivery

delude**
delusion
delusory
de malo
demand
demarcation
demeanor
dementia
  praecox
demesne**
demi
de minimis
demise**
demisi**
democracy
demolish
demonstrable
demonstrative
demote**
demotion
demur**
demure**
demurrage
demurrer
denarii
de natura
  brevium
dene**
deniable
denial
denigrate
denomination
denote**
denounce
de novo
dense**
density
dents**
denumeration
denunciation
denunciatory
deny
department
dependable
dependance**
dependence**
dependent
dependents**
depict
deplete

depletion
deponent
deportation
depose**
deposit
depositary**
deposition**
depositor**
depository**
depot
depots**
depraved
deprecate**
depreciate**
depreciation
depredation
deprive
de quo
deraign
deregulate
deregulation
derelict
de rien culpable
de rigueur
derivative
derivative tort
derogation
descend**
descendant
descent**
describe
description
desecrate
desegregate
desert
desertion
desiccate
desideratum
design
designate
designation
desirable
desire
desist
de son tort
despair
desperate**
desperation
despise
despoil

despondent
despotism
destitute
destroy
desuetude
detail
detain
detection
detention
deter**
deteriorate
determination
deterrence
detinue
detour**
detoxify
detract
detriment
detritus
deuces**
de una parte
deus ex machina
devastation
develop
devest**
deviate
device**
devious
devise**
devisee**
deviser**
devisor**
devolution
devolve
devote
devy
dew
diagnoses**
diagnosis**
diagram**
dialectal**
dialectical**
dialysis
diaphragm**
diary**
dica
dichotomy
dicta
dictate**
dictum

die**
dies**
dies non
diet**
Diet**
dieta**
difference**
different
differentia**
differential**
differentiate
difficult
difforciare
diffuse**
digest**
digesta**
Digests**
dignify
digression
diktat**
dilapidation
dilate**
dilatory
dilemma
diligence
dilute**
dilution
dime**
dimension
diminished
   capacity
diminution
dimissory
dinar**
dinner**
diocese
diplomat**
diplomate**
dipsomania
direct
direction
directive
director
directory
disability
disable
disabuse
disadvantaged
disaffect
disaffirm

disaffirmance
disagree
disallow
disappear
disappoint
disapprobation
disapprove**
disaster
disastrous
disavow
disbar
disbarment
disburse**
discern
discharge
disciplinary
disclaimer
disclose
disclosure
discomfit**
discomfort**
disconcert
discontinuance
discontinuous
discord
discount
discourage
discovert
discovery
discredit
discreet**
discrepancy
discrete**
discretion
discretionary
discriminate
discrimination
discriminator
disculpate
disculpation
discussion
disdain
disease**
disencumber
disenfranchise
disentailment
disfavor
disfigure
disfranchise
disgrace

disgruntled
disguise
disheritor
dishonest
dishonor
disillusion**
disincentive
disinclination
disingenuous
disinherison
disinherit
disinheritance
disinter**
disinterested
disintermediation
disinvestment
disjointed
disjunctive
   allegation
dislocation
disloyal
dismember
dismes**
dismiss
dismissal
disobedience
disoblige
disorderly
disorderly
   conduct
disparagatio**
disparage**
disparate**
disparity
dispassionate
dispatch
dispel
dispensation
dispense
disperse**
displace
display
dispono
disposable
dispose
disposition**
dispossess
disproof
disproportionate
disprove**

disputable
dispute
disqualification
disrate
disregard
disreputable
disrepute
disrespect
disruptive
dissatisfaction
disseise**
disseisin
disseisor
dissemble
disseminate
dissension
dissent**
dissenting
dissenting
   opinion
dissidence**
dissident
dissidents**
dissignare
dissipate
dissociate
dissolute
dissolution**
dissolve
dissuade
distance
distill
distinct
distinguish
distort
distrain
distrainee
distrainment
distraint
distress
distribute
distributive
district
distringere
disturb
disturbance
diverge
divers**
diverse**
diversification

diversion	domiciled	dowry	duel**
diversity	dominant	doze**	due process
divert	dominicum	draconian	dues
dives**	dominion	draco regis	dull**
divest**	dominus litis	draff**	duller**
divestiture	domus	draft**	dully**
divestment	donatarius	drain	duly**
divide	donatio**	dramatic	dum**
dividend	donation**	drastic	dumb**
divisible	donative	drawee	dummodo
division	donator	drawer	dummy
divisive	done**	drayage	dumping
divisor**	donee**	dredge	dun**
divorce**	donis	dreit-dreit	dunnage
divorcé**	donor	drilling	dunning
divorcée**	doom	drive in**	duodecima
divulge	doomsday pill	drive-in**	manus
do**	door**	driven**	duodenum
doable**	dormant	driver	duplex
docile	dorsum	droit	duplicate
docket	dosage	droop**	duplicitous
doctor	dose**	drop**	duplicity
doctrinal	dossier	drop off**	durable
doctrine	dotage	drop-off**	durance
document	dotal	dropout**	durante
documentary	dotard	drop out**	duration
doer**	dotation	drought**	duress
does**	double**	drown	Durham rule
doesn't	double jeopardy	drug	during
dogma	double time**	druggist	duties
dole**	double-time**	drunkard	duty
doll**	doubt	dual**	dye**
dollar**	doun**	dubious	dyeing**
dolor**	dour**	dubitable	dyes**
dolus	dovetail	dubitante	dying**
domain**	Dow, the	duces tecum**	dying declara-
domestic	dowable	due**	tion
relations	dower**	due care	dysentery**
domicile	dowment	due date	dyspepsia

E

each	earned income	earnings	earthy**
earmark	credit	earnings per	ease
earn**	earnest	share	easement
earned	earnest money	earthly**	easily

eavesdrop	elaborate	embryo	endangerment
ebb	elapse**	embryos	endeavor
ebullience	elder**	emend**	en demeure
eccentricity	elected	emenda	endocarditis
ecchymosis	election	emerge	endorse**
ecclesiastic	elective	emergency	endorsee**
echelon	electrocardiograph	emersed**	endorsement
echolalia	electrocution	emetic	endorser**
éclat	electroenceph-	emigrant**	endow
ecology	alogram	emigrate**	endurance
economic**	electronic	eminent**	enemy
economical**	eleemosynary	eminent domain	energy
economize	elegit	emissary	enervate**
e contra	elegy**	emission	enfait
ecumenical	elementary**	emit**	enfeoff
edema	elicit**	emollient**	enforce
edge	eligible	emolument**	enforceable
edible**	eliminate	emotion**	enfranchise
edict**	elision**	empanel	engage
edition**	elisor jury	empathize**	engender
editor**	elite	emphases**	engine
editus	ellipses**	emphasis**	engineer
educational	elongation**	emphysema	en gros**
educe**	elopement	empire**	enhanced
e'er**	eloquence	empirical	enigma
efface	elsewhere	emplead	enitia pars
effect**	elucidate	employ	enjoin
effective	elude**	emporium	enlarge
effectuate	elusion**	empower	en masse
efficacious	elusive**	emptor	enmity
efficiency	elusory**	empty	enormity
efficient	elute**	emulate	enrage
effluent**	eluvium**	enable**	enrich
efflux**	emanate	enabling clause	enrichment
effraction	emasculate	enact	enroll
eggregious	embargo	enactment	enrollment
egoism**	embark	enate	en route
egotism**	embarrass	enatic	ensconce
egress	embassage	en banc	enseal
egression**	embassy	en bloc	ens legis
eisne	embellish	enbrever	ensue
either**	embezzle	enceinte	ensure**
ejaculate	embezzlement	encephalogram	entail
eject	embodiment	enclose	entendment
ejection**	embolism	encourage	enter
ejectione**	embrace	encroach	enterceur
ejectment	embraceor or	encumber	enterprise
ejectum	embracer	encumbrance	entertainment
ejuration	embracery	endanger	entice

entire
entirety
entitle
entitlement
entity
entrapment
entreaty
entrebat
entrepôt
entrepreneur
entrust
entry
entry of
   judgment
enumerated
enumerated
   powers
enunciate**
envelop**
envelope**
en vie
environment
environs
envision
envoy
eo
ephemeral
epicene
epidemic
epidural
epilepsy
epiphysis
episode
epistolary
epitaph
epitome
epoch
equable**
equal
equality
equalize
equanimity
equatable**
equation
equilibrium
equip
equitable**
equity
equivalent
equivocal

equivocate
era**
erasable**
erasure
erect
ergo**
ergot**
eristic
erode
erotic**
err**
errand**
errant**
errata
erratic**
erratum
erroneous
error**
erupt
eruption**
escalator
escalator clause
escape
escapee
escheat
escheator
escrow
esnecy
esoteric**
espousals
esquire
essartum
essay**
essence
essential
essoin
establish
estate
estate tax
estimate
estimated tax
estop
estoppage
estoppel
estover
estrange
estray
estreat
estrepe
estrepement

estuary
et al.
et alii è contra
et alius
et allocatur
et cetera
eternal
ether**
ethic**
ethical
ethics
ethnic**
ethos
etiology
et non
et seq.**
et sic**
et uxor
eugenics
eulogy**
eunuch**
euphemism**
euphuism**
Eurocurrency
Eurodollars
euthanasia
evade
evaluate
evasio**
evasion**
evasive
event
eventual
eversion**
evert**
every
everyday**
every day**
everyone**
every one**
everything**
every thing**
evict
eviction
evidence
evidentiary
evil
evince
eviscerate
evocation**

evoke
evolution
evolved
ewage
ewe**
exacerbate
exaggerate
ex altera parte
examen**
examination
examine**
examinee
examiner
example
ex bonis
ex cathedra
ex causa
excavation
exceed**
excellence
except**
exceptio**
exception**
exceptionable**
exceptional**
excerpt**
excess**
excesses
exchange
exchequer
excisable
excise
excise tax
exclamation
exclude
exclusion
exclusionary
   rule
exclusive
ex colore
excommunication
excrement
excretion
exculpate
exculpation
exculpatory
ex curia
excusable
excusatory
excuse

ex delicto
ex dividend
ex dolo malo
execrate
execute
execution
executive
executor
executorship
executory
executress
executrices
executrix
exemplar
exemplification
exemplify
exempt
exemption
exercise**
ex facto
ex gratia
exhaustion
exhibit
exhibited
exhibition
exhort
exhumation
exhume
ex hypothesi
exigence
exigible
exile**

existence
exit
ex locato
ex maleficio
ex mora
ex officio
exonerate
exorbitant
exorcise**
exoteric**
exotic**
expansive**
ex parte
expatriation
expectancy
expedient
expediment
expeditation
expedite
expeditious
expel
expellee
expend
expendable
expendere
expenditure
expense
expenses
expensive**
experience
experiment
expert

expertise
expiration
expiration date
expire**
expiry**
explanation
expletive
expletory
explicate
explicit
exploitation
exploration
explosion
exponential
export
expose**
exposé**
exposition
ex post facto
expostulate
exposure
express
expressly
expromissio
expromissor
expropriation
ex proprio
expulsion
expunction
expunge
expurgation
ex relatione

ex rigore juris
extant**
extend**
extent**
extenuate
exterior
external
exterritorial**
exterritoriality**
extinguish
extinguishment
extortion
extortive
extradition
extraterrito-
    riality**
extravagant
extreme
extremis
extremity
extricate
extrinsic
exulare
ex una parte
ex utraque
    parte
ex voluntate
eye**
eyed**
eyewitness

F

fabricate
face
faces**
facet**
facial**
faciendo
facile**
facilitate
facility
facing
facsimile
fact**
facta**
faction**

factious**
factitious**
facto**
factorize
factory
facts**
factum
facultative
faculties
faculty
faggot
fail
failure
failure to indict

fain**
fair**
fair comment
fair hearing
fairly
fairness
fairness doctrine
fair use
fait**
faith
faitours
faker
falcare
fallacious

fallacy
fallback
fallible
Fallopian tube
fallout**
fall out**
fallow**
fallum
falsare
false
false arrest
falsehood
false imprison-
    ment

falsely
false pretense
falsification
falsify
falsus
fama
famacide
familia**
familiar**
family
fanatic
fanciful
Fannie Mae
fantasy
fardel
fare**
farleu
farmer
faro
farrier
farther**
fas**
fascinate
fascist
fast**
fastidious
fatal**
fatality
fate**
fated**
father**
fathers-in-law
fatuitas**
fatum
fatuous**
fatuus**
faucet**
fault
fautor
faux**
favor
favorable
favorite
fax**
faze**
fealty
fear
fearful
feasance**
feasant**

feasibility
feasible
feasor
feat**
featherbedding
feature
feces**
feckless
Fed, the
federal
Federal Court of
    Claims
Federal Reserve
federation
fee
fees
fee simple
feet**
feign**
felagus
fellatio
fellation
fellow**
felo de se
felon
felonice**
felonies**
felonious**
feloniously
felony
felony murder
female
feme
feme covert
feme sole
femicide
feminine
femme
fenatio
fence
fenestration
feod
feodal
feodary
feoffee**
feoffer or
    feoffor**
ferae**
feria**
ferment**

fermory
ferrator
ferret
ferrum
fertility
fertilize
fester
festum
fetal**
fête**
fêted**
feticide
fetid**
fetus
feud
feudal
feudum
fiancé**
fiancée**
fiasco
fiascoes or
    fiascos
fiat**
fiaunt
FICA
fiche**
fiction
fictitious**
fidelitas
fidelity
fides
fiducial
fiduciary
fief
field
fiend**
fight
fighting words
figment
figurehead
figures
filacer
filching
file**
filial
filibuster
filing**
Filipina**
Filipino**
filius

filling**
filum**
finagle
final
finance**
financial
financier
find**
finder's fee
finding
fine
fined**
finem facere
fineness**
finesse**
finger
finis**
finish**
finitude
fire
firearm
firebug
fireproof
firkin
firm
firma
firmly
first
first-degree
first instance
fisc
fiscal**
fish**
fisher**
fissure**
fists**
fit
fits**
fix
fixed costs
fixture
flaccid
flack
flaco
flag
flagitious
flagrans**
flagrant**
flagrante**
flagrante delicto

flair**
flam
flap**
flare**
flat
fleece**
flees**
flew**
flexible
flextime
flight
flimflam
float
float an issue
floating
floating-rate
flogging
floor broker
flop**
floppy disk
flotage
flounder**
flourish
flu**
fluctuate
flue**
flume
flummery
flummox
fluvius
flux
fluxus
flyma
foal
focus
fodder
foe**
foeneration
folgere
folio
follicle
follow**
follow-up
folly
foment**
fondle
fondling**
fool**
for**
forbade

forbear**
forbearance
force
forcible
forcible entry
fore**
forebear**
foreboding
forecast
fore-cited
foreclose
foreclosure
forego**
foregone
foreign
foreknowledge
foreman
forensic
   chemistry
forensic
   medicine
forequoted
foresee
foreseeability
foreseeable
foreseen
foresight
forestall
forestarius
forethought
forewarned
foreword**
forfeit
forfeitable
forfeiter
forfeiture
forgave
forge
forgery
forget
forgive
forgo**
forgone
forgot
forgotten
foris
forisfactura
forjurer
forma**
formal**

formality
formalize
formally**
formata brevia
formerly**
formidable
formula**
formulary**
formulate
fornicate
forswear
fort**
forte**
forfeiture
forth**
fortior**
fortiori**
fortuit
fortuitous
forty**
forum
forward**
fossatum
fosse
foster
fought**
foul**
foundation
founder**
foundling**
four**
Fourteenth
   Amendment
fourth**
Fourth
   Amendment
fowl**
foy
fractio
fraction**
fractional
fractious
fracture
fragmenta
fragrant**
frame-up
framework
franc**
franchise
franchise tax

franchisee
francus
frank**
fraternal
fratriage
fratricide
fraud**
fraudulent
   conveyance
fraught**
frays**
freak**
frectum
Freddie Mac
freehold
freelance
frees**
freeze**
freeze-out
freight**
freighter
freneticus
freoling
frequency
frequent
fresca
freshet
fretum
friable
friction
friend**
fright**
fringe
frivolous
frontage
frontager
front-end
froward**
frozen
frozen assets
fructus
fruit
fruition
fuel**
fugacious
fugam fecit
fugator
fugitation
fugitive
full**

full faith and
   credit
fulminate
function
fund
fundamental
fundamus
fundator

funeral**
funereal**
fungible
fungous**
fungus**
furandi animus
furiosus
furious

furnish
furor brevis
further**
furtherance
furthermore
furtive
furtum
fuse**

fuss**
fustis
future
futures
futures contract
futuri
fuze**
fuzz**

G

gabble**
gabel**
gadfly
gaff**
gaffe**
gafol
gag
gage**
gain
gainage
gainful
gait**
galling
gallon
gallows
galvanize
gambit
gamble**
gambol**
gaming
gamut
gap**
gape**
gaps**
garage
gardein
garene
garnish**
garnishee**
garnishment
garotte**
garret**
garrotte**
gas
gasps**
gassed**
gast**

gate**
gauge**
gauntlet
gavel
gays**
gaze**
geld**
gemot
gender
gender-neutral
genealogy
genera**
general**
general
   application
generality
generalize
generally
generation
generic
generous
gene splicing
genetic
genital**
genitalia
genitals
genius**
genocide
genre
gens**
genteel**
gentes**
gentile**
gentiles
gentle**
gentlemen**
gentle men**

gentry
gents**
genuine
genus**
gerens
geriatrics
german**
German**
germane**
germanus
gerrymander
gersume
gestate
gestation
gestum
getaway
get together**
get-together**
ghastly**
ghostly**
gibbet
gibe**
gigabyte
gild**
gilt**
gilt-edged
gimmick
girante
girth
gisement
gist
giveaway**
glamour stock
glance**
glands**
glans**
gleam**

glean**
gleba
glimmer
glom**
gloom**
glos**
gloss**
glum**
gnaw**
gobbledygook
godfather
going
golf**
gonorrhea
goon
gorilla**
govern
government
governor
grace
grade**
graduate
gradus
graffiti**
graffito**
graft**
grain
gram
grandfather
grandfather
   clause
grandjuror
grand jury
grandstand
grange
grangearius
grantee

grantor
graphed**
graphite**
grate**
gratification
gratis
gratis dictum
gratuitous
gratuity
gravamen
grave**
gravis
grayed**
graymail
great**
greenback
greenmail
gremium
gressume

greve**
grievance
grieve**
grievous
griff
grill**
grille**
grip**
gripe**
griper**
grippe**
gripper**
groan**
grocer**
groin**
groove**
grope**
gross**
grossement

grosser**
ground
groundless
groundwork
group**
grouse**
grove**
grown**
growth
grudge
gruesome
guarantee
guarantor
guaranty
guardian
guerpi
guerrilla**
guess
guessed**

guest**
Guiana**
guidance
guidelines
guild**
guile
guilt**
guilty
guinea**
Guinea**
guise**
gulf**
gunpoint
Guyana**
guys**
gynarchy
gynecologist

H

habeas corpus
habendum
habentes
    homines
habilis
habilitate
habit
habitancy
habitual
hable
hack**
haec**
haeres
hafne
haggle
hail**
hairy**
hale**
half**
half-truth
hall**
hallage
hallow**
hallucinate
hallucinogenic
halo**

halve**
halves**
handcuffs
handgun
handicapped
handiwork
handsale**
handsel**
handshake
handwriting
handyman**
handy man**
hang up**
hang-up**
hap
happenstance
harass
harassment
harbinger
harbor
hard**
hardship
harmful
harmless
harmony
harry**

hart**
hatch
haugh
haul**
haunch**
hauteur**
have**
haven**
havoc
hay-bote
hays**
hazard
haze**
head**
headland
headless**
headnote
headway
heal**
healer
health
healthy
hear**
heard**
hearing
hearsay

hearsay rule
heart**
hearth**
heat
heath**
heaven**
heavy-handed
hectare
he'd**
hedge
hedge-bote
hedging
heed**
heedless**
heel**
hegemony
heinous**
heir**
heir apparent
heiress
heirloom
heirlooms
hell**
he'll**
hematology
hematoma

hemiplegia	hierarchy	holographic will	housebreaking
hemophiliac	high**	holy**	householder
hence**	higher**	holy day**	housekeeper
henceforth	highest	homage	housing
henchman	high-flier	homagium	hovel
heptarchy	high grade**	home**	however**
herald	high-grade**	homicide	how ever**
herd**	high risk	homo	hubby**
here**	highway	homogeneous**	huckster
hereafter	higler	homogenous**	hue**
hereby	hijack	homologous	hui**
hereditaments	him**	homosexual	huis**
hereditary	Hindi**	hone**	human**
heredity	hindrance	honeste vivere	humane**
herein	Hindu**	honestus	humerus**
hereinafter	hire**	honesty	humorous**
hereinbefore	his	honeymoon	hunch**
hereinto	historical**	honor	hundred
hereof	history	honorable	hunter**
heresy	hitherto	honorary	hurdle**
hereto	hoar**	hooky**	hurricane
heretofore	hoard**	hooliganism	hurt
hereunto	hoarding	hopefully	hurtle**
hereupon	hoars**	hopeless	hurts**
herewith	hoarse**	hora	husband
heritable	hobby**	horde**	hybrid
hermeneutics	hoc**	horizontal	hygiene
hermetic	hock**	horrible	hymn**
hernia	hockey**	hors**	hyperbola**
heroin**	hold**	horse**	hyperbole**
heroine**	holder	hospitable**	hypercritical**
hers	holdup**	hospital**	hypnotic
hertz**	hold up**	hospitia	hypocrisy
herus	hole**	hostage	hypocritical**
hesitate	holed**	hostel**	hypostasis
heterosexual	holed up**	hostile**	hypotheca
hew**	holey**	hostile takeover	hypothecary
hiatus	holiday**	hostile witness	hypothecate
hidalgo	hollow**	hotchpot	hypothesis
hidden	holly**	hour**	hypothetical
hide**	holm**	house	hysterectomy
hie**	holocaust	houseboat**	hysteria
hied**	holograph	house-bote**	hysterical**

I

I**	id**	idea**	idem**
ibid.	ID**	ideal**	identic
ibidem	I'd**	idée fixe	identical

identifiable	illustrate	impecunious	imprest**
identify	image	impede	impretiabilis
ideo	imbecile	impediens	imprimatur
ideology	imbibe	impediments	imprimis
id est	imbrue**	impel	imprison
idiom	imbue**	impending	imprisonment
idiomatic	imitable**	impenitent	impristi
idiopathic	imitate	imperative	improbable
idiosyncrasy	immanent**	imperfect	impromptu
idle**	immaterial	imperil	improper
idol**	immature	impermissible	impropriety
ignite	immediate	impersonal	improved
ignominy	immemorial	impersonation	improvement
ignorance	immense	imperturbable	improvident
ignorant	immerse**	impervious	improvise
ignorantia	immersed**	impetuous	imprudence
ignoratio elenchi	immersion	impetus	imprudent**
ignore	immigrant**	impignorata	impudent**
ikbal	immigrate**	impinge	impugn
ikrah**	imminent**	implacable	impugned
ikrar**	immobilis	implant	impulse
ileum**	immoderate	implead	impulsive
I'll**	immolate	implements	impunity**
ill-advised	immoral**	implicate	impurity
illapse**	immorality	implied	imputation**
illation	immune	implied powers	imputative
illative	immunity**	implied warrant	impute
ill-disposed	immuno-	implore	imputed
illegal	suppressant	import	inability
illegality	immure**	important**	in absentia
illegible**	immutable	imports	inaccessible
illegitimacy	impact	importune	inaccurate
illegitimate	impair	impose	inaction
illeviable	impale	impossible**	inadequate
ill-fated	impanel	impostor**	inadmissible
ill-gotten	impaneling	imposts	in adversum
illicit**	impanelment	imposture**	inadvertence
illimitable	imparity	impotence	inadvisable
illiteracy	imparl	impotent**	inalienable
illiterate**	imparlance	impound	in alieno solo
illness	impart	impoverish	in alio loco
illocable	impartable**	impracticable**	inalterable
illogical**	impartial	impractical**	in ambiguo
illud**	impartible**	impregnable	inane**
illuminate	impassable**	impregnate	in apicibus juris
ill-usage	impassible**	imprescriptible	inapplicable
ill-used	impeach	impressed**	inappropriate
illusion**	impeachable	impressible	inapt**
illusive**	impeachment	impression	in articulo
illusory	impechiare	impressment	inasmuch as

inattentive	incompetence**	indebitatus	indistanter
inaudible	incompetent	indebtedness	indistinctive
inauspicious	incompetents**	indecent	indistinguishable
in autre droit	incomplete	indecipherable	indite**
in banco	incomprehensible	indecision	individual
in bonis	inconceivable	indeed	individually
incalculable	inconclusive	indefeasible	indivisible
in camera	incongruity	indefensible	indivisum
incapacitated	inconsequential	indefinite	indolence
in capita	inconsiderable	indelible**	indorsement
incarcerate	in consideration	indelicate**	indubitable
in casu proviso	in consimili casu	in delicto**	induce
in causa	inconsistent	indemnification	inducement
incautious	incontestability	indemnify	induciae
incendiary	incontinence	indemnity	induct
incentive	in contractibus	indemonstrable	indulgence
inception	incontrovertible	indent	indument
incessant	inconvenience	indentor	indurate
incest	incorporamus	indenture	industrial
incestuosi**	incorporate	independent	inebriate
incestuous**	incorporation	indescribable	inebriety
inchartare	in corpore**	indestructible	inedible**
in chief	incorporeal**	indeterminate	ineducable
inchoate	incorrect	index	ineffective
incidence**	incorrigible	Indian	ineffectual
incidental	incorruptible	indication	inefficient
incidentally	increase	indicative	inelastic
incidents**	incredulous	indices	ineligible**
incipient**	incredulity	indicia	ineluctable
incipitur	increment	indicium	inept**
incise	incrementum	indict**	ineptitude
incision	incriminate	indictable	inequable
incite**	incriminator	indictee	inequality
inciter**	incriminatory	indictio	inequity**
incivile	incroachment	indictment	inerrant
inclose	inculcate**	in diem	inert
inclosure	inculpate**	indigent	inertia
include	inculpation	indigestion	inertness
inclusion	inculpatory	indignity	inescapable
inclusive	incumbent	indirect	in esse
incognito	incumber	indiscreet**	in est de jure
incoherent	incumbrance	indiscrete**	inestimable
incombustible	incur	indiscretion	inevitable
income	incurable**	indiscriminate	inexact
in commendam	in curia	indispensable	inexactitude
incommensurate	incurrable**	indispensable	in excambio
in common	incursion	evidence	inexcusable
incommunicado	in custodia legis	indisposition	inexecutable
incompatible	inde	indissoluble	inexhaustible

inexistent	in flight**	in hoc	inoperable
in exitu	in-flight**	inhuman**	inoperative
inexorable	influence	inhumane**	in pais
inexpedient	influence	inimical**	in pari
inexpensive	peddling	inimitable**	in patiendo
inexperience	influx**	in infinitum	in perpetuity
inexplicable	in flux**	in initio	in personam
in extenso	informal	iniquity**	in pleno lumine
in extremis	informant	initial	in prender
in facie curiae	information	initial public	in principio
in faciendo	informed	offering	in propria
in fact	informer	initiate	input
infallible	in foro	initiative	inquest
infamia	infortunium	inject	inquirendo
infamous	infra**	in judicio	inquiry
infancy	infraction	injudicious	inquisition
infans	infrangible	injunction	in re
infanticide	infrastructure	injure**	in rebus
infatuate	in fraudem	in jure**	in rem
infection**	infrequent	injuries	insane
infectious	infringement	injurious	insanity
in feodo	infugare	injury**	inscription
infeoffment	in full	injustice	insecure
infer**	infusion	in jus vocare	inseminate
inferable	in futuro	in kind	insensible
inference	in genere	in law	insert**
inferential	ingenious**	in-law	inset**
inferior	ingenuitas	in limine	insider**
inferring	ingenuity	in litem	insidious**
infest**	ingenuous**	in loco	insight**
infidelis	ingest	in malam partem	in sight**
infidelity	ingratitude	inmate**	insignificant
in fieri	ingress	in medias res	insimul
in fine	ingrossator	in medico	insincere
infinite	inguinal	in mora	insinuate
infinitesimal	ingurgitate	in mortua manu	insinuation
infinitum	inhabit	innate**	insipient**
infirm	inhabitant	inner	insisted
infirmative	in hac parte	innervate**	insistence
infirmity	inhalant	innocence**	insistent
in flagrante	inhere	innocents**	in situ
delicto	inherent	innocuous	insobriety
inflame	inherent powers	in notis	insofar
inflammable	inherit	innovate**	insolate**
inflammatory	inheritance	innovation	insolation
inflation	inheritance tax	innuendo	insolence
inflect**	inheritor	innumerable	in solido
inflection**	inheritrix	inoculate**	in solo
inflict**	inhibition	in omnibus	insolvent**

209

inspect
inspection
inspector
in spite
instability
install
installment
instance**
instantaneous
instantly
instants**
in statu quo
instead
instigate
instill
instinct
instinctive
instirpare
in stirpes
institorial
institute
institution
instruct
instruction
instrument**
instrumenta**
instrumental**
insubordination
insubstantial
insufficient
insufficient
 evidence
insula
insular
insulate**
insult
insupportable
insuppressible
insurable
insurance**
insure**
insured
insurgent
intact
intangible
integer
integrate
integration
integrity

intellectual
 property
intelligence
intemperate
intend
intense**
intension**
intent
intention**
intentional
intents**
inter**
interagency**
inter alia
inter alios
interbank
intercede
intercession**
interchangeable
inter conjuges
intercourse
interdict
interesse**
interest**
interested
interface
interfere
interference
interim
interlineation
interlocking
interlocutory
interlopers
intermarriage
intermeddle
intermediary
intermediate
interment**
in terminis
intermission**
intermittent
intermixture
intern**
internal
Internal
 Revenue
 Code
international
interne**

internment**
inter pares**
inter partes**
interpellate**
interplead
interpleader
interpolate**
interpose
interposed
interpret
interpretation
interpreter
interracial
interregnum
interrogation
interrogatories
interrogatory
interrogee
interruption
intersection**
intersession**
intersperse
interspousal
interstate**
interstices
interstitial
interval
intervene
intervenor
intervention
interview
inter vivos
intestacy
intestate**
in testimonium
intimacy
intimate
intimidate
intol and uttol
intolerable
intolerance
in toto
intoxicated
intra**
intra-agency**
intractable
intra fidem
intransigent
intra parietes

intrastate**
intrauterine
intravenous
intra vires
intricate
intrigue
intrinsic
introduce
intromission**
introversion
intruder
intrusion
intrust
intuit
in turn**
inundation
inure**
in utero
in vacuo
invade**
invalid
invalidation
invaluable
invariable
invasion
invective
inveighed**
inveigle
invent
inventor**
inventory**
inventus
inverse
invest**
investigate
investigation
investigator
investiture
investment
investor
inveterate
invidious**
invigorate
in vinculis
inviolable
invisible
invitation
invitee
in vitro

invoice
invoke
involuntary
involuntary
    manslaughter
involve
invulnerable
in witness
    whereof
ion**
iota
ipse dixit
ipso facto
ipso jure
irascible**

irate
iron**
iron-safe clause
irrational
irrebutable or
    irrebuttable
irreconcilable
irrecoverable
irredeemable**
irreducible
irrefutable
irregular
irrelevant**
irremeable**
irremediable**

irremissible
irreparable
irrepealable
irrepleviable
irreproachable
irresistible
irresoluble
irresolvable
irrespective
irresponsible
irretrievable
irreverence
irreverent**
irrevocable
irrigation

irritable
irruption**
Islam**
isolate**
issuable
issue
item
itemize
iterate
itinerant
itinerary
its**
it's**

J

jactitation
jactivus
jactus
jail
Jane Doe
janitor
Jason clause
jay walking
jelled**
Jencks Act
jeopardize
jeopardy
jest**
jettison
jewel**
jewelry**
Jewish
Jewry**
jibe**
jobber
John Doe
joinder

join issue
joint
joint heir
joint tenancy
joint tort-feasors
jointure
jostle
jouir
joule**
jour
journal
journal entry
judex
judge
judgement or
    judgment
judgmental
    lapse
judicable
judicare
judicatio
judicator

judicatory
judicature
judices
judicial
judicial notice
judiciary
judicious
judicium
jugular
jump bail
junction
junior
junk
junket
junta**
junto**
jura**
jural
jurare
jurat
jurator
jure**

juridical
juris
jurisconsult
jurisdiction
jurisprudence
jurist
juror**
jury**
jus**
just**
justice
justice of the
    peace
justiciable
justification
justify
justitia
juvenile
juxtapose

K

kaia
kangaroo court
kaput**
karat**
karma**

keelage
kennel
Kenny method
kentledge
Keogh Plan

kerf
kernel**
key**
keyage
keycard

key man
    insurance
keyus
kickback
kidnapping

211

Kilberg doctrine
kill**
killer
kiln**
kindred
kintal
kintle
kiting

Klan**
kleptomania
knacker
knave
knee-jerk
knell
knew**
knife

knifepoint
knights
knock
know**
know-how
knowingly
knowledge
knowledgeable

known**
knows**
kosher
kraft**
kudos
kuleana
kyth

L

label**
labial**
labile**
labor
laboratory
laborer
labyrinth
labyrinthine
lacerate
laches**
lacks**
laconic
lacta
lacuna
lacus
lade**
lading
lag
lage-man
laid**
lain**
lair**
laissez-faire
laity
lam**
lamb**
landfill
landlady
landlord
land-reeve
lands
lane**
language
languish
Lanham
   Trademark
   Act

lapidation
lappage
laps**
lapse**
lapsed
laptop
larcenous
larceny
large**
largess **
largesse**
largest**
lascivious
latches**
latent
lateral
Latina**
Latino**
latitat
latitude
latrocination
laudanum
laudatory
laudum
launch
launder
laundering
launder money
lavish
lawbreaker
lawful
lawfulness
law journal
law review
lawsuit
lawyer
lax**

laxity
lay**
layer**
layman
layoff
lea**
leach**
lead**
leadership
leading
league
leakage
leal
lealte
lean**
learned
learning
   disability
lease
leaseback
leased**
leasehold
least**
leaute
leave
led**
ledger
ledges**
leech**
leet
legacy
legal
Legal Aid Society
legal eagle
legalese
legalism
legalistic

legality
legalization
legalize
legally
legal remedy
Legal Services
   Corporation
legare
legatary
legatee
legation**
legator
legatum
legem
legend
legerdemain
leges**
legislate
legislation
legislative
legislator
legist
legit
legitimacy
legitime
legwork
leisure
leitmotif
lemon law
lends**
leniency
lenient
lens**
lese majesty**
lesion
less**
lessa**

lessee**	licet	liter**	logjam
lessen**	licitness	litera**	loiter
lesser**	lie**	literacy	lone**
lesson**	liege	literal**	longanimity
lessor**	lien**	literary	longevity pay
lest**	lienee	litigable	long term**
lethal	lienor	litigant	long-term**
letter	lieu**	litigate	loo**
letter of the law	life**	litigationist	lookout**
levant et	lifehold	litigator	look out**
couchant	ligare	litigious	loophole
levee**	ligation**	litmus test	loose**
leverage	ligature	litre**	loosen
leveraged buyout	ligeance	litter**	loot**
leviable	light**	littering	looter
levy**	lightening**	littoral**	loquacious
lewd	lighter**	livable	lose**
lex	lightning**	live**	loser
lex domicilii	ligius	liveable	loss**
lex fori	likable	livelihood	lost**
Lexis	likeable	livery	lot
lex loci	likelihood	livestock	loud**
lex non scripta	likeness	livid	louse**
lex scripta	limb**	living	lout**
lex situs	limit	Lloyd's	loyal
lex terrae	limitation	loan**	loyalty
ley**	limited	loansharking	lubricant
liability	limn**	loath**	lucid
liable**	linage**	loathe**	lucrative
liaison	linchpin	lobbying	lucre
liar	Lindbergh Act	lobbyist	ludicrous
lib	linea	lobotomize	luggage
libation	lineage**	local**	lugubrious
libber**	lineal	locale**	lumbar**
libel**	lineaments	locality	lumber**
libelant	linear	locate	lumen
libelee	lineup**	locative calls	lumina
libelous	line up**	lockout**	lunacy
liber**	lingual	lock out**	lunatic
liberal	linkage	loco parentis	lunch
liberate	liquid	locus	lunge
liberties	liquidate	lodge**	lurid
liberty	liquidation	lodge a	luscious
libido	liquidity	complaint	lust
LIBOR**	liquor	lodger	lute**
libra	lira	lodgings	luxurious
library	lis**	logging	luxury
license	list**	logic	lye**
licensee	listing	logical	lying
licentious	lite pendente**	logistics	

213

M

mace
Machiavellian
machination
machinery
machismo
macho
maculate
madness
maelstrom
Mafia
mafioso
magazine
magic
magister
magisterial
magistracy
magistral
magistrate
magma**
magna**
Magna Carta or
  Magna
  Charta
magna culpa
magnanimous
magnate**
magnet**
magnify
magnitude
magnum opus
maiden
mail**
mail order
maim**
main**
mainframe
mainline
mainly
mainprise
mainstream
maintain
maintenance
majesty
major
majority
makeup**
make up**

mala
maladapted
maladies
maladjusted
maladroit
malady
malaise
malconduct
malcontent
mal de mer
maldistribution
male**
malediction
malefaction
malevolence
malfeasance
malfeasor
malfunction
malice
malice afore-
  thought
malicious
malign
malinger
mall**
malleable
Mallory Rule
malnutrition
malo
malpractice
maltreatment
malum
malversation
mammary
mammogram
manacles
manage**
manageable
manbote
mandamus
mandatary**
mandate
mandatory**
maneuver
manhandle
man-hour
mania**

maniac**
manic**
manifest**
manifestation
manifesto**
manifold
manipulate
Mann Act
manner**
manor**
mansion
manslaughter
mantel
manticulate
mantle
manual
manufacture
manumission
manumit
manuscript
mar**
marathon
marauder
mare**
mareschal
margin
margin account
marginal
marijuana
marina
marine
marital**
maritime
maritus
mark**
marked**
market**
marketable
markup
marque**
marriage**
marshal**
martial**
martial law
martyr
marvelous
Marxist

masculine
mask**
masochism
masquerade
mass**
massacre
massage**
masseur
masseuse
massif**
massive**
mass-produced
mastectomy
mastery
masturbate
materia**
materiel**
maternal
maternity
matriarch
matricide
matriculate
matrilineal
matrimonial
matrix
maturation
mature
maturity
maul**
maven
maxim
maximum
mayhem
mayor
McNabb-
  Mallory Rule
mea culpa
meager or
  meagre
mean**
meander
means
measurable
measure
mechanic
mechanic's lien
medal**

meddle**	mercantile	microprocessor	misapply
meddlesome	mercantile law	microstructure	misapprehension
median	mercat	midcourse	misappropriation
mediate	mercatum	middle	misbegotten
mediation**	mercenary	middleman	misbehavior
Medicaid	merchandise	mien**	miscalculate
medical	merchant	migrant	miscarriage
Medicare	merciful	migratory	miscegenation
medication**	merciless	mil**	miscellaneous
medicine	mercy	mile**	mischance
medico-legal	mercy of the	mill**	mischief
mediocre	court	milage	mischievous
meditate	mere	mileage	misconception
meditation**	merely	milestones	misconduct
medium	meretricious	militant**	misconstrue
meeting	merger	military	miscreant
meets**	merit	militate**	misdeed
megabyte	meritocracy	millimeter	misdemeanant
megalomania	meritorious	millionaire	misdemeanor
melancholia	merits	mimic	misdiagnose
melee	mesdames	minable	misdirection
melior	mese	minatory	mise
member	mesne**	mindful	miserable
membrum	message**	mindset	miserere
memoir**	messuage**	mineable	misery
memorandum	mestizo	miner**	misfeasance
memorial	meta**	mineral	misfeasor
memory**	metabolism	miniature	misfile
menace	metal**	minimal	misfit
ménage**	metallic	minimize	misfortune
ménage à trois	metamorphosis	minimum	misgiving
mendacious	metaphor	mining	misguided
mendacity**	metastasis	minion**	mishandle
mendicant	mete**	minister	mishap**
mendicity**	meter**	minor**	misinform
menial	metes**	minority	misinterpret
menopause	metes and	minus	misjoinder
mens**	bounds	minuscule	misjudge
mensa**	methadone	minute**	mislabel
menses**	methodology	minutes**	mislaid
mensis**	metric system	minutia**	misleading
mensor	metropolitan	minyan**	mismanage
mens rea	mettle**	mirage**	mismatch
mental	metus**	Miranda Rule	misnomer
mental anguish	Mexican divorce	mirandize	misogyny
mental cruelty	mezzanine	mirror	misplace
mente captus	michel-gemote	misadventure	misprision
mentition	microanalysis	misadvise	misprision of
Merc	microeconomics	misallocation	felony
mercable	microfilm	misapplication	misquote

215

misreading
misrecital
misrepresentation
misshape**
missives
misstatement
mistake
mistreat
mistress
mistrial
mistrust
misunderstand
misuse
mitigate
mitigating
mitigation
mittimus
mixed
mixture
M'Naghten Rule
mobile
mock
modal**
modal legacy
model**
modem
moderate
modern
modernize
modest
modicum
modify
modo et forma
modular
module**
modus
moerda

moiety
molest
mollify
momentary
momentous
momentum
monachism
monandry
moneta
monetary**
money
monitory**
monogamous
monolith
monopolize
monopoly
monopsony
monstrans de
  droit
monstrous
monumental
Moody's
moorage
moot**
moot case
mop-up
mora
moral**
morale**
morass
moratorium
moratur in lege
moreover
mores
morgue
moribund
Mormon

morning**
moron
morose
morphine
mors
mort
mortal
mortality
mortgage**
mortgagee**
mortgagor**
mortis causa
mortmain
mortuary
mortuus
Moslem**
mosque**
mote
mothers-in-law
motif**
motion
motivate
motive**
motorcycle
motor vehicle
mourning**
mouthpiece
movable
movant**
moveable
movement**
movent**
muddle
mugger
mug shot
mulatto
mulct

muliebrity
mulier
multa
multifarious
multilateral
multinational
multiple
multiplicity
multipurpose
multitude
mundane
municipal
municipal bond
munificent
muniments
munitions
murder
murderer
murderess
murdrum
museum
Muslim**
muster
mutable
mutation
mutatis
  mutandis
mute**
mutilate
mutual
mutual fund
mysterious
mystic
myth

N

nadir
NAFTA
naif
naive
naiveté
nameless
namely

Napoleonic Code
narc
narcissism
narcoanalysis
narcosis
narcotics
nark

narrate
narrative
nascent
NASDAQ
national
nationalization
native

Native American
natura brevium
natural
naturalization
naturalize
nature**
naught

nausea
nautical
naval**
navel**
navigable
navigate
near
nearby
nearsighted
nebulous
necessary
necessity
necrophilia
needless
needy
ne exeat
nefarious
negate
negation
negative
negative cash
    flow
neglect
negligence
negligent
negotiable
negotiate
Negro
neighbor
neighborhood
neither party
nemesis
nemo
neophyte
nephew
nepotism
nervous
nescience
net
network
neuroses**
neurosis**
neurotic
neutralize
nevertheless
new**
newborn
newlywed
newspaper

next
nexus
nicety
niche
nickname
nicotine
niece
night
nihil
nil
ninety
nisei**
nisi**
nisi prius
no**
noblesse oblige
nocent
nocturnal
noes**
no-fault
nolens volens
nolle prosequi
no-load
nolo contendere
nol pros
nomen
nominal
nominate
nominee
nomology
nomothetic
non**
non-ability
non-acceptance
nonacquiescence
non-admission
non-age
non-appearance
non-assessable
non-bailable
noncommittal
noncompetitive
noncompliance
non compos
    mentis
nonconforming
    use
non-continuous
noncontribution

noncumulative
nondeductible
non-delivery
nondescript
non-detachable
non-direction
non-disclosure
nondiscriminatory
none**
nonentity
nonexistent
nonfeasance
nonfeasor
non-forfeitable
non-functional
noninsurable
    risk
non-intercourse
non-intervention
nonjudgmental
nonlegal
non-merchant-
    able title
non-negotiable
nonobservance
non obstante
    veredicto
nonpareil
nonpartisan
nonpayment
non-profit
non pros
non prosequitur
nonrecourse
non-residence
nonsense
non sequitur
non-stock
nonsuit
non-support
non-tenure
non-user
non-waiver
    agreement
no one**
no-par
no-par value
nor**
normal

normative
nos**
nose**
no-strike clause
nostrum
nota
notable
notarial
notary
notary public
notation
noteworthy
notice
notify
noting
notion
notorious
notwithstanding
novation
novel
novelty
noverint
novice
novus homo
noxal
noxious
nuclear
nucleus
nuda
nude
nudum pactum
nugatory
nuisance
nulla bona
null and void
nullification
nullify
nullity
numerous
nuncio
nunc pro tunc
nuncupate
Nuremberg
    defense
nurture**
NYFE
nymphomania
NYSE

O

oar**
oasis
oath
obduracy
obedience
obeisance
obese
obey
obfuscate
obfuscatory
obit
obiter dictum
obituary
object**
objection
objection
    overruled
objective
objurgate
oblate
obligate
obligation
obligatory
oblige**
obligee**
obliger or
    obligor**
oblique
obliquity
obliterate
oblivious
obloquy
obreption
obrogation
obscene
obscure
obsequious
observant
observe
obsession
obsolescent
obsolete
obstacle
obstante
obstetrics
obstinate
obstriction**

obstruct**
obstruction**
obstruction of
    justice
obtain
obtention
obtrusive
obtuse**
obviate
obvious
occasion
occlude
occult
occupant
occupation
occupy
occur
occurred
occurrence
ocular
odd job
odd lot
odious
odor
odorless
oedipal
o'er**
offal**
off-color
offender
offense
offer
offering
offer of proof
offeror
off-grade
offhand
office
official
off-limits
offset
offspring
of record
of right
often
older**
olfactory

oligopoly
oligopsony
ombudsman
omen
omission
omit**
omnibus
omnipotent
omnipresence
omniscient
onanism
oncology
onerous
onetime**
one time**
ongoing
on time**
onus
onus probandi
open
open-end
opening
operable
operate
operative
ophthalmologist
opiate
opinion
opium
opponent
opportune
oppose
opposite**
oppress
oppressed**
opprobrious
oppugn
optician
optimal
optimism
optimum
option
optometrist
opus
or**
oracle**
oral**

orbit
orbiter**
orchestrate
ordain
ordeal
order**
ordinance**
ordinary
ordinary income
ordnance**
ordonnance**
ordure**
ore**
organ
organic
organization
orgy
orifice
origin
original
orphan
orthodox
orthopedics
oscillate
ostensible
ostentation
osteopath
ostracize
other
ought**
our**
ours
ouster
outage
outbreak
outburst
outcome
outer
outgo
outgrowth
outlaw
outlawry
outlay
outlet
outline
outlive
outlook

outmoded
out-of-court
out-of-pocket
outpatient
outpouring
output
outrage
outreach
outright
outset
outside
outstanding
ovarian
ovation
overall**
over all**
overassessment

overburden
overcharge
overcome
overcompensate
overdevelop
overdo**
overdose
overdraft
overdraw
overdue**
overemphasize
overestimate
overextend
overflow
overhaul
overhead
overhear

overlap
overlay
overload
overlook
overpower
overrate
overreach
override
overrule
overrun
overseas**
oversee
overseers**
oversees**
oversight
oversimplify
overt

over-the-counter
overthrow
overtime
overture
overturn
overuse
overvalue
overwhelm
ovoid**
ovum
owelty
owing
owner
oxygenize
oyer
oyez

P

PAC**
pacare
pace
pacify
pack**
package
packed**
pact**
pactum
padlock
paginate
paid-in
paid-up
pain**
painstaking
pairs**
pais
palatable
pale of the law
palimony
palliate
palliative
palpable
palpitate
palsy
paltry
pamphlet
panache

pandect
pandemic
pandemonium
pander
pane**
panel
panic
panicky
pannellation
panoply
paparazzi
paper
Pap smear
par
parachute
paradigm
paradox
paragon
paragraph
paralegal
parallel
paralysis
paralyze
parameter
paramount
paramour
paranoia
paraph

paraphernalia
paraphrase
paraprofessional
parasite
parcel
parcener
parchment
pardon
parens**
parent
parental
parenthesis
parents**
pares**
paresis
pariah
pari passu
parish**
par issue
parity**
parlay**
parley**
parliament
parochial
parol**
parole**
parolee**
parricide

parry
pars**
parsimony
partial
partible
participate
participatory
particular
particulars
parties
parties litigant
partisan
partition**
partner
party**
par value
passable**
passage
passbook
passed**
passenger
passers-by
passibility**
passible**
passim
passive
passive activity
passive income

passport
past**
paten**
patent**
patentee
pater
paternal
paternity
pathetic**
pathological
pathos**
patience
patiens**
patients**
patria
patricide
patrilineal
patrimony
patronage
pattern**
paucity
pauper
pause**
pawn**
pawner or
   pawnor
paws**
pax regis
payable
payment
payoff
payola
payroll**
pays
peace**
peaceful
peak**
peccable
peccadillo
peccant
peculation
peculiar**
pecunia**
pecuniary**
pedal**
pedantic
peddle**
peddler
pederasty
pedestrian

pediatrician
pedigree
pediment
peek**
peer**
peers
pejorative
pelfe
pell-mell
penal**
penalize
penal law
penalty
penance**
pend**
pendant**
pendants**
pendency
pendens**
pendent**
pendente lite**
penetrable
penile**
penis
penitent
penitentiary
pennants**
penned**
Pennoyer Rule
Pennsylvania
   Rule
penology
pension
pent**
penumbra
   doctrine
penury
peonage
people
per**
per accidens
peradventure
per annum
per autre vie
per capita
perceivable
percent
percentile
perception
per curiam

per diem
perdurable
peremption
peremptory**
perennial
perfect**
perfidious
perforate
perforce
perform
performance
   bond
perhaps
peril
period
periodical
peripheral
periphrasis
perish**
perjure
perjury
perks
permanent
permeable
per misadven-
   ture
permissible
permission
permissive
permit
permittee
permutation
per my et per
   tout
pernancy
pernicious
per os
per pais
perpetrate
perpetrator
perpetual
perpetuities
perplex
perquisite**
perquisites
per quod
per rectum
per se
persecute**
persevere

persistent
person
persona**
personal**
personality**
personalty**
personnel**
perspective**
perspicacious**
perspicuous**
persuade
pertain
pertinent
per tout et non
   per my
perturbation
pervade
per verba
perverse**
perversely
pervert
perverts**
per year
peso
pessurable wares
pesticide
petit**
petite**
petite assize
petitio principii
petition**
petitioner
pettifogger
petty**
peyote
phallic
pharmaceutical
pharmacist
pharmacology
phase**
phaseout
phlebitis
phenomenon
phial**
philander
philanthropy
Philippines**
philistine
philosopher
phobia

photographer
phrase**
phreak**
phylum**
physic**
physical**
physician
physiotherapy
physique**
pica**
picket
pickpocket
picture**
piece**
piecework
pied-à-terre
pier**
pigeonhole
piker**
pileup**
pile up**
pilfer
Pilipino**
pillage
pillar
pillory
pilot
pilotage
pinnacle
pious uses
pique**
piracy
pistil**
pistol**
pistole**
pitcher**
pitfall
pitiful
pitiless
pittance
pity
pix jury
place
placebo
placenta
placer
placit
plagiarize
plagiary
plaid**

plain**
plainclothesman
plaint**
plaintiff**
plaintive**
plan
plane**
planned**
plant**
plat**
plate**
plateau
platform
platitude
platonic
plausible
played**
plea
plea bargaining
plead**
pleader
plead guilty
pleading
pleadings
pleas**
please**
pleasure
pleat**
pledge
pledgee**
pledger or
    pledgor**
plenary
plene
plenipotentiary
pleural**
plevin
pliable
plot
plow back
ploy
plumber
plural**
pluralism
plurality
poach
pocket
podium
points
poison

poison pill
poker
pole**
polemic
police
policy**
polished
polite
politically
    correct
politics
polity**
poll**
pollutant
pollution
polyandry
polygamy
polygraph
polyopsony
polypoly
pompous
ponderable
pontiff
pontificate
Ponzi scheme
pool**
pooling
poor**
populace**
popular**
population
populist**
populous**
pore**
pores**
porn**
pornographic
pornography
porous
portable
portage
Portal-to-Portal
    Act
portend**
portent**
portentous
portfolio
portion**
portray
poseur**

position
positive
positive cash
    flow
posse
possess
possession
possibility**
possible
postage
postal
postdate
posted
posteriority
posterity
posthumous
posthypnotic
postmortem
postnatal
postnuptial
postoperative
postpartum
postpone
posttraumatic
post-trial
postulate
potable
potent**
potential
potion**
potpourri
pounce
pound
pour**
pour-over
pours**
poverty
power
powers
practicable**
practical**
practically
practice**
praecipe
praedial
praevaricator
pragmatic
praise**
praiseworthy
praxis**

prayer**
prays**
preamble
precarious
precatory
precaution
precede**
precedence**
precedent
precedents**
preceding**
precept
precinct
precious
precipe
precipitous
précis**
precise**
preclude
preconceive
precondition
precursor
predate
predatory
predecessor
predetermine
predicate**
predict**
prediction
predispose
preeminent
preemption
preemptory**
prefabricate
preface
prefect**
prefer**
prefer charges
preference
preferred
preferring
pregnancy
prejudge
prejudice
prejudicial
preliminary
prelude
premarital
premature
premeditate

premier**
premiere**
premises**
premium
premonition
premonitory
prenatal
prender
prendre
preoccupancy
preordain
prepaid
preparation
prepayment
prepense
preponderance
preposition**
preposterous
prerequisite**
prerogative
presage
prescience
prescribe**
prescript
prescription
presence**
present
presentation
pre-sentence
presenter
presentiment**
presently
presentment**
presents**
preservation
preserve**
preside
president
President of the
    United States
presidents**
presiding
presiding judge
pressure
presumably
presume
presumption
presumptive
presumptuous
presuppose

pretax
pretend**
pretense
pretention
preter legal
preterminal
pretermit
pretest**
pretext**
pretium
pre-trial
prevail
prevalent
prevarication
prevent
prevention
preview**
previous
preyer**
preys**
priapism
price
price earnings
    ratio
pride**
pried**
prima
primacy
prima donna
prima facie**
primage
primary
prime**
primer
primitive
principal**
principle**
prior
priori petenti
priority
prison
prisoner
privacy
private
privatize
privies
privilege
privileged
privileged com-
    munication

privity
privy
prize court
pro
probability
probable
probable cause
probate
probate judge
probatio**
probation**
probative
probity
problem
problematical
pro bono
procedural
procedure
proceed**
proceeding**
proceeds
process
processor
prochein
prochoice
proclaim
proclamation
proclivity
pro confesso
pro consilio
proconsul
procrastinate
procrustean
proctor
procurator
procure
procurement
procurer
prodigal**
prodigious**
prodigy**
proditor
produce
product
production
pro emptore
pro facto
profane
profanity
profess

profession
professional
professor
proffer**
proficient
profit**
profits
pro forma
profound
profuse
progenitor
progeny
prognosis
program
progression
progressive
prohibit
prohibition
prohibitory
pro indiviso
project
prolapse
pro legato
prolepsis
proles
prolicide
proliferate
prolific
prolixity
prolocutor
prologue**
prolongation
prominent
promiscuity
promiscuous
promise
promisee**
promises**
promisor**
promissor**
promissory**
promissory note
promote
prompt
promulgate
pronotary
prothonotary
pronounce
pronouncement
pronunciation

proof**
propaganda
propagate
propensity
proper**
properly
property
prophecy
prophet**
Prophet**
prophetic
prophylactic
propinquity
propitiate
propitious
proponent
proportionate
proposal
propose**
proposition**
pro possessore
propound
proprietary
proprietor
propriety
propter**
pro rata**
prorate**
pro re nata
prorogation
prorogue**
prosaic
proscribe**
proscribed
prose**
pro se**
prosecute**
prosecutor
prosecutorial
prosequi
prosequitur
pro solido
prospective**
prospectus
prosper
prosperity
prosperous
prostate**
prosthesis
prostitute

prostrate**
protagonist
pro tanto
protection
protegé**
pro tem
pro tempore
protest**
protestando
Protestant
protestation
protocol
prototype
protract
protrude
protuberant
proud
provable
prove**
provide
provided
province
provincial
provision
provisional
proviso
provisor
provocateur
provocation
provocative
provoke
provost
prowler
proximate
proximity
proxy
prudence
prudent
prurient interest
pseudo
pseudocyesis
pseudograph
pseudonym
psyche
psychedelic
psychiatrist
psychic**
psychoanalysis
psychoanalyst
psychological

psychology
psychoneurosis
psychopath
psychopathology
psychoses**
psychosis**
psychotherapy
psychotic
ptomaine
puberty
pubic**
public**
publicist
publicity
public law
publicly
publish
publisher
pudicity
pueblo
puerility
Puerto Rican
puffery
pugilist
pugnacious
puis
puisne**
puisne judge
pull**
pulling
pulmonary
pulsator
pummel
punctilious
punctuation
pundit
pungent
punishable
punishment
punitive
puny**
pupil
pur**
purchase
purchaser
pure**
purgation
purgative
purging
purity

purlieu
purloin
purpart**
purparty
purport**
purpose**
purposeful
purposeless
purposely
purprise

purr**
purse
purser
pursuant
pursue
pursuer
pursuit
pursuant
pur tant que
purus idiota

purvey**
purveyance
purveyor
purview**
pusher
push money
pusillanimous
put**
putative
putrid

puts and calls
putt**
pyramid
pyramiding
pyramid scheme
pyromania
pyrrhic
pyx jury

Q

qua**
quack
quackery
quadrant
quadrennium
quadripartite
quadripartitus
quadriplegia**
quadriplegic**
quadrumvirate
quadruplet
quadruplication
quae**
quaere**
quaerens
quaestio
quaestor
quaestus
quaff
quagmire
Quaker
qualification
qualified
qualifier
qualify

qualitative
quality
qualm
quamdiu
quando
   acciderint
quanti minoris
quantitative
quantity
quantum
quarantine
quare**
quarrel**
quarrelsome
quarry**
quart
quartage
quarter
quarterly
quarto die post
quash
quashing
quasi
quasi-judicial
quaver

quay**
queasy
queen's
queer**
que estate
quell
quench
querela**
querulous
query**
quest
question
questionable
queue**
quia
quibble
quick
quickening
quid pro quo
quiescent
quiet**
quietare
quietude
quietus
quintessence

quintessential
quintuplet
quirk
quit**
qui tam
quitclaim
quite**
quit rent
quittance
quitter
quixotic
quizzical
quoad hoc
quo animo
quod
quorum
quota**
quotable
quotation
quote**
quotidian
quotient verdict
quo warranto

R

rabbi
rabbinical
rabid
rabies
race

racial
racism
racist
rack
racked**

racket**
racketeer
racketeering
rack-rent
radar

radial
radiant
radiation
radical
radicals

radioactive	rarefied	real estate	recall
radiology	rarely	real estate tax	recallment
radius	rase	realign	recant
radon	rasure	realism	recapitalization
raffish	ratable	reality**	recapitulate
raffle	ratchet	realize**	recaption
raftage	rate	realized gain	recapture
rage	ratepayer	reallege	recede
raid	ratification	reallocate	receiptor
raider	ratify	reallot	receivable
railage	rating	realm	receive
railhead	ratio	Realtor**	receiver
railroad	ration	realty**	receivership
railside	rational**	reapply	recently
railway	rationale**	reapportionment	receptacle
Railway Labor	rationalization	reappraise	reception
Act	ratione	reapprehend	receptive
rain**	rattening	rear	receptor
rainmaker	raunch**	reargument	recess
raise**	raunchy	reason	recession
raising	ravage**	reasonable	recidivism
raison d'être	ravenous	reasonable	recipient
rake-off	ravish**	doubt	reciprocal
ramble	ravisher	reasoning	reciprocate
rambunctious	raw	reassert	reciprocity
ramification	raze**	reassess	recision
ramify	re	reassessment	recital
rampant	reach	reassign**	recite**
ramshackle	reachable	reassurance	reck**
rancelman	reacquire**	reattach	reckless
ranch**	reacquired	reattachment	reckless
rancid	reacquisition	rebait**	endangerment
rancor	reaction	rebate**	recklessly
rancorous	reactionary	rebel	recklessness
random	reactor	rebellion	reckon
range	read**	rebound**	reckoning
ranger	readers	rebuff	reclaim
rank	readily	rebuild	reclaimant
ranking	readjourn	rebus sic	reclamation
ransack	readjustment	stantibus	recluse**
ransom	readmittance	rebut	recodification
rap**	read-only	rebuttable	recognition
rape**	memory	rebuttal	recognizance
rapid	read-out	rebutter	recognize
rapine	ready and	recaption	recoil
rapist	willing	receiver	recollect
rapport	reaffirm	recess	recollection
rapprochement	reaffirmation	recession	recommence
rap sheet	reak**	recipient	recommend
rapture	real**	recalcitrant	recommendation

225

recommit
recompensable
reconcilable
reconcile
reconciliation
recondite
reconduction
reconfirm
reconnaissance
reconnoiter
reconsider
reconsideration
reconsign
reconstruct
reconstruction
recontinuance
recontrol
reconvene
reconventional
reconversion
reconvey
reconveyance
reconvict
record
recorder
recording
recordum
recount
recoup
recoupment
recourse
recover**
recoverable
recoveree**
recoverer**
recovery**
recreant
recreation
recriminate
recriminating
recrimination
recross examina-
    tion
recrudescence
recruit
rectal
rectification
rectify
rector
rectory

rectum
rectus in curia
recumbent
recuparatio
recuperate
recuperation
recusal
recusants
recusation
recuse**
recycle
red**
reddenda
reddendum
reddition
redeem
redeemable
redelivery
redemise
redemption
redetermination
redetermine
redevelop
red handed
red herring
redhibition
redhibitory
rediscount
redisseisin
redistribution
redistrict
reditus
redlining
redolent
redouble
redoubt**
redound**
redout**
redraft
redress
redressment
redubbers
reduce
reducible
reductio ad
    absurdum
reduction
redundancy
redundant
reduplicate

reed**
reefer**
reek**
reel**
reelect
reemploy
reenact
reentry
reestablish
reevaluate
reevaluation**
reeve
reexamination
reexchange
reexport
refer**
referee**
reference**
referendum
referring
refinance
refinement
reflect
reflection
reflexive
reform
reformation
reformatory
refraction
refrain
refresh
refreshing
refuge
refugee
refund
refunds
refurbish
refusal
refuse
refutation
regal
regale
regalia
regard
regarding
regency
regenerate
regeneration
regenerative
regent

regia via
regicide
regime**
regimen**
regiment**
regina
region
regional
register
registered
registrant
registration
registry
regnal years
regrant
regress
regressive
regressive tax
regret
regroup
regula**
regulable
regulae**
regular**
regularity
regularize
regulars
regulate
regulation
Regulation A
regurgitate
rehabilitate
rehabilitation
rehash
rehearing
rehearsal
rehypothecation
reif**
reify**
reign**
reimburse
rein**
reincarnate
reincorporate
reinforce
reinstate
reinstatement
reinsurance
reinsured
reinsurer

reintegration	remainder	renew	report
reinvest	remains	renewal	reportedly
reinvestment	remand	renominate	reporter
reinvigorate	remark	renounce	repose
reissue	remarkable	renovare	repossess
reiterate	remarriage	renovate	repossession
reject	remarry	renown	reprehensible
rejection	remedial	rent	represent
rejoice	remedies	rentable	representation
rejoin	remedy	rentage	representative
rejoinder	remember	rent-roll	representee
rejoining gratis	remembrance	rents	representor
rejuvenate	reminisce	renunciation	repress
relapse	reminiscent	renvoi	repression
relate	remise	reo absente	repressive
related	remiss	reopen	reprieve
relater	remission	reorder	reprimand
relation	remit	reorganization	reprisal
relations	remitment	reorganize	reprises
relationship	remittal	repair	reproach
relative	remittance	repairs	reprobate
relator**	remittee**	reparable	reprobation
relatrix	remitter**	reparation	reproduce
relaxant	remittitur**	repartee	reproduction
relaxare	remittor**	repatriation	reprove
relaxatio	remnant rule	repay	republic
release	remodel	repeal	republican
releasee	remonetization	repeat	republish
relegate	remonstrance	repel	repudiate
relent	remonstrate	repent	repudiation
relentless	remorse	repentant	repudiator
relevancy	remorseful	repertoire	repugnancy
relevant	remorseless	repetition	repugnant
reliable	remote	replace	repulse
reliance	removal	replacement	repulsion
relic	remove	replead	repulsive
reliction	remunerate	repleader	repurchase
relief**	remuneration	repledge	reputable
relies**	renaissance	replegiare	reputation
relieve**	rencounter	replenish	repute
religion	render	replete	reputed
religious	rendezvous	repleviable	request
relinquish	rendition	replevin	require**
relish	renegade	replevisor	requirement
relive**	renege	replevy	requisite
relocate	renegotiable	replica	requisition
relocation	renegotiate	replicant	requital
reluctance	renegotiation	replicate	requite
reluctant	Renegotiation	reply	res
rely	Act	repo	resalable

resale	respectively	reticence	reversal
rescind	respite	reticent	reverse
rescission	resplendent	retire	reversible
rescissory	respond	retiree	reversion
rescript	respondeat	retirement	reversionary
rescue	superior	retorsion	reversioner
research	respondent	retort	revert
resegregate	respondentia	retract	reverter
resegregation	responsibility	retraction	revest
resemblance	responsible	retraxit	review
resemble	responsive	retreat	reviewable
reservation	resseiser	retrial	revindicate
reserve	rest**	retribution	revise
reservoir	restaurant	retributive	revised
reset	restitution	retrieval	revision
resettlement	restorative	retrieve	revisit
resiance	restore	retro	revisor
resiant	restrain	retroactive	revitalize
reside	restraining	retrocede	revival
residence**	restraining	retrocession	revive
resident	order	retrogression	revivor
residential	restraint	retrospection	revocable
residents**	restrict	retrospective	revocation
residua	restricted	retry	revoke
residual	restriction	rette	revolt
residuary	restrictive	return	revolution
residue	restructure	returnable	revolutionary
residuum	rests	returnee	revolver
resight**	result	reunion	revolving
resign**	resultant	reunite	revulsion
resignation	resulting	reus	reward
resignee	resume**	revalidate	rework
resiliency	résumé**	revalorize	rewrite
resilient	resummons	revaluation**	rex**
res ipsa loquitur	resumption	reve	rezone
resist	resurgent	reveal**	rezoning
resistance	resurrect	revel**	rhetoric
resisting	resuscitate	revelation	rhetorical
res judicata	retail	revelatory	rhythm
resolute	retailer	revendication	ribald**
resolution	retain	revenge	ribaud**
resolve	retained	revenue	Richard Roe
resort	retainer	Revenue Ruling	RICO
resource	retaining	revenues	ricochet
resourceful	retaking	reverberate	rictus
resources	retaliation	revere	riddance
respect	retard	reverence**	rider
respectable	retardate	reverie**	ridgeling
respect for law	retardation	reverification	ridicule
respective	retention	reverify	ridiculous

rien
rigging the
  market
right**
righteous
rightful
right-handed
rights
right to know
right to life
right to work
rigid
rigidity
rigor
rigorous**
ringing
ringleader
riot
rioter
riotous
riotously
ripa
riparia
riparian
ripeness
  doctrine
rip off**
rip-off**
riposte
ripple effect
rising of court
risk**

risqué**
rite**
ritual
rival
rivalry
river
roadbed
roadway
rob
robber
robbery
robes
Robinson-
  Patman
robust
rock bottom
rod
rogare
rogatio
rogatory letters
rogue
roguery
roil**
role**
role model
roll**
rollback
roll call
rolled up
rolling
roll-over paper
rolls

Roman Catholic
romance
Roman law
romantic
rood of land
rookie
roomer**
root**
Rorschach test
rose-colored
roster
rota
rotate
rote**
rotten clause
roulette
round
rouse**
rousing
roust
rout**
route**
routine
routously
rowdy
rows**
roy
royal
royalties
royalty
rubber
rubella

Rubicon
ruble
rubric
ruckus
rudeness
rudimentary
ruin
ruinate
ruinous
rule
rule of law
rules
ruling
ruminate
rummage
rummager
rumor**
rumpus
rumrunning
runaway
rundown
run-in
runner
running
run-of-the-mill
runoff
rupture
ruse de guerre
Russian roulette
rusticum forum
rustler
ruthless

S

Sabbath
sabbatical
sabotage
saboteur
saccade
saccharin
saccharine
saccus
sacerdotal
sacrament
sacramentum
sacred
sacrifice

sacrilege
sacrosanct
sadism
sadomasochism
sadomasochist
saevitia
safe
safe-conduct
safecracker
safe deposit
safeguard
safekeeping
safety

sagacious
sagacity
sagaman
sages de la ley
said**
sail
sailing
sailors
saintly
sake
salable
salacious
salary

sale
sales
salesman
salespeople
saleswoman
Salic Law
saline
Sallie Mae
saloon
salubrious
salus
salutary
salutation

salute	save**	scintilla	sebastomania
salvage**	saver**	scion	S.E.C.**
salvation	saving	scire facias	secede
salve**	savings	scire feci	secession
salvo**	savior**	scite	seck**
salvor**	Saviour**	scofflaw	seclude
salvus plegius	savoir-faire**	scold	seclusion
Samaritan	savor**	sconce	second
sample	savvy	scope	secondary
sampler	sawed-off	scopophiliac	second-degree
sampling	scab	score	second-hand
sanatorium	scabrous	scorn	seconds
sanctimonious	scaffold	scot	secrecy
sanction	scald	scot-free	secret**
sanctuary	scale	scoundrel	secretariat
sanctum	scalper	scourge	secretary
sandbag	scamp	scrambling	secretary-
sandwich lease	scandal	scrawl	general
sane	scandalous	scream	secrete**
sanguine	matter	scriba	sect**
sanitarium	scant	scribe	secta
sanitary	scapegoat	scrip**	sectarian
sanitation	scar**	script**	section
sanitize	scarce**	scriptum	sectional
sanity	scarcity	scrivener	sects**
sans	scare**	scroll	secular
sapient	scares**	scruple	secularism
sarcasm	scarper	scrupulous	secundum
sarcastic	scars**	scrutable	secure
sardonic	scatological	scrutinize	secured
satanic	scavenger	scrutiny	securities
Satanism	scenario	scurrility	Securities (Act,
satellite	scene**	scurrilous	Commission)
satiable	scent**	sea**	security
satiate	scents**	seabed	secus
satire**	schedule	seal	sed**
satirical	scheduled	sealed	sedation
satisfaction	schematic	sealing**	sedative
satisfactory	scheme	seals	sedato animo
satisfied	schism	seamen**	sedentary
satisfy	schizophrenia	search	sedimentation
saturate	scholar	search and	sedition
Saturday night	scholarship	seizure	seditious
special	school	searcher	seduce
satyr**	schoolhouse	search warrant	seduction
saunkefin	schoolroom	seas**	seductive
saunter	science	seashore	see**
sauvagine	scienter	seasonal	seed**
savage**	scientist	seaward	seeming
savagery	scilicet	seaworthy	seen**

seepage	semiannual	sequence	sex**
sees**	semiautomatic	sequester	sexual
segment	semiconscious	sequestration	shackle
segregate	semilegal	sequestrator	shady
segregation	semimonthly	serf	shaft
seignior	seminal**	sergeant	shakedown
seigniorage	seminar**	serial**	shall
seisi	seminary**	seriately	sham
seisin**	semination	seriatim	shameful
seisina	semiofficial	series**	shanghai
seize**	semiprivate	serious**	shape up**
seizing**	semiskilled	serjeanty	shape-up**
seizor	semiweekly	serment	share**
seizure	semiyearly	serological	shareholder
select	semper paratus	serrated	shareowner
selection	senage	servant	sharif**
selectman	senate	serve	shark repellent
self-accusation	Senate	server	shear**
self-aggrandize-	senator	service	sheer**
ment	senescence	serviceable	sheik**
self-conscious	senile	servient	shelter
self-contradic-	senility	servility	shepardize
tory	senior	servitium	Shepard's
self-dealing	seniority	servitude	Citations
self-deception	sensational	servitus	sheriff**
self-defense	sense**	servus	Sherman
self-deprecating	senses**	sess	Antitrust Act
self-destruction	sensible	sessio	shield laws
self-determina-	sensitive	session**	shifting
tion	sensor**	sessions	shilling
self-employment	sensory	set	ship
self-evident	sensual	setback**	shipment
self-help	sensus**	set back**	shipper
self-imposed	sent**	set off**	shipping
self-incrimina-	sentence	set-off**	shipwreck
tion	sentencing	settle	shire
self-induced	sententia	settlement	shirk**
self-insurance	sentient	settler**	shock
self-interest	sentinel	settlor**	shone**
self-liquidating	sentry	setup**	shoot**
self-regulating	SEP	set up**	shop
self-restraint	separable	sever**	shop-books
self-righteous	separate**	severable	shopkeeper
self-serving	separation	several	shoplifting
sell**	separatists	severally	shore
seller**	septum	severance	short
sell short	sepulcher	severe**	shortchange
semblance	sequela	severity	short sale
semble	sequelae	sewage	short-term
semen**	sequels	sewer	shot

show cause	sine**	sloped**	solatium
shown**	sinecure	slopped**	sold
shriek**	single	slot machine	soldier
shrive	singular**	slough	sole**
shrub	sinister	slowdown**	solemn
shutdown	sinking fund	slow down**	solemnity
shut in**	sin tax**	slum	solicit
shut-in**	si prius	slumlord	solicitation
shyster	sir**	slur	solicitor
si**	sister	slush fund	solicitous
sic**	sit down**	small	solid
sick**	sit-down**	smattering	solidarity**
sickness	site**	smear	solidary**
sickout	sit in**	smelting	solidity**
side**	sit-in**	smile**	solidum
sidewalk	siting	Smith Act	solitary
siege	situate	smuggling	solitude
sighed**	situation	smut	solon
sight**	situs	snare	solvency
sign**	skeleton bill	snatch	solvent**
signal	skeptic	snatcher	solvit**
signatory	skeptical	sneak thief	some**
signature	skepticism	sniper	somnambulism
signed	skid	so**	somnolence
signet	skill	soakage	son**
significant	skillful	soar**	sons-in-law
signification	skimpy	sober	soon
signify	skin search	sobriety	soot**
si ita est	skip bail	sobriquet	sophist
silence	skiptracing	socager	sophistication
silent	skyjack	so-called	sophistry
silicon**	slacker	social	sophomore
silicone**	slains	socialism	soporific
silver	slander	Social Security	sordid**
similar	slanderer	sociedad**	sore**
similarity	slanderous	société**	sores**
simile**	slate	société anon-	sororicide
similiter	slaughter	yme**	sors**
simony	slave	society**	sorted**
simple	slavery	sociopath	sou**
simplex	slay**	sodality**	sough
simpliciter	sleigh**	sodomite	soul**
simplicity	sleight**	sodomy	sound
simulate**	sleuth	softcore	sounding
simulated	slice	software	soundness
simulation	slick	soil	source**
simul cum	sliding scale	soit	sous**
simultaneous	slight**	sojourning	southern
simultaneously	slip	solace	souvenir
since	slope	solar	sovereign

sovereignty
soviet
sow**
spacious**
Spanish
spare
sparingly
spasm
spasmodic
spat
spatial
spawn
speak
speaker
Speaker of the
  House
speaking
special
specialist
specialize
specialty
specie**
species**
specifiable
specific
specifically
specification
specific
  performance
specify
specimen
specious**
spectacular
specter or
  spectre
spectrograph
speculate
speculation
speculative
speculum
speech
speedy
spellbound
spelling
spend
spendthrift
sperate**
sperm
spew
spillage

spilt**
spin-off
spinal
spineless
spinster
spiritual
spital
spittle
split**
split-off
spoil
spoilable
spokesman
spokesperson
spokeswoman
spoliation
spoliator
spondeo
sponsions
sponsor
sponsorship
spontaneity
spontaneous
sporadic
spot
spousals
spouse
sprain
sprawl
spread
spreadsheet
spree
sprinkling trust
spurious
spurn
spy
squalid
squalor
square
squatter
squatter's rights
squeeze-out
squire
squirearchy
stab
stability
stabilize
stable
stagflation
stagnant

stagnate
stagnum
stake**
stakeholder
stakeout
stale
stallage
stalwart
stamp
stance
stand
stand-alone
standard
Standard and
  Poor's
standardize
standby**
stand by**
standing
staple
starboard
star-chamber
stare decisis
stark
starvation
stash
state
stated
State Depart-
  ment
statehood
statehouse
statement
statesman
stateswoman
statewide
stating
station
stationary**
stationery**
statist**
statistics
statue**
stature**
status**
statute**
statute law
statute of
  limitations
Statute of Wills

statutory
statutory rape
statutum
staunch
stave
stay
steadfast
steady
steak**
steal**
stealth
steamship
steel**
steerage
steerer
steering
  committee
stellar
stenography
steonographer
stepbrother
stepchild
stepdaughter
step-down
stepfather
stepmother
step-parent
steppingstone
stepsister
stepson
stereotype
sterility
sterilization
sterilize
sterling
steroid
stet processus
stevedore
steward
stewardess
sticker
stickler
stifle
stifling a
  prosecution
stigma
stigmatize
stiletto
still
stillborn

stimulant	stranding	structure**	sublessee
stimulate**	stranger	struggle	sublessor
sting	strangle	strumpet	subletting
stint	strangulate	strung-out	sublicense
stipend	strangulation	strychnine	sublimate
stipendiary	stratagem	stubborn	sublime
stipes	strategic	studded**	submerge
stipulate	strategy	studied**	submergence
stipulated	stratify	studious	subminimum
stipulation	stratocracy	stultify	wage
stirpes	stratum	stumble	submission
stochastic	straw	stumbling block	submit
stock	stray	stump	submittal
stock certificate	stream	stumpage	sub modo
stockholder	streamline	stupefacient	submortgage
stockholders	street	stupefaction	sub nom
stocks	streetwalker	stupefy	sub nomine
stodgy	streetwise	stupendous	subnormal
stoic	strength	stupor	subnotations
stolen	strengthen	stuprum	suboptimal
stoned	strenuous	sturgeon	subordinate
stonewall	stretcher	style	subordinated
stop	stricken	stymie	subordination
stopgap	strict	suable	suborn
stop-limit order	strict construc-	suasion	subornation
stop-loss order	tion	sua sponte	suborner
stoppage	stricter**	sub	subpartner
storage	stricti juris	subagent	subpoena
store	strictissimi juris	subaltern	subpoena duces
storehouse	strictly	Subchapter S	tecum
storekeeper	stricto jure	sub colore juris	sub potestate
storeroom	strictum jus	subcommission	subrogation
storm	stricture**	subcommittee	subrogee
stowage	strident	sub conditione	subrogor
stowaway	strife	subconscious	sub rosa
stowe	strike	subcontract	subscribe
straddle	strikebreaker	subcontractor	subscribed
straddles	striking	subculture	subscriber
straggler	stringent	sub curia	subscription
straight**	strip	subdivide	subsequent
straightforward	strip-mining	subdivision	subservient
straight-laced	strive	subduct	subside**
straight-line	stroke	subdue	subsidiary
strained	strong	subirrigate	subsidize
strait**	strong arm**	subject	subsidy**
straitjacket	strong-arm**	subjection	sub silentio
strait-laced	strong-minded	subjective	subsist
stramineus	stronghold	sub judice	subsistence
homo	struck	subjugate	subsoil
strand	structural	sublease	substance

234

substandard
substantial
substantially
substantiate
substantive
substitute
substituted
substitution
substitutional
substitutionary
substraction
subsume
subtenant
subterfuge
subterranean
subtle
subtraction
suburb**
suburban
subversion
subversive
succession
successive
successor
succinct
succor**
succumb
sucker**
sudden
suddenly
sue**
suffer
sufferable
sufferance
suffering
suffice
sufficiency
sufficient
suffocate
suffrage
suggest
suggestion
suggestive
sui
suicidal
suicide
suit**
suitable
suite**
suitor

suitors
sullen
sultry
sum**
summa**
summarily
summarize
summary**
summary court-
   martial
summation
summer**
summery**
summing up
summit
summon
summons
summum jus
sumptuous
sun**
Sunday
sunder
sundries
sundry
sunset law
sunshine law
sunstroke
suo**
superable
superannuate
superb**
supercargo
supercilious
superficial
superfluous
superimpose
superintend
superintendent
superior
superior court
superiority
superlative
supernatural
supernumeraries
supernumerary
supersede
supersedeas
superseding
superseniority
supersession

superstition
superstitious
supervening
supervention
supervise
supervision
supervisor
supervisory
supplant
supplement
supplemental
supplementary
supplicant
supplicate
supplier
supplies
supply
support
supportable
supportive
suppose
supposed
supposition
suppress
suppression
supra
supremacist
supremacy
supreme
Supreme Court
Supreme
   Judicial
   Court
sur**
surcharge
sure**
surcharge
sure**
surely**
surety
surface
surfeit
surgeon
Surgeon General
surgery
surgical
surly**
surmise
surmount
surname

surpass
surplus
surprise
surrebut
surrebuttal
surrebutter
surrejoin
surrejoinder
surrender
surrenderee
surrenderor
surreption
surreptitious
surrogacy
surrogate
surrogate's
   court
surround
surrounding
surtax
surveil
surveillance
survey
surveyor
survival
survivalist
survive
surivership
surviving
survivor
survivorship
susceptible
suspect
suspended
suspense
suspension
suspensive
suspensory
suspicion
suspicious
sustain
sustenance
suture
suzerainty
swallow
swamp
swath
sway
swear
swearing

sweat equity
sweating
sweatshop
sweeping
sweepstakes
sweeteners
sweetheart
   contract
swell
swelter
swerve
swill
swindle
swindler
swindling

switch
switchblade
switchyard
   doctrine
swoon
sworn
sybarite
sycophant
syllabus
syllogism
sylvan
symbol**
symbolic
symbolize
symmetry

sympathetic
   strike
sympathize
sympathy
symptomatic
symptoms
synallagmatic
   contract
synchronism
synchronization
synchronize
syndicalism
syndicate
syndicating
syndrome

synergism
syngraph
synod
synonymous
synopsis
syntax**
syntheses**
synthesis**
synthesize**
syphilis
syphilitic
system
systematic
systematize

T

tabernacle
tabetic dementia
table
tableau
tablet
tabloid
taboo
tabula
tabular
tabulate
tacit**
tacite
taciturn
tack
tacked**
tacking
tacks**
tact**
tactic
tactless
Taft-Hartley Act
tail**
tailage
tails**
taint
take
takedown
take-home pay
takeoff**

take off**
takeover**
take over**
taker
taking
talc**
tale**
tales**
talesman
talisman
talk**
tall**
tallage
tallagium
tally
Talmud
talweg
tame
tamper**
tampering
tampon
tam quam
tandem
tangent
tangible
tank
tankage
tantalize
tantamount

tantrum
tape
tape recorder
taping**
tapping**
tardy
tare**
target
tariff
tarnish
tarpaulin
task
taskmaster
tasksetter
taskwork
tasteful
tasteless
tattoo
taught**
taunt
taut**
tautologous
tautology
tavern
taverner
tawdry
tax**
taxable
taxable income

taxation
tax break
tax dodge
taxes**
tax evasion
tax exempt
tax haven
taxi
taxicab
taxing
taxis**
taxless
tax lien
taxpayer
T-bill
T-bond
teach
teacher
team**
teamster
teamwork
tear**
tear gas
tearing of will
technical
technicality
technically
technician
technique

tedious
tedium
teem**
teenager
teeter**
teetotaler
telecast
telecommunica-
   tions
telegenic
telegram
telegraph
telepathy
telephone
telethon
Teletype
teletypewriter
television
telex
teller
telltale
temerarious
temerity
temper**
temperament
temperamental
temperance
tempest
tempestuous
Templars
template
temple
temporalis
temporality
temporal lords
temporary
Temporary
   Emergency
   Court of
   Appeals
temporary
   restraining
   order
tempore
temporize
tempt
temptation
tempus
tenable
tenacious

tenacity
tenancy
tenant**
tenants
tenantship
tencon
tend
tendency
tendentious
tender
tender offer
tenement
tenent**
tenere**
tenet**
tenor**
ten-percenter
tense**
tensile
tension
tentative
tents**
tenuit
tenuity
tenura
tenure**
tenured faculty
term
termagant
termer**
Termes de la
   Ley
terminable
terminal
terminate
termination
terminer
termini
terminology
terminus
termless
termor**
terms
tern**
terra**
terre-tenant
terrible
terrific
terrify
territorial

territoriality
territory
terror**
terrorist
terroristic
terse
tertiary
tertium quid
test
testable
testacy
testament
testamentary
testate
testation
testator
testatrix
testatum
teste of a writ
testes**
testicle
testify
testimonial
testimonium
testimony
testis**
test-tube
tête-à-tête
tetrarch
text
textbook
textual
texture
Thai**
than**
thane
thanelands
thaneship
thankful
thankless
theater
theatre
theft
their**
theirs**
theme
then**
thence
thenceforth
thenceforward

theocracy
theology
theoretical
theorize
theory
therapeutic
   abortion
therapist
therapy
there**
thereabout
thereafter
thereamong
thereat
thereby
therefor**
therefore**
therefrom
therein
thereinafter
thereinbefore
thereof
thereon
there's**
thereto
theretofore
thereunder
thereuntil
thereunto
thereupon
therewith
thesaurus
theses**
thesis**
they're**
thief
thieve
thievery
thin
things
think
thinkable
thin-skinned
third
third party
thirds
Thirteenth
   Amendment
thorny
thorough

thoroughfare
thoroughgoing
thoroughly
thought
thoughtful
thoughtless
thrash**
thread**
threat**
threatening
three-mile limit
thresh**
threshold
threw**
throes**
through**
throughout
throughput
throughway
Throwback Rule
throw out
throws**
thrust
thug
thumbprint
thunder
thus
tic**
tick**
ticker tape
ticket
tidal
tide**
tideland
tidewater
tidy
tie**
tied**
tie in**
tie-in**
tie-in arrange-
    ment
tiel
tier**
tie up**
tie-up**
tight
tillable
tillage
timber**

timberland
timberlode
timbre**
time
timekeeper
timely
time-price
    differential
timeserver
timeshare
timetable
timework
timid
tinpenny
tip-off
tipper**
tippler**
tipster
tipsy
tirade
tireless
tiresome
titan**
titanic
tithe-free
tither
tithes
tithing
titian**
titillate**
titivate**
title
titleholder
titter**
titular
T-note
to**
tobacco
tobacconist
tocsin**
toed**
together
toiled**
toilsome
token
told**
tolerance
tolerant
tolerate
toleration

toll**
tollbooth
tolled**
toller
tollgate
tolls
tomb**
tombstone
tome**
tomorrow
ton**
tone**
tong**
tongue**
tonnage
tonsure
tontine
too**
tool**
top-heavy
topography**
topple
top-secret
Torah
torment
torpedo doctrine
torpor
Torrens title
    system
tort**
torte**
tort-feasor
tortious**
tortuous**
torture
torturous**
Tory
total
totalitarian
totality
totalize
Totten Trust
touch-and-go
touchstone
tour d'echelle
tour de force
tourn
tournament
tout
towable

towage
toward
towed**
tower
to wit
town
township
toxemia
toxic
toxical
toxicant**
toxicate**
toxicity
toxicology
toxicomania
toxicosis
toxify
toxigenic
toxin**
toxoid
tracer
trachea
tracing
tracked**
tracks
tract**
tractable
traction
tractor
trade
trade in**
trade-in**
trademark
trade off**
trade-off**
trader**
tradesman
trading
traditio
tradition
traditional
traditionary
    evidence
traduce
traduction
traffic
trafficker
trafficking
tragedy
tragic

trail**
trailblazer
trailer
train
trainee
trainload
traipse
trait
traitor**
trajectory
trammel
trammer
trample
tramway
trance
tranquilizer
transact
transaction
transactional
transatlantic
transceiver
transcend
transcendent
transcribe
transcript
transfer
transferable
transferee
transference
transferor
transfigure
transfix
transform
transformation
transgression
transgressor
transient
transire
transit
transition
transitive
transitory
translate
translation
translator
translucent
transmission
transmittal
transmutation
transparent

transpire
transplant
transport
transportation
transpose
transposition
transsexual
transshipment
transverse
transvestite
trap
trassans
trassatus
trauma
traumatic
traumatism
traumatize
travail**
travel**
traveled
traveler's check
traveling
travelled
traverse
traverse jury
traverser
travesty
treacherous
treachery
treadmill
treadwheel
treason
treasure**
Treasurer of the
    United States
treasure-trove
treasury**
Treasury**
treaties**
treatise**
treatment
treaty
treble
tremble
tremendous
tremor**
tremulous
trenchant
trend
trendsetter

trendy
trepidation
trespass
trespasser
triable
triad**
triage
trial**
trial jury
triangulate
triangulated
triarchy
triaxial
tribadism
tribal
tribe
tribulation
tribunal
tribune
tributary
tribute
trichinosis
trick
trickery
trickle
trickle-down
trickster
tried**
trier of fact
trifle
trifling
trigger
Trinity Term
trinkets
triors
tripartite
triple tax-
    exempt
triple witching
    hour
triplicate
tripod
triumphant
triumvirate
trivia**
trivial**
troglodyte
Trojan horse
trolley
tronage

troop**
troupe**
troops
trophy
trouble
troublemaker
troubleshooter
troublesome
trover
troy weight
truancy
truant
truce
truck
truckload
truculence
truculent
true
tried
true bill
trumped-up
trumpery
truncate
truncheon
trussed**
trust**
trust-busting
trustee**
trusteeship
Trust Indenture
    Act
trustor
trustworthy
trusty**
truth
truthful
Truth-in-
    Lending Act
try
tryout**
try out**
tsar
tub
tubular
Tucker Act
Tudor
tuition
tulle**
tumescence
tumid

tumor
tumultuous
tun**
tune**
tuning
tunnage
tunnel
tu quoque
  argument
turbary
turbid
turbulent
turf and twig
turgid

turn**
turncoat
turn down
turnkey
turnout**
turn out**
turnover**
turn over**
turnpike
turntable
turpis
turpitude
turpitudo
tutelage

tutelary
tuteur**
tutor**
tutorship
tutrix
twenty-percent
  rule
twinge
twist
twitch
two**
two-faced
two-issue rule

tying
typecast
typewriter
typhoid fever
typical
typify
typography**
typology
tyrannical
tyrant
tyranny
tythe
tything

U

ubi jus, ibi
  remedium
ubiquitous
ubiquity
uglify
ugly
ullage
ulterior
ultima ratio
ultimus haeres
ultra
ultraism
umbilical
umbrage
umbrella
umpirage
umpire**
unabashed
unabated
unable**
unabridged
unacceptable
unaccompanied
unaccountable
unaccrued
unacknowledged
unadjusted
unadorned
unadulterated
unadvised
unaffiliated
unallowed

unalterable
unambiguous
un-American
unamortized
unanimity
unanimous
unanimous
  verdict
unanswerable
unanticipated
unappealable
unappropriated
unarguable
unarmed
unarticulated
unascertained
unassailable
unassigned**
unassisted
unassuming
unattached
unattested
unaudited
unauthorized
unavailable
una voce
unavoidable
unaware**
unawares**
unbalanced
unbearable
unbecoming

unbeknown
unbelievable
unbiased
unborn
unbounded
unbreakable
unbridled
unbroken
uncalled-for
uncanny
uncensored
uncertainty
unchallenged
unchanged
uncharitable
uncharted
unchaste
uncivilized
unclaimed
unclassified
uncle
unclean
unclear
unclothe
uncollected
uncollectible
uncomfortable
uncompelled
uncompensated
uncomplicated
uncomplying
uncompromising

unconcealed
unconcerned
unconditional
unconscionable
unconscious
unconstitutional
unconstrained
uncontaminated
uncontested
uncontradicted
uncontrollable
uncontroverted
uncontrovertible
unconventional
uncooperative
uncorroborated
uncouth
uncover
unction
unctuous
undamaged
undated
undaunted
undecided
undefended
undeniable
undenied
under
underachieve
underage
underassessment
underboss

undercapitalized
undercover
undercut
underdeveloped
underdrawn
underemployed
underemployment
underestimate
undergo
undergraduate
underground
undergrowth
underhanded
underinsured
underlay**
under-lease
underlet
underlie**
underlying
undermine
underneath
undernourished
underpaid
underpinning
underpriced
underrepresented
underscore
undersecretary
undersell
undersexed
under-sheriff
undersigned
undersized
understand
understanding
understate
understatement
understood
undersubscribed
undertake
undertaker
undertaking
under-tenant
under-the-table
undertone
undertook
undervaluation
underway
underworld
underwrite

underwriter
undeserved
undesirable
undeterminable
undetermined
undeveloped
undiagnosed
undignified
undirected
undisbursed
undischarged
undisciplined
undisclosed
undisposed
undisputed
undistributed
undivided
undo**
undocumented
undue**
unduly
undying
unearned
unearth
uneasy
unedited
uneducated
unemancipated
unemotional
unemployed
unemployment
unemployment
    compensation
unenclosed
unencumbered
unenforceable
unentered
unentitled
unequal
unequivocal
unerring
unessential
unethical
uneventful
unexceptionable**
unexceptional**
unexecuted
unexercised
unexpected
unexpended

unexpired
unexplained
unexpressed
unfair
unfaithful
unfamiliar
unfashionable
unfathomable
unfavorable
unfinished
unfit
unflappable
unflattering
unfocused
unforeseeable
unforeseen
unforgetable
unforgivable
unfortunate
unfortunately
unfounded
unfriendly
unfulfilled
unfunded
ungainly
ungodly
ungovernable
ungraded
ungrateful
unguarded
unhappy
unharmed
unhealthy
unhindered
Uniat
Uniate
unidentifiable
unifactoral
unified
uniform
Uniform
    Commercial
    Code
uniformity
unify
unilateral
unimpaired
unimpeachable
unimproved
    land

uninclosed
unincorporated
uninfected
uninformative
uninhabitable
uninhibited
uninspected
uninspired
uninsurable
uninsured
unintelligible
unintended
unintentional
uninterested
uninterrupted
union
unionization
unionize
Union Jack
unique**
unissued
unit**
unitary
unite**
United Nations
United States
unitization
unitize
universal
university
unjust
unjust enrich-
    ment
unjustifiable
unkempt
unknowingly
unknown
unlawful
unlawfully
unleash
unless
unlicensed
unlikelihood
unlikely
unlimited
unliquidated
unlisted
unlivable
unload
unloading

unlucky	unrecorded	unthinkable	urinalysis
unmanageable	unrecovered	unthinking	urn**
unmarketable	unredressed	until	usable
unmarried	unregulated	untimely	usage
unmentionable	unrelated	untouchable	usance
unmerciful	unrelenting	untoward	use
unmistakable	unrepresented	untried	useable
unmitigated	unresponsive	untrue	used to
unmoral**	unrestrained	untruthful	usee
unnamed	unrestricted	unusable	useful
unnatural	unrightful	unusual	useless
unnecessary	unruly	unverified	user
unneeded	unsafe	unvoiced	usher
unnegotiable	unsanitary	unwanted**	using
unnoticed	unsatisfactory	unwarranted	usque
unnumbered	unsavory	unwary	usual
unoccupied	unscathed	unwholesome	usufruct
unofficial	unscheduled	unwilling	usura**
unorganized	unscrupulous	unwitting	usurer**
unorthodox	unsealed	unwonted**	usurious
unpaid	unsecured	unworthy	usurp
unpalatable	unseemly	unwritten	usurpation
unpatented	unselfish	unyielding	usurper
unprecedented	unsettled	upbeat	usury**
unpredictable	unsightly	upbringing	uterine
unprejudiced	unsigned**	upheaval	uterus
unpremeditated	unskilled	uphold	utility
unpretentious	unsophisticated	upkeep	utilization
unprincipled	unsound	uplift	utilize
unproductive	unspeakable	uproar	utmost
unprofessional	unstoppable	upset price	utopia
unprofitable	unstudied	upshot	utter
unproven	unsuccessful	up-to-date	utterance
unprovoked	unsuitable	upturn	utterly
unpunished	unsupervised	urban**	uxor
unqualified	unsuspecting	urbane**	uxoricide
unquess	unsworn	ure	uxorious
unquestionable	untaxed	urgency	
unreasonable	untenable	urgent	

V

vacancy	vaccine	vagabond	vain**
vacant	vacillate	vagary	vainglory
vacate	vacuity	vagina	vale**
vacation**	vacuous	vagrancy	valediction
vacatur	vacuum	vagrant	valentia
vaccination	vadium	vague	valet**

valetudinary	venality	versatile	videocassette
valiant	venaria	verses**	videotape
valid**	venatio	versus**	viduity
validate	vend	vertical	vie**
validity	vendee	vertiginous	vies**
valley	vendetta	vertigo	vi et armis
valor	vendible	verus	view
valorize	vendition	very**	viewers
valorous	venditor	vested	vigil
valuable**	venditrix	vestige	vigilance
valuate	vendor	vestigial	vigilant
valuation	vendue	vestigium	vigilanteism or
value	veneer**	vestry	vigilantism
value added tax	venemous	vestura	vignette
valueless	venerable	vesture	vigor
valuer	veneration	veteran	vigorish**
vandal	venereal disease	vetera statuta	vigorous**
vandalism	venery	veterinarian	vile**
vandalize	vengeance	veto	vilify
vanguard	vengeful	vetoes	village
vanish	venia**	vex	villein
vanquish	venial**	vexari	villeinage
vantage	venire**	vexata quaestio	villenous
variable	venire facias	vexation	judgment
variance	venireman	vexatious	vinagium
variant	venit	via**	vindicare
variation	venter	viability	vindicate
variety	ventilate	viable	vindicated
various	ventilation	viaduct	vindication
vary**	venture	vial**	vindicator
vascular	venue	vicarial	vindicatory
vasectomy	veracity**	vicarious	vindictive
vassal	veranda	vicar	vine**
vastum	verandah	vice**	vinous
vaudeville	veray	viceroy	vintage
vavasor or	verba	vice versa	vintner
vavasour	verbal	vicinage	violable
vector	verbatim	vicinity	violation
veer**	verbiage	vicious**	violative
vegetable	verderer	vicissitude	violator
vegetative	verderor	vicontiel	violence
vehement	verdict	victim	violent
vehicle	veredictum	victimize	violently
vehicular	verge**	victimless	vir**
veies**	verification	victory	virago**
veil**	verified	victual	viral
veilings	verify	victus	vires**
vein**	verisimilitude	vide	virgata
velocity	verity	videlicet	virge**
venal**	vernacular	video	virgin

243

virginity
Virgo**
virgo intacta**
viricide
virile
virility
virtual
virtue
virtuous
virtute
virulence
virulent
virus**
vis**
visa**
vis-à-vis
visceral
viscount
viscous
vise**
visible
visionary

visit
visitation
visitor
visne**
visor**
visual
visus
vital
vitamin
vitiate
vitiligate
vitreous
vitriol
vituperate
vivarium
vivary
viva voce
vivid
vividly
vivum vadium
viz**
vocabula artis

vocabulary
vocation**
vociferous
voco
vogue
voice
voiceprint
void
voidable
voidance
voir dire
volatile
volatility
volens
volition
volitional
Volstead Act
voluble**
volume
voluminous
voluntarily
voluntary

volunteer
voluptuous
vomit
voracious
voracity**
voter
voting
vouch
vouchee
voucher
vouching
vouchsafe
vox populi
voyage
voyeur
voyeurism
vulgar
vulgarity
vulnerable
vulva
vying

W

wacreour
wad**
wade**
wadia
waffle
wage
wageless
wager
wagering
wages
Wagner Act
wagon
waif**
wail**
wainable
wainage
waist**
wait**
waive**
waiver**
wale**
walk in**
walk-in**

walkout**
walk out**
walkup**
walk up**
wall**
wallow
Walsh-Healey
   Act
wampum
wand**
wander**
wangle**
want**
wanton**
wantonness
war**
ward**
warda
warden
warder
wards
ware**
warehouse

warehouseman
warehousemen's
   lien
warfare
warmonger
warm up**
warm-up**
warn**
warning
warp
warpath
warrant
warrantable
warrantee**
warranties
warrantor**
warranty**
warred**
warren
Warsaw
   Convention
wary**
wash

washout**
wash out**
wash sale
wasp**
WASP**
waste**
watt**
wastage
wasteful
wasting
wastrel
watch
watchdog
watchful
watchman
watchword
water
waterborne
watered stock
waterfront
Watergate
waterlogged
watershed

watertight	well-done	wherewithal	wild
waterway	well-founded	whether**	wildcatter
waterworks	well-grounded	which**	wilding
waul**	wellhead	whichever	Wild's Case
wave**	well-meaning	whichsoever	will
waver**	well-spoken	Whig	wile**
wavering	well-to-do	while**	willful
wax**	well-wisher	whim	willingly
waxen	welsh**	whimper	windfall
way**	welsher	whimsy	window
way-bill	wen**	whine**	windstorm
waylay	we're**	whiplash	windup**
ways and means	wetback	whipping	wind up**
wayward	wether**	whipsaw	wine**
weak**	wetland	whirlwind	winner
weak-minded	we've**	whiskey	winsome
weakness	whack	whisper	winter
weal**	whacks**	whit**	wipeout**
wealth	whale**	white	wipe out**
wealthy	whaler	white-collar	wiretap
weapon	wharf	white-collar	wiretapping
wear**	wharfage	crime	wisdom
wear and tear	Wharton Rule	white knight	wishful
wearing apparel	what**	whitewash**	wistful
wearisome	whatever	white wash**	wit**
weary**	whatsoever	whither	witam
weather**	wheel**	whoever	witch**
weathering	wheeler-dealer	whole**	with**
weave**	wheelright	wholesale	withal
Webb-Pomerene	whelm	wholesaler	withdraw
Act	whelps	wholesome	withdrawal
wed**	when**	wholly**	withdrawing
we'd**	whence**	whomever	withhold
wedding	whenever	whomsoever**	withholding
wedlock	when issued	whore**	withholding tax
weed**	where**	who're**	within
week**	whereabouts	whored**	without
weekday	whereafter	whorehouse	withstand
weekly	whereas	whoremaster	witness
weigh**	whereby	whores**	witnessing part
weighed**	wherefore	who's**	witting
weight**	wherefrom	whose**	wittingly
weighty	whereof	whosesoever**	wive
weir**	whereon	whosoever**	wizened
weird	wheresoever	widget	wobble
welfare	whereto	widow	woebegone
we'll**	whereunder	widower	woman**
well-appointed	whereupon	widowhood	women**
well-being	wherever	width**	women's rights
well-disposed	wherewith	wife	wonder**

245

wonderful
wondrous
wont**
won't**
wonton**
wood**
woodwork
woodworker
word processing
words
wore**
work
workday
worker
workers'
  compensation
working
workload
workman

workmen's
  compensation
workout**
work out**
workshop
world
World Court
worldly
worn**
worrisome
worship
worsted
worth
worthless**
worth less**
worthwhile
worthy
would**
would-be

wound
wounded
  feelings
wrangle**
wrap**
wrath
wrathful
wreak**
wreck**
wreckage
wrecker
wreckfree
wrench
wrest**
wrestling
wright**
wrinkle
wrist
wristdrop

writ
write down**
write-down**
write in**
write-in**
write off**
write-off**
write up**
write-up**
writing
writ of
  certiorari
written
wrongdoer
wrongful
wrongfully
wrong
wrote**

X-Y-Z

xenomania
xenophobia
xerography
X-rated
x-ray
yacht
yard
yardmaster
yea and nay
year
yearend
years

year to year
yeas and nays
yea-sayer
yeast
yellow-dog
  contract
yen-denomin-
  ated
yeoman
yesterday
Yick Wo
  doctrine

Yiddish
yield
yield to maturity
yoke**
yolk**
yore**
you**
youngster
your**
you're**
yours
youth

youthful
zany
zealot
zealotry
zealous
zenith
zero coupon
  bond
zigzagged
zone
zoning
zygote